David Brazier

David Brazier — Buddhist name: Dharmavidya —is the head and founder of Amida Shu and the Amida Order. He is president of the International Zen Therapy Institute. His root teachers have been in Japanese Zen and Pureland Buddhism. He has written a dozen books, on Buddhism, philosophy and psychology. He lives in central France.

Authentic Life
Buddhist Teachings and Stories
ISBN 978-0-9931317-6-9

Published by Woodsmoke Press 2019
Copyright © 2019 David Brazier

David Brazier asserts the moral right to be identified as the author of this work.
All rights reserved.

Design: Kaspalita Thompson
Typeface: Gentium Book Basic

Woodsmoke Press
Amida Mandala
34 Worcester Road
Malvern
WR14 4AA

kaspa@woodsmokepress.com

Praise for *Authentic Life: Buddhist Stories and Teachings*

"Referencing a wide range of themes across numerous Buddhist traditions and historical contexts, the author offers a fresh vision and insights on a wide range of spiritual and religious topics. Brazier's statement, "When meditation is about awareness and no longer about rapture, I am dismayed" symbolizes the spirit of this impressive book."

~ Kenneth Kenshin Tanaka, Professor Emeritus, Musashino University and Past President, International Association of Shin Buddhist Studies

"These pages are crammed with both wisdom and heart. Brazier has long decades of Buddhist practice and study behind him, and yet always writes from a place of freshness and humility. This allows us to join him with our own questions, and find our answers as he finds his. Suitable both for long-term practitioners and those brand new to Buddhism, this book will help you to find your own refuge."

~Satya Robyn, Buddhist Priest and author of *Coming Home: Refuge in Pureland Buddhism*

Praise for *Not Everything is Impermanent*

"This is a book by a true Bodhisattva - an awake awakening being - who brings his compassion and insight to those with troubled hearts everywhere. He guides us all to become what he calls myokonin, "ordinary, fallible persons shining with simple faith." And he makes perfectly clear why "there is no reason not to be loving, compassionate and wise." Instead of our living within fear and the narrow specificity of hate, David Brazier presents us with a way to grasp and experience the vastness of love."

~ Rev. Saigyo Terrance Keenan, author of *St. Nadie in Winter: Zen Encounters with Loneliness*

"Engaged Buddhism is one of the movements that is key to the interdependent transformation of consciousness and society on which the survival of our species and the development of an enlightened society depends. David Brazier is an important agent and catalyzer of that movement. Let us profit from his contribution to the transformation in question."

~ Elías Capriles, author of *The Beyond Mind Papers: Transpersonal and Metatranspersonal Theory*

"*Not Everything is Impermanent* is an enriching discourse, a symphony with interlacing refrains of truth. It is written beautifully, and nuanced with all of the hopefulness that English allows. The Ivory Tower is made accessible here – a very down-to-earth and practical guide indeed. As our planet shrinks in its virtual reality, such works are bridges of understanding among people. The more that we are able to see through each other's eyes, the greater are the prospects of peace. Like learning a new language, this book proposes a new philosophy that not only stretches a student outwards to the other, but reveals in finer detail the structure of his own being. I highly recommend this book for the use of those who would offer realistic compassion to neighbour, client or otherwise."

~ Colleen G. Dick, M.S. Holistic Nutrition and Health

"A fine dharma book, full of essence teachings, through the medium of Buddhism and psychotherapy. Rich in anecdote, it guides the reader on a radical path of awakening."

~ Roshi Joan Halifax, Founder and Abbot of Upaya Zen Center

"David Brazier is a lucid and brilliant writer. This book offers a generous selection of poignant observations about our lives, guiding us as a friend would to live with greater vibrancy, wholeness, and humility. Filled with profound and practical gems of wisdom, Brazier shows how the path toward liberation involves fully embracing our humanness rather than futilely trying to transcend it. Reading this book will help you feel more comfortable with your humanity in a way that will further genuine spiritual growth. One of the clearest books I've seen on the importance of integrating our humanity with our spiritual practice."

~ John Amodeo, author of *Dancing with Fire:
A Mindful Way to Loving Relationships* and *Love & Betrayal*

"In this book David Brazier shows an extra-ordinary, even mysterious, ability to re-discover both the meanings of Buddhist teachings and the inner drivers of our feelings and demeanours. He gently takes the reader by hand on a fascinating voyage, supported by a secure knowledge base and a close intimacy with human experience."

~ Massimo Tomassini, Mindfulness Trainer at the Pundarika centre

Authentic Life
Buddhist Teachings and Stories

David Brazier

Previous books by David Brazier

A Guide to Psychodrama

Beyond Carl Rogers:
Towards a psychotherapy for the 21st century

Zen Therapy

The Feeling Buddha

The New Buddhism

Who Loves Dies Well

Her Mother's Eyes and Other Poems

Love and its Disappointment:
the meaning of life, therapy and art

Not Everything is Impermanent

Buddhism is a Religion

Questions in the Sand

The Dark Side of the Mirror

Contents

Introduction by Kaspalita Thompson	i
On Verbal and Meditative Nembutsu	1
Religious Consciousness: The Buddha's Basic Teaching on How to Be a Noble One	7
Nembutsu as Trikaya Buddhism	13
Ya Ya Ya	18
On Becoming Ippen	25
Refuge	34
Prayers of the Heart	36
The Koan of Shakyamuni	42
Faith is Enlightenment, Enlightenment is Faith	46
The Meaning of Tathagata	50
Five Points on Impermanence	54
Dragon Pearl – The Story of Nagarjuna	56
More Awe	63
Your Sutra	70
Dependant Origination is Other Power	72
Understanding the Skandhas	81
Dogen	88
Dilemmas About Dogen or Dogen's Dilemmas	92

Here and There With Saigyo	97
Dogen and Saigyo	100
The Equivalence of Three Buddhist Principles	103
In Less Than a Day	107
What Is Samadhi For?	109
Some Thoughts about Ambapali	115
Vijnana and Ayatana	122
Self Psychology East and West	129
Letting It Go	132
Samadhi Soup	135
Fo Tao Li: The Ideal Life	138
Unpredictable Relationship	141
Can a Tile Be a Mirror?	146
Realising Anger	148
More on Anger	152
Decay of the Body	159
Praying for All Lineages	161
Shariputra and His Brother Enter the Way	163
Buddha's Last Words	166
Two Famous Koans	172
Why Is It So Hard to Be Natural?	175
Crazyana	181
Dealing With Emotion: The Fixless Fix	187

Punyayashas: Buddha Child on Golden Ground	193
Three Aspects of Delusion and Enlightenment	198
Buddha's Ambivalence About Meditation	203
Effacement	210
Bencho: Successor of Honen	217
Getting Out of Prison	221
Anshin: Part One ~ It's Alright	226
Anshin: Part Two ~ Domestic Bliss?	231
Anshin: Part Three ~ Symbolism of My Island Home	236
Anshin: Part Four ~ The Judgement of the Oracle	240
Anshin: Part Five ~ Four Sukhas	244
Anshin: Part Six ~ Faith in Therapy	248
Anshin: Part Seven ~ Practical Application	251
Eightfold What?	253
Love and Destiny: The Way of Ashvaghosha	257
The Merit of a Fan	263
Grandmotherly Mind	265
Does the Dharma Need Updating?	268
Training in Buddhism	290
Styles of Buddhist Training	296

The Samadhi of Equality	302
The Robe	306
Overcoming Weakness and Discovering No Birth: The Story of Parsva	308
Mindful Foundation	313
Ju-Nen Contemplation	320
The Night of Enlightenment	323
Sila, Samadhi and Prajna	328
Kyo Ju Kai Mon: Ten Precept Teaching	332
Reflecting the Ocean of Truth: The Koan of Kapimala	337
Dialectic Within the Teaching and Within the Sangha	339
Dharma Based Alternative Society	341
Singularity and Community	344
Teachers, Disciples and Students	347
Respecting Difference	355
Dualities and Nondualities	358

Introduction

Dharmavidya (the Buddhist name of David Brazier) lives in central France, in an old farmhouse surrounded by thirty acres of meadow, scrub and woodland. The dharma hall is a barn thirty feet high without any doors. In the summers I have spent there, swifts flew in and out of the barn and dormice chattered high up on the roof beams above the Buddha.

The community there ebbs and flows like the seasons. Sometimes Dharmavidya is there on his own, living the life of a holy hermit. Sometimes communities form of disciples, or volunteers, or some mix of the two.

At the start of 2016, when many of these teachings were first written, there was a small community around Dharmavidya. 2016 was also the year of Dharmavidya's first pulmonary embolism, and he spent much of the year in recovery. All of these things colour the teachings in their own way, as do the many years of Dharmavidya's spiritual practice and training.

During this time he was also beginning the process of researching and writing his book on Dogen's Genjokoan, *The Dark Side of the Mirror*. There are shared themes and resonances between that book and these short teachings. Connections between them include ideas like effacement and working with how the mind actually is, rather than how we would like to be.

Many of the teachings in this collection come from Dharmavidya's reflections on the typical life of a Buddhist trainee, particularly the Buddhist trainees in our tradition, and even more specifically the life of the trainees and volunteers in the community in France at that time. Some of the teachings and stories here are completely accessible to beginners, and some assume some knowledge of our Pureland tradition.

Reading at the edge of our comprehension can be useful sometimes. When I first started studying and practicing Buddhism there were some teachings that made intuitive sense straight away, and some teachings that I couldn't understand and yet held me in their gaze. Those more difficult teachings rewarded re-reading and deep thinking. I encourage you to engage with the more challenging chapters of this book in the same way.

At the heart of this book is the *nembutsu*, the practice of taking refuge in an Other Power that is wise, loving and kind, particularly through saying the name of Amida Buddha. This practice recognises our fallible human nature — that we are beings of greed, ill-will and ignorance as much as anything else — and that there is something that beings such as us can rely on.

The outpouring of love from the Buddha to us, and through us to others is the foundation of Dharmavidya's faith and practice, and the bedrock of the teachings and stories in this collection. In some chapters it is explicit, and in the others less so. I hope you will see how this deep religious truth shines through the whole book, and enjoy reading and contemplating these teachings, as much as I enjoyed collecting them.

With deep gratitude to Dharmavidya, my teacher.

Acharya Kaspalita Thompson

On Verbal and Meditative Nembutsu

The primary practice of Pureland Buddhism is called nembutsu (nien fo in Chinese), which literally means "mindfulness of Buddha". Sometimes such mindfulness is interpreted as meaning "keeping Buddha in mind" and sometimes as "saying the Name of Buddha".

Many people who write about the development of Pureland Buddhism in Japan and its history assert that verbal nembutsu developed out of meditative nembutsu. By the latter we mean a purely mental activity of saying the words inwardly, or of visualising the image of Amitabha, or any of the other images listed in the Contemplation Sutra. The general drift of such writings is that the verbal nembutsu came to be considered more practical for ordinary people in the "Dharma-ending Age".

It is generally said that it was Shan Tao in particular who interpreted references to "mindfulness of Amitabha" in the sutras as referring to verbal utterance of the Name. Earlier practitioners, such as Lu Shan Hui Yuan, who founded the first White Lotus Society in China for Pureland practice in 400 CE, are said to have done a meditative nembutsu only, based on the Pratyutpanna Samadhi Sutra.

My own view is that this makes too sharp a division. I am sure that from the very earliest times Buddhists have praised and invoked the Buddhas in a wide variety of ways and that the practice of circumambulating stupas while reciting the Buddha's Name must date at least from immediately after the demise of Shakyamuni. There are indications that the worship of Buddha relics was established even during the lifetime of the sage. A person does not have to be dead for relics to exist, as we know from the practice of lovers keeping a lock of hair of their beloved in a locket. So I think that calling and contemplating have always existed side by side and rather than thinking of one replacing the other we should regard them as complementary.

In China, it was common — normal even — to practise Ch'an (Zen) and Jing Tu (Pureland) concurrently. This is called "dual practice" and to this day is a fairly standard way of doing Buddhism in China. Buddhism is taken to consist of a number of schools that are not mutually exclusive, but rather are complementary. There are several philosophical schools that expound the Dharma from the viewpoint of particular sutras — Lotus, Avatamsaka, etc — a Vinaya school that sets out monastic discipline and Buddhist ethics, and the two practice schools, Ch'an and Jing Tu. These are all seen as, as it were, segments of the same cake. When Buddhism went to Japan, the founders were often people who had only received one of these segments and the particular circumstances of Japanese culture at the time resulted in Buddhism developing differently there, such that, in

Japan, Buddhism is divided into separate denominations and while it is possible for the individual practitioner to practise more than one variety concurrently, this is not general.

A result of these circumstances is that Zen and Pureland are more distinct in Japan than in China. In China there was a tendency for nembutsu (the main practice of Pureland) to be considered as a form of meditation (the main practice of Zen) and for meditation to be seen as a contemplation of Buddha Nature identified with Amitabha and, therefore, as not unrelated to nembutsu.

Consequently, there was a tendency in China to look at nembutsu practice in terms of its technique, whereas in Japan there is more of an assertion that nembutsu has nothing to do with technique. We do not need to get hung up on these differences nor take sides, but it is interesting to reflect upon what Buddhists in different circumstances have done to try to make their practice more profound or effective.

Thus, for instance, some Chinese masters recommend that when saying the nembutsu out loud it is good to do one or more of the following:

- visualise Amitabha and/or the Pureland.
- make the effort to hear the sound of your own voice so that you say and hear the nembutsu simultaneously.
- say the nembutsu continuously so that there is no time gap between the end of one and

the start of the next into which stray distracting thoughts may enter.
- coordinate the words with the breathing or with the steps in walking or with the bodily movements of making prostrations.

These and other similar technical refinements can make the practice more concentrated and can fulfil the principle of practising nien fo with "body, speech and mind".

The Chinese were interested in techniques of this kind because they saw the objective of the exercise as being to arrive at "the nembutsu samadhi" — a state of rapturous absorption in the grace of Amitabha. In this there is clearly a "self-power" element.

The Japanese, on the other hand, took the logic of "other-power" further. The idea of a nembutsu samadhi was not eschewed, but it was seen as something granted rather than something achieved. Furthermore, while the arrival of such a samadhi was seen as a confirmation of Amida's grace, it was not regarded as necessary. A person can enter the Pure Land without ever having experienced the samadhi. However, when Honen was asked why he chose Tao Cho, Tan Luan and Shan Tao as exemplars rather than choosing other Pureland masters of old, he said that it was because they had experienced the samadhi whereas others had not. He himself experienced the samadhi in a particularly major way near to the end of his life.

In our *Summary of Faith and Practice** we say that our nembutsu is not done as a form of meditation. In our approach, rather, meditation is done as a form of nembutsu. When the selection of nembutsu as primary practice has been made, other forms of practice naturally become forms of nembutsu. Nembutsu thus becomes a form of "unremitting mindfulness" as taught by Shakyamuni Buddha, not because one remains consciously attentive to nembutsu every wakeful hour but because it is so integrated into one that it has become second nature. This means that Amitabha is in our life whether we are thinking about him or not. This is what is called "anshin" — peaceful mind or settled faith. It is a state of complete assurance.

This is a state of "joy and ease" rather than one of intense effort. It colours all the sentiments of one's life and, in particular, takes away the fear of death. By doing so it affects our emotional life in a variety of beneficial ways. We then naturally express what arises and such expression is practice. In this condition, practice is not a means of arriving at any particular state, it is a natural and easy expression of faith and gratitude already established. Whether that expression takes a verbal, kinetic or contemplative form makes no difference. There are a myriad ways to express love, faith and devotion.

---

* page 1, Nien Fo Book: The service book of Amida Shu, Amida Shu, 2018

There is no need to worry if all of the foregoing is not yet clear to you. It will all be explained as we go on. Later, you can come back and reread this beginning and it will then speak to you more clearly. This is an approach to Buddhism that goes directly to the heart and to the deeper dimension of our being. We acquire it more by the feel than by intellectual understanding.

Religious Consciousness: The Buddha's Basic Teaching on How to Be a Noble One

The term mindfulness can be constructed as "religious consciousness". I would like to say a little more about this here by making reference to the Longer Discourses of the Buddha, the Digha Nikaya. In Buddha's terminology, it is what one needs in order to be a "noble one".

Buddha's First Concern

By noble one, in the life and discipline of the Tathagata, we mean a person who follows a holy life. The Buddha's primary concern seems to have been to teach people how to do this. He approached the matter from different directions with different people. He was familiar with the range of different theories of the teachers and philosophers of his time, but he did not think that strong adherence to any of them was the key to success. Yet he did have a strong sense of the spiritual and the holy and a connection with the Buddhas of the past and the future who all work to help beings live out the holy life. His, was, therefore, a middle way, and a sense of serving a perennial wisdom that transcended particular philosophies, honouring what they pointed at rather than the details of the mode of pointing. He did not regard philosophy and metaphysics as useless — it could inspire a person to holiness — but he saw the danger of dogmatism and of getting lost in theory.

On the other hand, he was not simply a moralist. He taught right and wrong, but not in isolation from the mental culture that is necessary to underpin and give rise to it. Nor is such culture simply some kind of technique. What he taught was an attitude of life wholly directed to the sacred substance and purpose of life, death and existence.

Fruits of the Holy Life

In the second book of the Digha Nikaya, the Samañña Phala Sutta, which we can loosely translate as "The Fruits of the Holy Life", he sets out his stall on this matter.

He talks about how one should regard things in this world so as to avoid becoming entranced by them. Delight in them but do not get carried away by them. No matter whether we are talking about sights, sounds, smells, tastes, tangible things, or things imagined, he advocates that one avoid such an engagement with it as might lead either to covetousness or dejection.

Seeing Deeply

Then he takes the same principle a step further and uses the term mindful. The Sanskrit term smriti (Pali sati) that we translate as "mindfulness" is related to the word for remember and it refers to what one has taken to heart, the things one keeps within that act as a guide and protection for one's life. If one is mindful of what is really important, one will not go astray. This is the original meaning. It is somewhat different from what people make of the term mindfulness these days.

Buddha says that in everything one does, "in going forth or coming back" one should have in mind all that is wrapt up therein, in other words, the ethical and spiritual significance.

"Also in looking forward or looking back, in stretching out an arm or pulling it in again, in eating, drinking, masticating, swallowing, obeying the calls of nature, in going, standing or sitting, in sleeping, waking, speaking or being silent," be aware of all that it really means.

There is a contemporary trend that has got hold of the lesser half of this injunction and lost touch with the greater half. The lesser half is the stress upon every possible action. The greater half is to know what it means. T.W.Rhys Davids in one of the first translations of this text from the Pali says in a footnote to this particular verse, that it is the Buddhist analogue to St. Paul's 'Whether, therefore, ye eat or drink, or whatsoever ye do, do all to the glory of God' (I Cor. x.31.).

What is being talked about here is not self-conscious awareness of the present moment or body-scanning or any other mechanical technique, beneficial as some of those techniques might be for certain medical purposes. What is being talked about is religious consciousness, having a consciousness of the high purpose and meaning of everything that one does because everything that one does is part of the holy life within a holy cosmic vision and exists for that purpose.

Loss of Spirit

When people are cut off from their sacred life they become either avaricious or dejected and this leads to fear, resentment, aggressiveness and all manner of evils. Buddha does not teach morality as the goal, but he sees clearly that moral or immoral behaviour is a sign of how closely connected or not a person is with the holy life.

Naturally Honouring Heaven

We said earlier that the Buddha took a middle path in regard to philosophy. He recognises that there exist many kinds of metaphysics in the world. On the one hand he does not want people to get lost in the jungle of competing views, but, on the other hand, he does not advocate a secular rejection of them either. Rather, he points out that a person who practises the holy life in the way he suggests naturally honours all gods, naturally stores up treasure in whatever heavens there may be, naturally avoids the hells and lower regions, naturally creates conditions for a good rebirth and so on. He does not want us to argue about which metaphysic is the correct one because, whichever it is, the practical implication is the same. A person needs a religious consciousness as a foundation and the Buddha calls this by the term that has come to be translated as mindfulness.

Free As a Bird

A person who has such a consciousness is not entrapped by the things of the world but can enjoy them in freedom. He has few physical needs, few enough that he can take them with him wherever he goes, just as a bird carries its wings. He wants us to be free as birds. Then there will be a deep contentment.

Such people hanker not and are free of ill-will and ill-temper. Being light and inspired they do not fall into laziness, fretfulness or worry. The Rhys Davids translation says that they have a "serene heart" and are free from "irritability and vexation of spirit". They have "passed beyond perplexity".

Be of Good Cheer

It seems clear to me that this kind of religious consciousness was regarded by the Buddha as an invaluable treasure. The Buddha used a lot of very down to earth examples to make his point. In this case, he says that such a person would feel like one who used always to be in debt but due to a sudden business success can now say, "'I used to have to carry on my business by getting into debt, but it has gone so well with me that I have paid off what I owed, and have a surplus left over to maintain a wife'. And he would be of good cheer at that, would be glad of heart at that."

Buddha is pointing out that there are times when the ordinary person from time to time, due to good fortune, experiences freedom, happiness and good cheer, but, of course, this is dependent upon factors largely outside of his control whereas the person who has religious consciousness has such joy of heart in any situation whatever. Whatever the situation, he sees the deep meaningfulness of life. He feels in connection with the Tao, the gods, Amida Buddha, Olympus and all. He rejoices with them all.

Nembutsu as Trikaya Buddhism

In Mahayana Buddhism there is a teaching common to all schools called the trikaya. Tri means three. Kaya means body. So the Three Treasures, in which Buddhists take refuge, have these three bodies or manifestations.

Master Keizan wrote: "In the Three Treasures, Buddha, Dharma and Sangha, there are three merits. The first is the true source of the three treasures. The second is the presence in the past of Shakyamuni Buddha and the third is the presence at the present time."

Dharmakaya

The first is the true source, which is the dharmakaya, the Tao, the Unborn, that which is not impermanent, endlessly functioning, ceaselessly giving rise to pure inspiration. This is Dharma in its absolute mode, without beginning and without end. It is the fundamental truth of the universe and all possible universes. It is true, was true and will be true whether anybody knows it or not. Still it needs expression. It invites us but is not coercive. It is an open field within which all wonders appear. Those with few desires sense it and feel its wonder. Those with many desires see the surface of things, but even for them the dharmakaya is mysteriously working.

Nirmanakaya

The second is the appearance of Buddha in the world, the nirmanakaya, concrete physical manifestation in the material world of the sage who teaches the Dharma to all who have but little dust in their eyes and who is compassionate indiscriminately to all beings. A Buddha appearing in the world is born at a certain time, enlightened at a certain time, teaches in particular places and times, and dies when the time comes. This kaya is a historical event. Such a happening, however, is shot through with dharmakaya. The Buddha does not live for self. He is a mortal body but magnified by the spirit of all the Buddhas of all times. In the Larger Pureland Sutra, Ananda asks Shakyamuni how it is that he looks so radiant and asks if it is a sign that Shakyamuni has been communing with all the other Buddhas of past, present and future, and Shakyamuni affirms that this is so. Buddha is a mortal, but an extraordinary one. What had he got that others lack? The inspiration of the true source and communion with all those who manifest that source no matter where or when.

Sambhogakaya

The third is the appearance at the present time. This is the sambhogakaya, the spiritual manifestation of the Three Jewels in manifold forms, visions, dreams, and signs. This is what has been put into the world by the appearance of a Buddha in the past. Buddha does not die when Buddha's body dies. Thus, where dharmakaya is without beginning or end and nirmanakaya has a beginning and end, sambhogakaya has a beginning but no end. Once the Dharma is in the world it is forever, appearing in innumerable ways. Sambhogakaya is the bridge between the dharmakaya and the foolish being. It is Shakyamuni still with us. It is Amida Buddha's all acceptance. It is the solace of Quan Shi Yin and Samantabhadra, the wisdom of Manjushri and the saving power of Kshitigharba. Sambhoga means enjoyment. This is how we ordinary beings of the present enjoy the spiritual life. The nirmanakaya died long ago and the dharmakaya is only directly perceptible to the enlightened. It is through the sambhogakaya that Buddhist religious consciousness is made manifest. The central figure on the main altar of most Buddhist temples in the orient is some representation of the sambhogkaya.

The Religious Consciousness of Buddhists

This, therefore, is the religious vision of Mahayana Buddhism. This vision, in one way or another, is what the devotee keeps in mind and is open to. This is mindfulness or religious consciousness. It keeps the practitioner open in such a way that the Tao can function and form her or him. Sometimes the devotee is conscious of what is happening and sometimes not, but once they have entered the path much happens, both wittingly and unwittingly.

Practice is Encounter

Delusion and enlightenment are qualities of encounter. The ten thousand things enlighten us. When we encounter one another, delusion and enlightenment are both present and absent. When we encounter the Buddhas, similarly. Faith (shraddha — literally "heartedness") is what enables a person to stay in this flow of encounters, in which delusion and light alternate and through which Dharma enters the world. Thus how we encounter others is our practice. Yet in every encounter we are stirred up. Rising passion (samudaya) overwhelms us. How can we turn such passion into the path? When religious consciousness is already established, we are meeting the sambhogakaya every moment.

The Key to Practice

How then is it to be established? One needs a key. Each school of spirituality provides keys of various kinds. For Pureland Buddhists the key is nembutsu. The nembutsu is to call on Amida Buddha, who is the embodiment of the sambhogakaya. Namo Amida Bu!

Good things happen — Namo Amida Bu! Bad things happen — Namo Amida Bu. Meeting a friend — Namo Amida Bu. Encountering an enemy — Namo Amida Bu. Seeing a stranger — Namo Amida Bu.

In the nembutsu are the three bodies of Buddha, the three bodies of Dharma, the three bodies of Sangha. Therefore, in the nembutsu is all merit. Thus, in all encounters is all merit.

Although we talk of the effectiveness of this or that method, the great masters were enlightened in moments of encounter. When any aspect of the trikaya is present in our encounter with another, then the Dharma Light is present. Keep turning the key and the sambhogakaya will take up residence in your heart. Then all will happen naturally. Namo Amida Bu.

Ya Ya Ya

The First Sutra

The Majjhima Nikaya is an important collection of Buddha's teachings. The very first sutta in that collection is, therefore, of some special importance. However one rarely hears it mentioned. This may be in part because it is highly repetitive and because the point it makes is a very simple one. However, both these facts tell us that this point was fundamental. Buddha wants to push the point home because everything else depends upon it.

The sutra is called Mulapariyaya. Mula refers to something being basic or fundamental and pariyaya means going on and on, repetition. You can almost hear it in the word — ya-ya-ya. This sutra exposes our basic ya-ya-ya, and it is at the beginning because it is the root of all the rest.

I notice that in the Ñanamoli and Bodhi translation, which is the most commonly used one now in English, it says in the introductory summary that this sutra is too difficult for a beginner to understand and, therefore, to not pay too much attention initially but come back to it later. I think this is not correct. You can make it complicated if you want to, but doing so avoids the main argument.

A Cup of Tea

The basic purpose of the sutra is to make clear the difference between an enlightened person and a worldling. This, after all, is what Buddha's teaching was about. The Buddha tells us that the enlightened person and the worldling may both experience the elements, earth, air, fire and water as what they are. This now sounds esoteric, but what he is saying is that both experience ordinary life in the material world. A cup is a cup (earth). The tea in it is tea (water). The steam above it is steam (air). The cup is hot (fire) to both of them. The elements are just all in a cup of tea. Enlightenment does not mean that one no longer can enjoy a cup of tea, nor does it mean that one sees the tea in an especially different way. Buddha says that both "see earth as earth as it is."

Now, this is a first very simple point. I don't know how many times I have read in spiritual books or heard in talks by spiritual people, that the enlightened person sees things as they are whereas the worldling does not. Not so, says the Buddha. Both see the same earth and see it as it is.

The Main Point: Self

What then is the difference? The difference is that the worldling then goes on to think, "I like tea, this tea is mine, I am a tea drinker" or he or she goes on to think, "Tea is not to my taste," or "Where is my tea?" or "I'm not a tea drinker," or things of this kind and when he thinks these kinds of things they are of importance to him or her. They are important because to the worldling the self is more important than the tea.

Both experience earth as earth, tea as tea and so on, but to the worldling what matters is his own relationship to it and what it says about himself, whereas, for the enlightened person, these thoughts do not occur, or if something like them occurs it is in a purely objective sense. In other words he is able to investigate the taste of tea without becoming self-invested in the matter.

This is the basic teaching of non-self. It is not that non-self is a mental state. Non-self means other. The enlightened person is focussed on the other, whether the other is a person, a cup of tea, the earth element, whatever.

Not a Technique

It is true, of course, that the enlightened person does, therefore, often have a fuller experience of things than the worldling who is so lost in fantasies about him or herself that much of life passes in a blur. By extension, if you get the worldling to do attentional exercises and really focus upon the cup of tea, then he will get a momentary sample of how an enlightened person experiences a cup of tea.

However, the ability to taste tea in the here and now is not enlightenment — anybody can do it. This will not make him an awakened sage. Why not? Because he will then start to think things like "I'm quite good at this mindfulness business," or "I'm not the kind of person who can do these exercises," or "Doing this exercise was my idea in the first place," or "I've now got mindfulness in my repertoire so I'll now be a happier and more effective person," or other things like that, which are all self-infested, whereas the enlightened person will not get drawn into such thoughts.

Worldly People Talk to God too

In the sutra, the Buddha goes further. Not only does the worlding experience the cup of tea as a cup of tea, she might also experience God as God or all the gods as gods, or see angels as angels or heaven as heaven and so on. So it is not that the enlightened person necessarily sees higher things that the worldling does not see. It is not that the enlightened person has interviews with God whereas the worldling does not.

What is the difference, then? The difference is that the enlightened person does not then get self-infatuated over the idea, "I'm the kind of person who talks with gods." They don't contrive to drop into the conversation, as if it were nothing, "Well, as God told me,..." He does not think, "I must be a rather special person that God speaks to me." When the god Brahma Sahampati told Shakyamuni to go forth for the good of the many, for the salvation of gods and humans, he did not think "That must mean I'm a special kind of guy," he just thought, "Yes, you're right, OK, here goes."

If you are a signed up modern Buddhist you might not appreciate this bit about gods, of course, but in the sutra Buddha then goes on to list all the higher dhyanas in similar fashion. Dhyanas are the stages of meditative absorption. The worldling may experience the fifth dhyana and know it for what it is, may experience the sixth dhyana, even the seventh dhyana. A deluded person may experience the eighth and final dhyana, know it for what it is, and still be completely deluded.

Again, we can ask, how many spiritual books tell us that the difference between the truly spiritual person and the non-spiritual one is that the spiritual one experiences these higher states and the worldly one doesn't? Not so, says the Buddha. All these dhyana states are available to the worldling and, furthermore, the worldling sees them for what they are as they really are. It says so in the sutra in so many words. Ñanamoli and Bodhi translate these higher dhyanas as "infinite space," "infinite consciousness," and "neither perception nor non-perception" — the lot. You can experience all eight dhyanas and still be a complete worldling.

So what is the real difference? The real difference is that the enlightened person does not go on to think "These dhyanas are mine, now," does not just let it slip out, "Well, when I was in the seventh dhyana, you know..." He does not become self-invested and the dhyanas do not become self-infested. She may think "So what is this dhyana? Why? How? What now?" but she is not caught in it in terms of sensual gratification, conceit or opinionatedness.

Ego Vermin

These three are the main dimensions of ego from the Buddhist point of view: 1. sensual indulgence or preciousness in the derogatory sense of the term, 2. conceit, which may be positive or negative, i.e. I am better or I am worse, and includes all the range of exaggerated self-identities, pride and embarrassment that we so easily fall into and 3. opinionatedness, which is undue attachment to fixed views. These three are our ya-ya-ya.

So, enlightenment is characterised by non-ego, not by the attainment of higher states, participating in religious or worldly experiences of a particular quality, being able to be in the here and now, knowing the elements each as it is, or anything of the kind. It is to not invest self in everything we touch. Self is the vermin of the mind and our mind vermin get out and infect the world.

Liberation

We can imagine that Buddha had to deal with a lot of people who came to him telling him about their spiritual attainments, or all the divine visions and firework shows they had witnessed, the practices they had mastered, or rehearsing to him their strongly held beliefs or opinions about this, that or the other. He did not agree. He did not refute. His point was and is: that is not the point.

The point is the personal trip that one is on in telling such things, whether one is telling oneself or telling others. What Buddha is saying in this first sutra is that all kinds of experiences are available to worldly people and spiritual people alike, that being spiritually awakened is not a matter of getting the right experience, talking to God, doing the right meditation, perfecting awareness, or whatever; it is a matter of not tripping out on it, whatever it is. There is life. There is the experience of life, sacred beyond ordinary comprehension. Then there is the ya-ya-ya that goes on and on by which we feed the vermin of ego and thus infest the world.

On Becoming Ippen

Ippen is known as the founder of the Ji Shu, an important school of Pureland Buddhism. Here I will tell the story of his early life up to the time when he took the name Ippen. In following this story we can understand some of his spiritual realisations and dilemmas.

Early Life and First Going Forth

Ippen was born on the island of Shikoku in the south of Japan. He came from a samurai family that had seen both glory and defeat. His father, Michihiro, gave up the samurai life and became a Buddhist priest in order to pray for members of his family who had died in the wars. Michihiro's Dharma name was Nyobutsu.

Nyobutsu went to Kyoto and became a disciple of Shōkū (1177-1247), who was a leading disciple of Honen (1133-1212), the founder of the Pureland School (Jodo Shu) in Japan. When he returned to Shikoku Nyobutsu married and set up a Pureland temple. His second son was born in 1239 and called Shōjumaru. This boy was the one who would be later known as Ippen.

In 1248 Nyobutsu's wife, Shōjumaru's mother, died. Shortly afterwards, aged nine, Shōjumaru became a monk in the Tendai School. In 1251 he travelled to the main island of Japan to study Pureland with Shōdatsu

(1203-1279) another important disciple of Shōkū and a friend of Nyobutsu.

Second Going Forth: The Non-duality of Ten and One

In 1263 Nyobutsu died and Shōjumaru went back home to assume family responsibilities. He married and became immersed in family life. However, one day, while playing with children spinning a top, he had an awakening moment. He realised that samsara is like the top. If you keep whipping it it keeps spinning, but if you stop whipping it it slows down, falls over and stops.

In 1271, Shōjumaru, now 32 years old, was caught up in a violent incident in which he nearly lost his life. Attacked by four armed men and seriously wounded he fought back, disarmed one of the assailants and fled. At this point he decided to once again go forth from the household life and he went once again to see Shōdatsu. This meeting seems to have led him to reassess the practice he had formerly done with this teacher, coming to the conclusion that it had been a period of self-power effort on his part.

He left Shōdatsu and went on to the temple of Zenkōji at Nagano, a temple associated with Shōkū, the teacher of Shōdatsu and Nyobutsu. During his retreat at Zenkōji Shōjumaru made a copy of the painting of the White Path between the Rivers of Fire and Water, an important Pureland icon. This retreat had a profound effect upon him and we can see the seeds of much of his later work in his experience there. At Zenkōji he met hijiri (wandering holy men) and he encountered the practice of distributing fuda, papers on which the six syllables of the nembutsu were printed. The Zenkōji temple still exists and I have visited it. It is closely associated with the notion that it is the ordinary deluded person who is saved by Amida.

He then returned to Shikoku and made himself a hermitage hut. He placed the painting on the east wall. He then dedicated himself to continuous nembutsu practice for three years, imitating, thereby, a three year retreat that had been done many years before by Shōkū. During this time he summed up his understanding in the following verse, entitled "The Non-duality of Ten and One"

> Perfect enlightenment ten kalpas
>   old pervades the realm of sentient
>   beings.
>
> In ichinen is birth in Amida's land.
>
> When ten and one are not different,
>   no-birth is actualised.
>
> When land and realm are the same,
>   we sit in Amida's great
>   congregation.

I have left the word ichinen untranslated because it can be rendered in several over-lapping ways. Ichi means one or singular. Nen, as in nembutsu, means thought, remembrance and mindfulness. So ichinen can mean one thought moment, or wholehearted mindfulness, or a single recitation of nembutsu, or simply sincerity of heart.

It is a key term in Ippen's teaching often carrying all of these meanings simultaneously.

The non-duality of ten and one means the unity of immediacy and eternity. Ten refers to Amida's enlightenment which transcends time and space while one refers to the singularity of a moment of pure hearted utterance of the Name. The meaning is very close to William Blake's "to see a World in a Grain of Sand... and Eternity in an hour." This is one way of expressing religious consciousness transcending particular doctrines.

Becoming a Hijiri

Shōjumaru then left his hermitage and went deeper into the mountains to an area noted for yamabushi (mountain ascetics) in order to pray for clarity and guidance. He is said to have had many important dreams during this time.

After this further retreat he returned home briefly, gathered together some basic essentials and a few key scriptures and then took to the road, never again to live in a house. He set out together with three companions who are believed to have included his wife and daughter.

They first went to Shitennō-ji, a Pureland pilgrimage site (in present day Osaka). Here he conceived the intention to spread the nembutsu to the whole population of the country. Honen said that Amida vows to save every person who says the nembutsu even once. Shōjumaru, therefore, resolved to save beings by getting them to utter the nembutsu once. "Once nembutsu" or "One time nembutsu" is, in Japanese, ippen nembutsu.

He adopted the practice of approaching people, saying the nembutsu, inviting them to say it, then giving them a fuda. They could then, if they wished, use the fuda as an object of worship in a home shrine.

In his thinking, the one utterance automatically invoked the ten kalpas of Amida's enlightenment. In other words, one moment of sincerity was direct connection with an eternity of grace. The fuda constituted evidence of the person's acceptance by Amida and also, of course, connected the practitioner with the holy man.

The Arising of Great Doubt

From Shitennō-ji a pilgrimage route led to Mount Koya and it was natural for the party to go on. Koya is the holy mountain of Shingon Buddhism and is where the founder of Shingon, Kukai is entombed and believed to be still alive in deep samadhi waiting for the arrival of Maitreya, the Buddha of the future. Shingon means "true word" and in the thirteenth century for many people the true word was the nembutsu. Koya was thus, at that time, another great centre for hijiri and a natural place for the group of four to go to pay respect to the great bodhisattva.
Beyond Mount Koya, in a southerly direction, the pilgrimage trail goes toward the great Shinto shrine of Kumano. At this stage of Japanese history, the supreme deity of Shinto had come to be regarded by many as a manifestation of Amida Buddha, so widely had the

nembutsu teaching spread. On the way to Kumano, however, an incident occurred that threw Shōjumaru into doubt.

On the road he met a Ritsu monk. Ritsu is the vinaya school of Japanese Buddhism. Ippen offered the monk a fuda, saying, "Accept this, awaken ichinen, say Namu Amida Butsu." The monk said, "I cannot do so. At present ichinen faith does not arise in me. If I take the fuda I will be breaking my precept against telling a lie."

Shōjumaru said, "Don't you believe the Buddha's teaching? Please take the fuda," but the monk replied "I have no doubt about the teaching but there is nothing I can do about the fact that faith does not arise in me."

By this time a goodly crowd of pilgrims had gathered around. Ippen realised that if the monk did not take the fuda the others would not do so either. He therefore said to the monk, "Even if you don't have faith, please accept the fuda." The monk did so and in due course so did the other pilgrims. The whole incident had, however, thrown Shōjumaru into a turmoil.

Some of the dilemma here turns on the meaning of ichinen. Ichinen can mean one nembutsu, so the request can be taken as, "Please say one nembutsu and I will give you a fuda." However the monk takes ichinen to mean "with sincerity of heart" and he realises that as yet he does not find such faith in himself. Rather than be dishonest, he elects not to receive the fuda. Is nembutsu only real when uttered with sincere faith?

Encountering the God

Shōjumaru was much affected by this incident and believed that it must have happened for a reason. He went on to Kumano and prayed there for guidance. Was his mission misguided? Was he asking people to be insincere and colluding in lies by getting all and sundry to say the nembutsu? Should the monk have taken the fuda or not? What a bundle of dilemmas!

Sitting in the main hall at Kumano, he had a vision. A yamabushi with white hair and a long hood appeared before him. Behind him a host of other yamabushi all prostrated. Shōjumaru realised that this must be the deity of the shrine. The yamabushi god spoke, "Hijiri! Spreading the yuzu nembutsu*, why do you do so in the wrong manner? It is not through your effort that sentient beings attain birth (in the Pure Land). In Amida Buddha's complete enlightenment ten kalpas ago all that was needed for the salvation of beings was already settled and is Namo Amida Butsu. Do not discriminate between the pure and the impure. Give the fuda regardless of whether people have faith of not."

The vision faded away and Shōjumaru found himself surrounded by many children who had come to receive fuda. They took the slips of paper and all ran off saying "Namu Amida Butsu! Namu Amida Butsu!"

---

* yuzu nembutsu: a form of nembutsu in which practitioners believed their recitation would help others.

From this time on Shōjumaru called himself Ippen and it is by this name that we know him to this day. In the single moment, there is no self-power. The vision at the Kumano Shrine finally broke Ippen's attachment to self-power. Even though he had transcended his desire to practice for his own salvation, still he had been stuck with a different kind of hubris, the belief that by his power he could save all others.

Some Reflections

Ippen gives us a fascinating example of a faith that cares little or nothing for sectarian boundaries. He follows his father's Pureland faith, but initially does so in a Tendai temple. Later he studies with Pureland teachers and has a major revelation at Zenkōji but goes on to have further insights at the Shingon mountain and his most impressive experience occurs in a temple that is not even Buddhist. He can be said to bring together the Way of the Buddhas and the Way of the Gods. He is also sensitive to holy places and makes his whole life into a pilgrimage.

The succession of stages in his early spiritual development show us a series of steps from self-power to other-power. At the Tendai temple and under Shōdatsu he studied nembutsu teachings but when he later reflects upon it he sees that he did so in a self-power manner. When he goes to Zenkōji he receives a more direct inspiration of the spirit of Shōkū and this precipitates him into doing his own hermitage nembutsu retreat with the White Path icon. This leads him to a doctrinal conviction expressed in the non-duality of ten and one, which releases him from the need to seek his own individual salvation, but he realises that he still needs guidance and goes off into the mountains where he finds some further resolve. This leads him to the hijiri path and he sets out on his endless pilgrimage, hoping to live up to the ideal of saving all sentient beings. Then he has the encounter with the Ritsu monk (Quan Yin in disguise?) which leads him to his pivotal encounter at the Kumano Shrine where he faces the ambition involved even in this high ideal.

Each person has a path and the stories of great exemplars show us examples. Each of us has to walk his own way, but the kinds of challenges and dilemmas that we encounter are essentially similar. Whether we say nembutsu or sit in zazen, whether we recite the mantras of Shingon or say the prayers of Shinto, whether we live in a house, a temple or walk the highroad as a hijiri, we all face the barriers created by pride, ambition and conceit and the challenges of loss, violence, attachment, separation and failure. In becoming Ippen, Shōjumaru found his own way to celebrate ten kalpas of perfect enlightenment in each single utterance of the Holy Name.

Refuge

In the Ekottaragama Sutra it says:

> Beings who take refuge in Buddha
>
> Do not fall into lower rebirth
>
> They cease from excess and dwell with humans and gods
>
> And will arrive at nirvana
>
> The essence of Buddhism is refuge

Dogen Zenji says:

> "What the Buddhist patriarchs have authentically transmitted is reverence for Buddha, Dharma and Sangha. If we do not take refuge in them, we do not revere them and if we do not revere them we do not take refuge in them."
> Kie Sanbo in Nichijima and Cross 1999 Shobogenzo, Book 4

Many people these days think that Buddhism is a form of personal growth or a method of self enhancement. This is in order that one can protect oneself. However, the main thing in Buddhism is to give up protecting oneself and take refuge in Buddha. Then one can go forth with open hands and an open heart and no matter what befalls, one will arrive at nirvana in the end, not by one's own power, but because those who have such faith naturally receive boundless grace.

Prayers of the Heart

Nembutsu and the Jesus Prayer

In a previous chapter I wrote of the nembutsu as a key by which to access the trikaya Buddha. I said that other spiritual paths have other keys. One such is surely the Jesus Prayer of Christians.

The form of this prayer is:

> Lord Jesus Christ, son of God, have mercy upon me a sinner.

It is sometimes shortened to:

> Jesus have mercy.

or:

> Lord, make haste to save me.

I think we can readily see a close similarity between the nembutsu and the Jesus Prayer. Both act as a link between the ordinary being and the spiritual world of saving power.

In the case of Buddhists this saving power is attributed to Amitabha Buddha (Amida). In the case of Christians it is attributed to Jesus on behalf of God.

In terms of the logic of the trikaya, Jesus on Earth is the nirmanakaya while Jesus in heaven is a form of sambhogakaya, manifesting to the ordinary believer as the Holy Spirit.

"Namo" literally means "I call upon". When we say "Namo" one is indicating oneself as the one calling, "I call", as the foolish being in need of enlightenment and salvation. In Christianity this is equivalent to "me a sinner". In Japanese, the nearest term to sinner is akunin, literally "bad-person", and Pureland Buddhists often use this term to indicate the kind of person that is the special object of Amida's love.

Christians use the term "mercy" because they have a concept of a judgement. This is a little different from Buddhism, since in Buddhism there is no judge, but it is certainly the case that Amida is believed to rescue beings who through their own foolishness would otherwise fall foul of the terrible consequences of karma.

There is, therefore, an important parallelism between these two practices. Both are seen as forms of unceasing prayer and practised as such.

As far as we know the Jesus Prayer originates in the sixth century when it was taught in Egypt by Diadochos. He taught it as a means of arriving at inner peace. In Buddhist terms, we can say that it was a form of samatha meditation leading to anshin. Anshin literally means peaceful mind, with the implication of settled faith.

Was the Christian practice influenced by Buddhism? We do not know. It is possible. Religions are always borrowing from one another and, in the time before the rise of Islam, there probably was Buddhist influence in Egypt. We cannot say. It does not really matter because what impresses is the manner in which these parallel practices have won the allegiance of millions of practitioners in both religions over the centuries during periods when the two religions had no contact with one another, so even if there were an unknown common origin it has stood the test of time in both domains separately.

For Christians this is the way to draw near to God. It is called the Prayer of the Heart. For Buddhists this is the way to allow Amida into our hearts and thereby connect ourselves with all the Buddhas. It is the most direct expression of shraddha (shinjin) which is faith.

In the Taoist classic it says "with desire, one sees boundaries; without desire, one sees into its wonder". Forms differ. The core is the same. Emphasising difference we demonstrate our superficiality. When we go beyond attachment to this or that group we see into the wonderful foundation of it all.

Radiant Face

In the morning service at Amida Shu temples and gatherings there is a passage that begins "Your radiant face, like a mountain peak catching the first burst of morning light, has awesome and unequalled majesty." It's the first verse of a short text called Tan Butsu Ge*, which is a section of the Larger Pureland Sutra.

'Tan Butsu Ge' literally means Song in Praise of the Buddha. In this case it is the Buddha Lokeshvararaja who lived an immense time ago in an altogether different world, perhaps a different universe. The song is sung in the sutra by Dharmakara Bodhisattva who subsequently, much much later, becomes Amitabha Buddha. It expresses his delight and astonishment on meeting the Buddha and tells how he is inspired by this meeting to enter the Buddha Way.

Radiant Appearance

This story of Dharmakara meeting Lokeshvararaja is told by the Buddha Shakyamuni to Ananda. The incident reflects the opening of the encounter between Ananda and Shakyamuni themselves. Ananda similarly has been struck by the radiant appearance of Shakyamuni. He says, "Oh Blessed One, I do not ever recall seeing the Tathagata so serene, purified, cleansed and radiant as I do today. This thought occurs to me 'Today the Tathagata dwells in the sphere of the most rare Dharma! The sphere of the Buddhas! ...The Buddhas of the three times contemplate one another. Could it be that you are now bringing to mind all the other Buddhas? Are you gazing upon the tathagatas, arhats, Samyak Sambuddhas of the past, the future, and the present?' Is that why your august

---

*Page 6, Nien Fo Book: The service book of Amida Shu, Amida Shu, 2018

presence shines with such radiance today?" and the Buddha replies, "You are right, Ananda, you are right."

You can tell a lot from a face. My companions here tell me that they can tell when my illness[*] is worse and when it is less bad because they can see it in my face. When I am bad, my energy withdraws inside and the face darkens. When I am well the opposite happens. Sometimes we see somebody that we are familiar with and we think, "Either he is in love, or he just won the lottery." A radiance is evident to everybody.

Such radiance tells us the inner state of a person. It is also infectious. In the famous Fred Astair song, *They Can't Take That Away From Me*, one of the things he treasures is "The way your face just beams." When somebody has that radiance we all benefit, feel lifted and liberated. This is the effect that a Buddha has.

Receiving and Giving

How is it that a Buddha is so often radiant? The sutra tells us. The Buddha is radiant because he is receiving radiance himself. He has a mind full of the Buddhas of past, future and present. This is the real meaning of mindfulness. What energy comes out of us depends upon what energy goes into us and this is substantially a question of what we have in mind. Sometimes the mind is necessarily preoccupied with pressing difficulties. Sometimes it is full

---

[*] Written in 2016, when Dharmavidya was recovering from a pulmonary embolism.

of the joy of love. The more troubles we carry around, the less opportunity we have to soak up the love.

The Buddha, therefore, recommended a simple life so as to give more space to contemplate the myriad Buddhas. In the Pratyutpanna Samadhi Sutra it says that the person who practises the samadhi sees Buddhas everywhere. This is religious consciousness — it is what all good religions instil. The terminology may vary but the basic inculcation of an openness to divine light is universally the same. Allowing in the radiant face that smiles upon us from every direction results in our own face lightening up. In this way we can all be mirrors for the moonlight of the Dharma. In this way we bring happiness to one another — "their hearts will lighten and be joyful, happy and at ease."

We say that in the scriptures, light is a symbol for wisdom, but it is more than just a symbol and not just a metaphor — there really is light in the face of a person who receives the Dharma, just as there is spring in her step and song in her voice. Similarly, Tan Butsu Ge talks about "The melody of your enlightenment." This radiance is a kind of visual music and when we are affected by it we want to sing, just as Dharmakara sings in the sutra. The other day when we were all in the Aphrodite Field together and the sun was shining his smiling face upon us, we started chanting, and the song of Buddha's enlightenment filled the world. Tan Butsu Ge.

The Koan of Shakyamuni

The Importance of Being Disturbed

When we look at the life of Shakyamuni Buddha, we see that his early life was consumed in self-indulgence. Then we read the story of the 'Four Sights'. He went out of his palace and saw a sick person, an old person, a corpse, and then a holy man. The first three sights disturbed him deeply and the fourth gave him the idea that he could be a better person than he was.

So we can say that Gotama's question was, "Why is there birth, old age, sickness and death?" But then we can ask why was this his question? Why was he so troubled by what he saw that day? The answer is that this was a reality that he had been hiding from. Self-indulgence is one way of hiding. Why did he feel the need to hide from this question? Because of the question behind the question which, in his case, was, "Why did my mother have to die?" His mother had died seven days after his birth.

Koan Means a Universal Spiritual Problem in Personal Form

When we phrase it this way, we can see how the koan refers to a universal problem (impermanence) yet manifests in a deeply personal matter (his mother's death). Why did my mother have to die has two aspects. "Why did this happen to me?" and "Am I guilty?"

The second of these questions then led Siddhartha into several years of penance. He joined the ascetics and practised torturing himself in an effort to neutralise or pay off his bad karma.

The two questions are like two sides of a coin. If you look at your own question you will probably find that it breaks down in a similar way, one half being to do with self-pity and the other with self-condemnation.

You have probably learnt that koans are insoluble spiritual riddles. In a sense this is true, but we should not let that idea fool us about how personal, penetrating and significant they are. Was Siddhartha guilty? His birth brought about his mother's death. So, in one sense yes and in one sense no. Why did it happen to him? Fate? Bad luck? Karma? There is no clear answer.

Koans Defeat Us

Thus koans are not something that we solve. It is truer to say that they are the things that defeat us. That defeat is what we need. Until the ego is defeated it will go on running our life. When the ego has been defeated, there is no need to go on grousing about life any more, and also no need to get oneself fixed. Thus a huge amount of energy that is normally wasted is saved and can be applied in more constructive ways.

When he was enlightened, Shakyamuni realised that it was not a question of how life was treating him, but of how he was treating it. In order to treat it well, he needed to have the faith to drop the idea that he himself needed fixing before he could do anything. Being set on curing one's own guilt complex could go on for the rest of this lifetime, at the end of which one would just feel more guilty because of having wasted so much time that could have been spent doing better things.

All the practices he had adopted up to that point had been designed to sort himself out by paying off his own karma or attaining particular mind states. In the enlightenment experience he realised that Mara would always be there, that you could experience all the higher mind states and still be deluded, and that moods and emotions come and go like the weather depending on conditions.

Fixing by Not Fixing

Suddenly seeing all this, seeing that all the products of Mara were just life's decorations, understanding the difference between things that come and go according to conditions on the one hand and things that remain eternally true on the other, enabled him to reorient his life. From then on he was able to enjoy life for what it is and help others in a natural way. He was no longer frightened of life because he was no longer trying and failing to make it into something different.

In a sense, he fixed himself by giving up the idea of fixing himself and/or fixing the world. After that he was able to live a constructive life, a noble life in the world as it is, which included many good deeds for others. It also included going home and making his peace with the family he had walked out on some years before. Instead of using up all his time indulging or torturing himself he founded a religious movement that would endure more than 25 centuries, helped innumerable other people, gave teachings that would inspire whole civilisations, and became one of the most loved and respected people on the planet.

Faith is Enlightenment, Enlightenment is Faith

Generally, in Buddhist circles, it is said that you need faith in order to enter upon the Dharma Way but when you have progressed you don't need faith anymore because it is replaced by knowledge and wisdom, but... Faith is wisdom and complete wisdom is complete faith.

What Do You Know?

In the common view, knowledge and faith are taken as mutually exclusive. Faith is what you need when you don't know. So when you know you won't need faith. However, what is it that you come to know? In fact, you come to really, really know that you don't know. So faith is IT.

Right now you think that you don't know, but a big part of you thinks that you are really clever as clever, and God or mummy or whoever just hasn't realised yet just how clever you are. The well of self-conceit is very deep.

The Pit

How are we to deal with this deep well? There are many spiritual practices that purport to tell us how to fill in the well and concrete over the top. People join and start digging. After a while of shovelling earth into the pit they stop and have a look and it looks as big as ever. Then the instructor says, "Well, it takes a long time." In fact, a few myriad kalpas, so keep digging. Right? Wrong. The pit has no bottom.

Well, it is certainly true that those practices will give you something — many things in fact — self-discipline, patience, stress-relief, and so on, just as shovelling into a bottomless pit will strengthen your muscles and, maybe, teach you some patience — and those things are all certainly worth having. After a while most people who go on practising are doing so for those benefits primarily, but something is still missing. Filling in the well can come to be a rather fixed focus and in becoming attached to one's practice one runs the risk of becoming intolerant, and rather narrow.

Getting Too Square

Buddhism in the West started to flourish in the hippy period — it was a happy part of flower power — but now that it is putting down roots, in contrast to the early days, it already has the reputation of being somewhat puritanical. Buddhists are those people who won't let you have any fun anymore. It's no longer a happening — it risks becoming squarer than square.

Is there another way? The puritan streak is a function of believing that one can do God's job oneself. At the end of that road God has been forgotten altogether, and, unfortunately, the world is no more spiritual than before. That is not what Buddha taught. In Buddhism we don't say God, we say Dharma and the Dharmakaya, we say the Buddha Tao, the Unborn, Amaravati, there are any number of names for the Nameless. It is not naming it that matters, it is having faith in it.

Clinging is Anxiety

The Buddhist texts talk a lot about giving up clinging. Clinging, and its associated anxiety, is the opposite of faith. It is like being in the swimming pool and being unwilling to let go of the rail on the side. In order to float one has to relax. When you can float you can say "I have faith that the water will hold me up," or you can say "I know from experience that the water will hold me up." It is the same thing. Faith and knowledge merge. Our faith is based on experience and when it is solid we call it knowledge.

The puritan impulse, however, is really a clinging to false certainty. One becomes overly convinced that one is on the right track and by one's own effort one can achieve everything necessary. This was the condition of Shakyamuni during his period of asceticism. Deep down he thought he knew better than his parents, his teachers, his companions, everybody. Result — disaster.

The person of wise faith knows that they do not know where the road is taking them. They know something is happening and they are willing, that's all. With willingness, one can play one's part. Then things happen. But one can never pre-determine the outcome —

there are too many variables. Nonetheless, as all the ancient texts say, there are bigger forces at work and one can trust them. They are reliable.

Vast Ignorance

In awakening, faith is not replaced by wisdom, wisdom is faith. Faith is not replaced by knowledge — the knowledge that one gains is knowledge of the immensity of one's ignorance. That is what truly boggles the mind and allows faith to find its proper place. When one has been completely boggled in this way, there is no need to fill in the well. Throw down the shovel. Or use it as a dancing partner. Be like the characters in the Pratyutpanna Samadhi Sutra who, when they hear the Dharma, are so ecstatic they dance on tip toe. That's faith. That is also dhyana, samadhi, and liberation.

Go pick flowers, then visit each other's wells and decorate them, and laugh and laugh. Then the gods will give you wings.

The Meaning of Tathagata

The Sanskrit word Tathagata is one of the common epithets of Buddha. In Japanese it is 'Nyorai'.

The word can be construed as Tatha-gata or as Tatha-agata.

Tatha is sometimes rendered into English as the neologism "Thusness" which renders the word into a sort of English without making the meaning particularly clear and leaving a nice ambiguity.

If you want a rather secular, materialistic interpretation of Buddhism, then you can take thusness as meaning "things as they are" and say that the tathagata is one who sees things as they actually are — however you think that that is.

However, in the context of Indian religion this probably does not work unless by "things as they actually are" you mean how they are in the eyes of God. The word Tatha derives from "tat" which in common speech means "that". At first sight this look innocuous enough. However, the key slogan of traditional Indian religion is "Tat tvam asi" which means "Thou art That" where That means God, Brahma.

The basic meaning of this slogan is that the fundamental part of a person is a fragment of God and the purpose of religion is that all those fragments be ultimately reunited with Brahma. There can be little doubt that the Buddhist use of Tat and Tatha were framed within this kind of perspective but with a shift of meaning.

In Pali, we also say "Namo Tassa". Here Tassa is also a derivative of the same root. This phrase means "I take refuge in That One", That One being the Buddha. All of these phrases attribute a divine dimension to Buddha. Modern people do not like this and try to argue their way around it. They prefer to emphasise that Siddhartha Gotama was a human being. This is due to the intense humanism of our age. However, it is a misreading of Buddhism. Buddhism does not think of divinity in the same way as we are used to in monotheistic religions, but nonetheless, it is the spiritual presence of Buddha that is considered important — more important than God, in fact.

What impressed his followers in Asian history was not how human he was but precisely the other aspect — how divine, or more-than-divine, he seemed. Clearly he had something about him that was not common, not ordinary, not just like everybody else, and that "something" is what is called Tat or Tatha — "That" or "Thatness". It is That in which Buddhists take refuge.

Now let us look at the other half of the word Tathagata. "Gata" means gone. If we read the whole word this way then it means that the Buddha has gone to the transcendent domain, the spiritual world, the sphere that Buddhists are forbidden to speculate about but which clearly is intended to be taken as being wonderful, marvellous and consummate, the goal of the spiritual life.

So if Buddha is the "One Gone to That Domain" then our task is to exert ourselves to do what he did and follow. This is the self-power approach to Buddhism. The rousing slogan of this philosophy is "The Buddhas do but point the way; thou must walk the path alone; strive on with diligence."

However, Tathagata can also be scanned as Tatha-agata. Agata means come. Now, in this approach, Buddha is the one who has come from the transcendent realm. In this view, Buddha has come to help and save us. This is the other-power perspective on Buddhism. When Buddha comes to us in this way, our part is to receive him, be grateful, open ourselves, be humble and receptive. The Japanese term Nyorai definitely means Tatha-agata, since "rai" in Japanese means "come". So Japanese Buddhism, not just in the Pureland Schools, is shot through with an other-power perspective. The slogan here is, perhaps, the haiku of Honen Shonin that reads: "The moon shines into every hamlet in the land, but only those who gaze upon it carry it in their hearts."

Of course, although particular schools of Buddhism may have different emphases, some mix of self-power and other-power is always apparent in practice. They are like the yang and yin of Buddhism. Tathagata comes to us, Tathagata walks ahead, sometimes glancing back. Tathagata urges us forward along the narrow path. There are many images, each picking up a different aspect of how we are helped. Different people need different things and the same person has different needs at different stages. The Buddhas are not limited by our concepts. Their compassion extends limitlessly.

Five Points on Impermanence

Buddhism makes much of 'impermanence'. This has several aspects to it.

1. These teachings tell us that all the conditions that we meet within samsara are fragile. Whatever circumstances we may build our expectations upon, they can never be wholly relied upon. Simply recognising this can lead us to be more 'philosophical' when things do not work out as we expect. You might campaign for one thing and the other eventuates — are you going to mope, or grasp the nettle?

2. The Buddha saw beings 'rising and falling according to their deeds'. Sometimes people seem to be doing well, yet are unhappy inside. Sometimes others seem to be doing badly, yet have inner strength. It is difficult to tell the inner story but it manifests in what people actually do. Actions speak louder than words. As conditions unfold over time each person is tested and the quality of their life bears fruit. Sometimes one gets one's comeuppance. We can have sympathy.

3. Teachings on impermanence also impart urgency. Time is short. We only have this human body for a brief period. It is no use waiting for the right conditions to show up. This is it. If we are going to have a meaningful life, this is the time to get on with it.

4. Whatever disaster befalls, whatever terrible circumstance arises, it will pass. A storm rarely lasts all day. Therefore we should cultivate patience. Don't get caught up in ignoble words and deeds that are but the froth of the moment. Take a longer term view.

5. Impermanence offers no permanent succour. While engaging with impermanent conditions, it is also important to seek a more reliable refuge. Not everything is impermanent. Buddhism orients us to nirvana. By having faith that transcends the impermanent world we find the core of the Dharma.

These five points, to be philosophical, to have sympathy, to not waste time, to be patient and to seek a true refuge go the heart of the matter.

Dragon Pearl – The Story of Nagarjuna

Nagarjuna is counted as one of the most important and influential thinkers in Buddhist history and all the major schools of Mahayana Buddhism claim him as a founding figure. On the one hand, he can be seen as an original thinker who put into circulation the ideas that later became the core of Mahayana — emptiness, altruism and other-power — yet, on the other hand, it is equally possible to portray him as simply having, with great skill, reiterated the essence of what had been taught by Shakyamuni Buddha, thereby correcting the course of Buddhism and putting it back on track.

There are many stories and legends concerning Nagarjuna. It is said that he was from a rich family and, as a young man, was a bit of a playboy. One day he and two friends decided to climb over the wall of the raja's palace and go to see the women in the harem. According to the story they had found a way to make themselves invisible. However, the guards got wind of what was happening and slashed the air with their swords. Nagarjuna's two friends were both killed. This incident had a deeply troubling and sobering effect upon him.

He decided to turn to religion and began to study. He studied every religion trying to find the meaning of life. In particular, he wanted to find his true nature which he thought of as a kind of precious and eternal pearl within himself. Gradually he became very learned in matters of religion. However, he was dedicated only to his own salvation. To this end he retreated to a hermitage deep in the mountains.

One day the Buddhist sage Kapimala (Japanese: Kabimora) was travelling in the area. The king of the region had given Kapimala the use of a hall some distance from the royal palace in which to practise and teach. Kapimala gave teachings to animals as well as humans and one day he gave the refuges to a python. From the python, Kapimala heard of Nagarjuna as a hermit living at an isolated place much deeper in the mountains where there were no people. Nagarjuna taught the animals and dragons. The name Naga-arjuna implies "triumphant over dragons." If we want to put a symbolic meaning on this we can say that Nagarjuna was concerned with mastering his own dragons in his search for his own inner nature — the bright pearl that he believed was to be found within himself.

Kapimala went to see Nagarjuna. When they met, Nagarjuna wondered if Kapimala was a true sage or not and whether he had found the pearl. Kapimala realised what was on Nagarjuna's mind and said to him that he should not worry about whether he, Kapimala, was an enlighened sage or not, but that he, Nagarjuna, should become a proper monk. We will come back to the inner meaning of this conversation in a minute.

Nagarjuna questioned Kapimala about whether he had the pearl that Nagarjuna was seeking. Kapimala did have the pearl. Nagarjuna wanted to know what the pearl was like. Kapimala said that the pearl was not like anything. This pearl could take any form whatsoever. The jewels of the ordinary world all have aspects, and consequently are not real jewels, but the pearl of the Dharma was beyond having fixed aspects.

The point of all this conversation is that a real monk is, from the perspective of Kapimala, somebody who lives to help others and is willing to take on whatever is necessary in order to do so. He is not somebody who spends his time chasing after his own enlightenment, own Buddha Nature, own realisations or peak experiences or anything of the kind. Nor is he somebody who has overcome all his own dragons and become a great saint necessarily. Nagarjuna wants to know if Kapimala has done what Nagarjuna is trying to do — achieve complete self-mastery and Buddhahood — but Kapimala says, "it really does not matter whether I am such a saint or not. What matters is that you become a proper monk and stop chasing your own spiritual ambition. The pearl that you seek is not the kind that you are looking for. Furthermore, although it is true that this pearl is the most precious in all the world, it is also true that all the world is this pearl." He means that for the true monk there is nothing in the world that is outside of the Dharma, nothing that cannot be the cause and means of saving sentient beings.

Nagarjuna was greatly enlightened by his encounter with Kapimala who evidently did not care whether people regarded him as enlightened or not but was still possessed of the precious pearl of Dharma that has no fixed aspects. This idea of aspectlessness became a central feature of Nagarjuna's teaching in the future. He called it emptiness (shunya). He saw that all systems of rational ideas, even Buddhist ones, become incoherent if you push them to their ultimate conclusion and so can never be a basis for the kind of self-validation that he had been seeking. Broadly Buddhism is concerned with cause and effect, but nothing can be said to be wholly caused by something else nor not caused by anything else. There is an essential freedom. However, although these ideas seem ontological, for Nagarjuna they are soteriological. He is not really setting out a philosophy of the nature of being, but rather one of how people are to be rescued from slavery to their own egotism, which so often takes the form of attachment to views and opinions (drishti).

Like so many other great sages we can see Nagarjuna's enlightenment as falling into two stages. The first stage occurs when his friends are killed. He comes up against impermanence in a way that cuts very deep. At this point he gives up his old ways and devotes himself to religion. He then adopts a method by which he hopes to arrive at his own salvation. Eventually he has his encounter with Kapimala who shows him how his self-power path is missing the point.

Now Nagarjuna became such a great sage — perhaps second in Buddhism only to the Buddha himself — because he realised just how subtle delusion can become. He saw his own spiritual materialism and his teaching thereafter included the most devastating demolition of such self-justifying rationalisation in the whole of Buddhist philosophy.

Nagarjuna's insights were the foundation of Mahayana Buddhist philosophy. It is said that he travelled into the depth of the ocean and received the Prajna Paramita literature from the king of the dragons (Nagas). Interpreting this psychologically we can say that he explored his unconscious and, instead of finding the pearl he thought he was looking for, that would be a kind of ultimate self-justification, what he came up with was shunyata, the essence of prajna paramita, complete freedom from attachment to self-power.

Shunyata, in Nagarjuna's philosophy, is the opposite of svabhava. You can find a huge amount of literature upon these two concepts. Much of this literature takes an ontological rather than a soteriological perspective but, I suggest, in doing so misses the point. Svabhava is not about the presence or absence of a self-defining essence in entities in the world, it is simply another term for self-power. Sva means self and bhava means becoming. Nagarjuna had been trying to make himself into a saint until he met Kapimala. He hoped by doing so to extinguish the passions that had got his friends killed and so very nearly brought disaster to himself. Kapimala had the jewel of the Dharma but was not interested in whether he was a saint or not. The self-creation project (svabhava) was just an irrelevance.

Much of Nagarjuna's writing is in the most extreme level of abstraction and therefore of wide application, but the application that is most pertinent is to the personal spiritual path. When he says that 'there is nothing that arises from itself yet to say that something arises from something else that is not itself is equally incoherent', he is, among other things, saying that one does not wake up spiritually completely by your own effort, yet even if you are awakened by an encounter with somebody else - as he had been - you do not become that person or identical to that person, nor is that person responsible for what has happened to you. The spiritual awakening of each person is unique and yet not independent. One relies upon other power. One does not become the other, one is not the other, and yet what one comes to be is not produced independently of the other either.

Nagarjuna's shunyata is freedom within conditions, not because conditions limit freedom but because conditions are the bright pearl, the substance of the activity that we call Dharma, nirvana appearing in the world. One can always look at the conditioned aspect and see conventional truth (saṃvṛti), or one can look at the unconditioned or ultimate (paramārtha). To live the spiritual life you need both. Again, this is a practical point about the spiritual life. As a "proper monk" in Kapimala's sense, one should be able to deploy all ordinary circumstances in the service of ultimate ends. Religion is about ultimate purposes alive within ordinary life.

According to the Pureland tradition, it was also Nagarjuna who originated the idea of an easy path and a difficult path. Again we can see how this relates to his own life and experience. The difficult path was what he attempted in his hermitage in the mountains, trying to cut off his human nature and defeat all his dragons. That is svabhava, self-power, and it is, as he said, as difficult as crossing the Himalayas on foot unaided. The easy path is one in which one gives up the quest for personal perfection, receives the jewel freely bestowed by the Buddhas, and lives a life of faith, finding the Dharma manifest in all the miscellaneous circumstances of life. Rather than crossing the Himalayas on foot, this is like being carried along by boat.

Centuries later Zen Master Gensa was noted for the phrase "The whole universe in ten directions is one bright pearl" and he used this expression to test the understanding of his students. Those who come into spiritual practice are often, like the young Nagarjuna, thinking that they can find the pearl within themselves, but as Dogen says in Ikka no Myoju "as the mind is not personal, why should we worry whether we have got a right pearl or not got one — even such worry is not separate from the one bright pearl."

More Awe

The End of Awareness

The first stage of Buddhism coming to the West is about finished now. This first stage is the consciousness stage. It has been all about awareness, mindfulness, consciousness, attention, and alertness. We should all be very tired by now. If we have been doing all this attention practice for all these years, then a big part of us must be craving for sleep.

It Would Be Better to Dream More

To sleep, to sleep, perchance to dream. Ever since Hamlet, modern humans have feared the unconscious. We know that Buddhism is about overcoming the ego, but all this consciousness training is essentially just drilling ourselves in more and more clinging to the ego-ideal. It would be better to dream more.

The Unconscious Stage

The next stage, therefore, is the unconscious stage. Some people have already got a little bit of this but mostly the consciousness movement has just got more and more extreme. The idea that consciousness itself is the goal is a kind of madness. Saying that consciousness is the answer to the spiritual problem is like saying that words are the answer to the problem of literature or numbers are the answer to economics. It does not really mean anything. Consciousness is part of life, not the answer to it, a tool, not a goal.

Nearly all the important things in life go on unconsciously most of the time. We meet somebody. "Hello, who are you?" "I'm John." "Nice to meet you, I'm Jane." What does it mean? John is not conscious of who or what John is and Jane is not conscious of who or what Jane is. These are just labels. Also, 'nice to meet you' is a secret code, but does anybody consciously know what it means? They are players on an unconscious stage.

Perhaps it means, 'This is really boring, but I must not let that show,' or, perhaps it means, 'I'm looking for somebody to have a baby with and I'd like to try you out,' or, perhaps it means, 'You remind me of somebody I have unfinished business with and I'd like to hook you into my game so that I can finally get some satisfaction for my neurotic obsession.' Or, it could mean all sorts of things. Even if a clairvoyant could work out which of these it means on this particular occasion, you can be pretty confident that neither John nor Jane know.

We Do Not Know Who or What We Are

- So tell me who you are really.

- I'm an accountant.

- No, I mean who you are, not what you do between nine and six.

- I'm one third Irish, half Norwegian and the rest I don't know.

- No, I mean who you are, not where your ancestors lived.

- etc.

We can describe what goes on in our life, but we do not know who or what we are. The source of all these goings on reveals itself to us only piecemeal.

So is there any question that is going to get real satisfaction here? Even if there were, would the other be able to answer it?

The Collector

It's the same with conscious Buddhism. We collect a lot of names and affiliations and chunks of history — so what? There is a lovely story about a man coming to see Trungpa Rinpoche and saying, "I have done the whole Mahamudra and then I did the whole Ati Yoga Supreme Teaching. What do you recommend that I do now?" and Rinpoche said, "I'll teach you to meditate."

However, nowadays even meditation has fallen into the same programmatic trap. To meditate used to mean to contemplate sacred mystery. Now it means get in control and fix your stress. Unfortunately, that is just another trip.

Mostly people think that to work with the unconscious means to make it conscious and do away with it but that is like thinking that the way to work with plants is to pull them up and examine the roots in order to make them grow better. When the plants have been pulled up and separated from the medium in which they flourish we might think we have achieved something, but that is not the way to grow good flowers.

Growing Flowers

What are the flowers of Buddhism? Gratitude, generosity, openness, good-heartedness, calm, enthusiasm, faith, love, compassion. You know about all this, but do you know it — does it make your hair curl, stop you in your tracks, stand you on your head? When these qualities are real, not just theory, not contrived, they amaze. Buddhism is not a programme in gratitude development: it is a confrontation with Mara in which flowers appear in the sky.

Real gratitude wells up. It comes from a dark abyss. That dark abyss is what Buddhists call shunyata. Shunya-ta means empty-ness. Giving it a name makes no difference to the fact that we have no idea what goes on in there. However, we can be sure that whatever it is, it is a threat to the ego ideal. All this consciousness stuff is mostly about being better at defending the ego ideal from the onslaught of shunyatya, when what should be happening is co-operation.

Welling Up

What we do have some experience of is that things well up. Welling up is a palpable phenomenon. Good things, bad things, all kinds of things, well up. According to Buddhism, welling up (samudaya) is a natural response to sukha and dukkha, to blessings and afflictions — and they are going on all the time. So the first thing one can do is to stop being frightened of what's welling up and start being interested.

Awareness can play a part here, but you don't do this in order to improve awareness skills. Nor do you do it in order to push what has welled up back down again, nor in order to classify, dissect and dispose of it, nor in order to learn how best to hide what has welled up. No, you do it like receiving a Christmas present. "Oh, wow, what's this? Thanks, what do you do with it? Oh, it's like some sort of puppy. Hello fella... do you want to play? Ow! It bit my ankle. Oh, I guess he's just having fun. Well, whoever gave me this, thank you very much!" Life is like that. There is something going on in consciousness all the time, but it is arriving from somewhere else and it has a life of its own.

Consciousness itself is the least of it. It is not the gift that matters, it is the giver and the spirit of the gift and the giver of life is the abyss — shunyata. We have to trust that the spirit of the gift from the abyss is beneficent. That's religion.

Breaking Up the Concrete

What comes into consciousness comes from that deep, dark place — from the Tao, the primeval stirrings of life itself. It is important to revere shunyata. All those old fashioned religious sounding words — reverence, worship, faith, awe, grace, wonder, devotion, prayer, revelation and so on — are part of a big tool kit for working with the abyss. They have gone out of fashion because what is currently a la mode is the attempt to seal off the void with concrete.

This is the final development of materialism. Materialism is about concrete: concrete techniques, concrete results, concrete profit, concrete concepts, concrete posture. But Buddhism is not posturing. It has become as if consciousness were all there is, or all that is worthy of respect, which is like honouring the servant and ignoring the lord of the house.

Consciousness Is a Bubble in a Stream, a Star at Dawn

Materialism is reaching its limit, but somehow it has recruited a large part of Buddhism in the West into its frame. When meditation is about awareness and no longer about rapture, I am dismayed. When it is an artificial procedure, rather than astonishment and wonder, I am lost. Perhaps the word practice should be scrapped altogether. Concrete looks very solid, but when it breaks up it just returns to dust and pebbles.

Where Now?

So how are we to go forward from here? Perhaps we should start by praying.

> — I don't know who I am praying to,
> but whoever or whatever you are,
> please give me a lead.

If you make such a prayer sincerely, an answer will come: not immediately and not in the form you expect, but when you look back not long after you should be able to see that something happened. That is what I mean by working with the abyss. That kind of work is real practice. In real practice, one is not in control. One is dealing with something mysterious. You don't know who or what is on the other end of the line. This helps you to realise that, actually, you don't know who is on this end either. Yet something is going on. Something important is happening.

Names don't matter much. You can say 'the gods' or 'all the Buddhas' or 'Heaven' or 'Mother Mary' or whatever. If you call the wrong deity, you can be sure She will pass the message on. You don't have to be an expert on what happens down there in order to give them a call.

Consciousness is a bubble in a stream, a star at dawn. In the case of the bubble, it's the stream that matters. In the case of the star it's the cosmos that matters. Infinite sacred mystery. Trust it. Worship it. It won't let you down.

Your Sutra

There are many Buddhist sutras. The sutras are mostly the words of Buddha. There are also a few that are spoken by great disciples. Then there is literature on the discipline for renunciants called the Vinaya and a philosophical literature written soon after the death of Shakyamuni called the Abhidharma. In addition, there are commentaries written by the great ancestors of the Buddhist tradition. These include many hugely important original works such as the Senchaku of Honen Shonin, the Shobogenzo of Dogen Zenji and the Transmission of the Lamp by Atisha. The total literature is vast.

Consequently each school of Buddhism has its favoured scriptures from within the whole. Some schools favour the Nikayas. Some favour the Lotus Sutra. The Pureland Schools favour the Pureland Sutras and so on. In Amida Shu we favour the Pureland Sutras, but also the Lotus Sutra and take the whole range of Buddhist literature as an important resource.

The word 'sutra' means a 'thread'. When you have a surgical operation, they stitch up the wound with 'sutures'. It is the same word spelt differently. So each sutra speaks to a theme or thread of conversation, which brings out the fact that the majority of sutras started out as memories of significant conversations, particularly conversations between Shakyamuni and an enquirer. These conversations were responses to issues raised by the enquirer. The matter got sewn up not just by the meaning of the words spoken, but also by the manner and deeper communication that took place.

All these threads tell us some aspect of the Dharma, but as the different people that Shakyamuni talked to were diverse and had diverse concerns, so the conversations went different ways. Hence there are many threads.

Now, of course, this means that were you yourself to encounter the Buddha there could ensue a conversation that would then give rise to a new sutra, one especially tailored to your particular case or koan. Everyone should make a prayer to hear that sutra.

Dependant Origination is Other Power

When Siddhartha Gotama became enlightened and so became Shakyamuni Buddha what he realised was dependent origination, pratitya samutpada. Consequently, the precise meaning of dependent origination has been a subject of debate throughout Buddhist history.

Dependent Origination Became Other Power

At some point in the transmission of Buddhism in China, the term other power was coined as a more graphic way of explaining dependent origination. It was probably Tan Luan who made this shift of terminology. Some people say that by doing so he was creating a new revisionist form of doctrine and that, therefore, the Pureland Schools that derive therefrom are later philosophies, related to but distinct from the teaching of Shakyamuni. Others say that Tan Luan had rightly discerned the true meaning of Buddha's enlightenment and restored the original Buddhism. For those who take the latter view, Pureland is by no means a later development, but is the most original form of Buddhism deriving directly from the primary realisation of Shakyamuni at the source of his ministry. I am in the latter camp and here I would like to say a few things in support and explication of this perspective.

Shakyamuni Was a Spoilt Kid

Let us first look at the life of Siddhartha Gotama. The story begins with his pampered youth followed by his first going forth and his extreme asceticism. When that period of ascetic exertion ended in failure he experienced enlightenment. What does this mean?

He was pampered, at least in part, because his mother had died giving birth to him and his father and step-mother compensated for the loss. This circumstance must generate a psychological problem. To know that one's birth has occasioned the death of one's mother is not easy. To then be treated to every kind of luxury to boot only exacerbates the existential guilt. It is no wonder that he felt an urge to punish and torture himself. However, he will not have rationalised this to himself in this way. He saw it as a quest to end his own suffering and find a solution to the problem of disease, decay and death. This rationalisation is, of course, only a small remove from the psychological diagnosis I have just offered, but it does couch the whole thing in a religious frame.

He Tried Self-power and It Failed

The religion of the time included the notion that one could purify oneself of past karma by voluntarily undergoing penance. In the process one also gained mastery over the body and it was apparent that it was the fact of having a body that caused one to go through disease, decay and death. Therefore, the body was, in a sense, the guilty party, so it was not inappropriate that it be punished. This logic became particularly powerful in the Jain religion, in some forms of yoga, later in medieval Christianity and in some other historical religions.

We can see this ascetic approach as an attempt at mastery, of the body, of mind over matter, of oneself over one's fate. It is svabhava — self-generation, self-power.

It did not work. Shakyamuni did not become enlightened by his self-power practice. He did not become enlightened by torturing his body, by sitting still for almost unendurable periods, by starving himself, nor by any comparable discipline. By these disciplines he did gain a certain worldly reputation as a great ascetic and this brought him respect among other ascetics, but he did not become enlightened. Nor did he become enlightened by ethical restraint. He did not become enlightened by following the Eightfold Path, for instance. None of these things served to enlighten him. Each had some intrinsic results, some of which were beneficial in a relative sense. It is like learning to run a four minute mile. Doing so may make you fit which might be a good thing and might damage your joints which might be a bad thing, but it will not make you enlightened, unless it happens to make you realise what a fool you are.

Shakyamuni became enlightened when he gave up, when he realised that what he had been doing did not work. The self-power project failed. Of course, one can say that, in a certain sense, he did realise the futility of self-power so profoundly because of the dedication with which he had pursued it, but that is a bit like saying that you will appreciate good food more if you have nearly died of self-poisoning several times. It is no recommendation for poisoning oneself.

So He Woke Up to Other Power and Called It Dependent Origination

In any case, when we see Shakyamuni's enlightenment in this way it makes perfect sense to say that what he discovered was the opposite of self-power.

So, if we take this to be the case and say that Tan Luan was right, then when the Buddha said "Until I understood dependent arising I was not enlightened. It was only when I did fully understand dependent arising that I considered myself enlightened." He is saying "Until I understood Other Power I was not enlightened, it was only when I did fully understand Other Power that I was enlightened." Now, if we assert this, then there are some points we still have to clarify.

Adventitious Light

Let us have a closer look at the term Shakyamuni used. Pratitya means "having depended". Samutpada means that something steps up. Samutpada is very close in meaning to the second Truth for Noble Ones — samudaya. There are a number of translations currently used in English versions of Buddhist texts — dependent arising, co-dependent arising, inter-dependent co-arising and so on. Each of these implies a slightly different bias on the part of the particular translator. It is, however, possible to see Siddhartha's choice of words as descriptive of what had happened to him. He had depended (upon a notion of self-efficacy) until something new stepped up. His awakening was spontaneous, but it happened in a circumstance. The circumstance was his own error coupled with a trigger that nudged him into a different perspective. It took something outside of his self, something outside of his old perspective, to do the trick. So two things are necessary, error and trigger — foolishness and other power.

Other Power Has Many Appearances

When we talk about other power in Pureland we generally mean the power of Amitabha Buddha. However, the term other power as it stands is not so limited. It simply implies any power that is not self. Amitabha Buddha can take on any form necessary. What Shakyamuni abandoned was self-power, svabhava. The opposite of svabhava in the philosophy of Nagarjuna is shunyata, emptiness. Shunyata means emptiness of self, ego, svabhava, conceit. It also means that things are not limited to one inherent identity. The relevance of this last point is that anything can serve as the trigger. Amitabha is not attached to being Amitabha.

One of the difficulties of interpreting Buddhism is that many of the key teachings are expressed in the negative. Dependent origination is generally expounded as a means of showing how one bad state arises from another. Shakyamuni's life, however, became a matter of one good state arising from another. Where the term dependent origination is commonly expounded to show bad arising from bad, other power is expounded as good arising from good. Other power, then, is the positive form of dependent origination and dependent origination, as we commonly encounter it in Buddhist texts, is the negative of other power. Similarly, other power is a positive way of saying shunyata.

When one is empty of self one is full of grace. It does not make much difference which Buddha the grace emanates from or what disguise they are wearing at the time. As Dogen says, in the end it is just Buddhas together with Buddhas and the universe is one bright pearl — forgetting the self one is enlightened by everything and, as in the Pratyutpanna Samadhi wherever one looks one sees Buddhas.

The positive form of dependent origination, therefore, is that everything becomes a suitable circumstance for awakening when one is no longer self-obsessed. This is the core message of Shakyamuni and of all Buddhas. This is the meaning of "sarva dharma anatma" — all that is fundamentally true is empty of self.

Everybody Errs but Nobody Does So Intentionally

The subtlety of Buddhist philosophy lies in its distinguishing the relation between self and other as not being deterministic yet not being wholly a matter of independence either. As Thich Nhat Hanh says, one is "made of non-self elements," yet one is not simply a product of deterministic cause-effect processes. One is not enlightened wholly "from within", yet one is not enlightened in a deterministic way either. There is, in fact, no technique, method or circumstance that can guarantee or determine spiritual awakening, yet, equally, none that could not be a sufficient trigger if the situation were ripe enough. It has something in common with an accident, yet nor is it purely random. It often occurs, as it did for Shakyamuni and for Nagarjuna when, for some reason or other, one realises that one had got matters entirely wrong and when one looks back on it one can see that the error was some form of svabhava, conceit, but one was incapable of seeing it when one was in the midst of it. Nobody errs intentionally.

Faith is Encounter

The circumstance that triggers such a realisation is commonly an inter-personal encounter of some kind, which is to say meeting an other. All the time we are in the midst of others, but do we really meet them? Much of the time our supposed encounter with others is mostly a matter of us massaging our own projections and conceits and trying to use the other as a prop (lakshana) for our self-justification project. However, occasionally, real encounters occur and something new really steps up. This takes faith and magnifies it. In really encountering what is other one has to let go, to fall without a parachute, as it were.

In the case of Nagarjuna it was his encounter with Kapimala. Many people will say that Shakyamuni became enlightened without such an encounter, but in *The Feeling Buddha*[*] I suggest that the critical encounter for Siddhartha Gotama was that with Sujata who showed him unselfconscious kindness. What these two personages have in common is that neither Sujata nor Kapimala were caught up in the conceit of self. This conceit of self — svabhava — was to become the main target of Shakyamuni's critique.

All the Teachings Express One Truth

So, I think Tan Luan was right. Dependent origination and other power are equivalent terms and the shift from the former to the latter assists us in seeing the Dharma in positive rather than negative terms. This approach unifies all the major teachings and roots Other Power Buddhism in the original enlightenment of all the Buddhas. That one chooses to turn toward one particular Buddha makes practical sense, but to worship one is to worship them all — there is no quarrel between Buddhas.

Beginning With Self-Power is Inevitable

It is natural enough that people take it when reading that Buddhism is all about eliminating the conceit of self that this means that they are to achieve some such elimination by some effort and method and looking for such methods they seize upon particular practices or formulas such as particular meditations, disciplines, or the Eightfold Path

---

[*] Brazier, D. *The Feeling Buddha* Robinson 2012

or whatever. It is natural enough, but it misses the core. It gets hold of the wrong end of the snake. It introduces personal ambition into spirituality and generates spiritual materialism. Perhaps it is inevitable. However, it only bears fruit when it fails and fails in a sufficiently strong way. Such a reversal is always, in some fashion, an encounter with other power.

Short of this, what can one do but have faith, have gratitude for the presence of the Dharma, the example of the great sages who have gone before us and shone a light. That light is our other power. One day, just as it did to Siddhartha Gotama and to Nagarjuna, it will knock us off our pedestal.

Understanding the Skandhas

Buddhist Analytical Psychology

One of the most basic Buddhist teachings is that of the skandhas. There are five skandhas and the teaching can be understood in various ways. Here I am going to talk about it from a psychological point of view. I am also going to suggest some alternative translations for some of the key terms to those that are commonly used.

Why are the commonly used translations misleading? Most of the material about the skandhas that you will read in popular books about Buddhism translates the skandha terms using such words as feelings, perception, consciousness, and so on which are all characteristics of any living human being. Now the skandhas are presented in the texts as something that the Buddha would prefer that we get rid of. I do not think that the Buddha wanted us to get rid of feelings, perception and consciousness. Therefore I have gone back to looking more closely at the original words and come up with a rather different sense of what they actually mean.

Again, the skandhas are commonly presented as a list of elements with no strong relation one to another. However, in most cases when Buddha presents a list it is in a specific order because each element conditions the next one in the list. This general principle of identifying chains of conditioning is a broad and fundamental one that we see right through the teachings of Buddha and I believe that it is intended in the skandha teaching too.

So, with those introductory caveats, let us look at the skandhas themselves. There are five. They are rupa, vedana, samjna, samskara and vijnana. They are always given in that order, though it is possible also to see them as a circle. Rupa conditions vedana, vedana samjna, samjna samskara, samskara vijnana, and vijnana, the last skandha, conditions rupa, the first. Thus the five can be seen as a circle, not just as a sequence.

Rupa

The narrow meaning of rupa is an idol or icon. Thus, the statue upon the altar is called a Buddha rupa. In English we tend to say idol when we are being negative and icon when we are being positive. However, it is not just religious images that are covered by these terms. There are things we idolise and things that are iconic. The term rupa can be taken as having a wide significance. All kinds of things in our experience have some degree of this special quality. We are surrounded by things — forms and appearances — that have some degree of power over us. This can be as trivial as the smell of coffee or as significant as the person one is married to. Rupa signifies any form or appearance that exercises a degree of fascination over or provokes reaction in us.

Vedana

Veda means knowledge. Thus vedana, commonly translated as "feeling", actually means knowingness. Knowingness is prejudice. The dictionary says "affecting, implying, or deliberately revealing shrewd knowledge of secret or private information." So one might say that a person gave a knowing look, meaning that his face revealed that he has prior knowledge about something. Vedana has double valency, for and against. When we have a prejudice it is for or against something. This does constitute a kind of feeling, but the term feeling is broader than vedana. Feelings have much more than two valencies — they come is a vast array of different colours and tones. Vedana means that when a person perceives something that is a rupa for them it immediately arouses some prior knowledge that disposes them for or against that object. Seeing a piece of chocolate, one might be attracted. Seeing a spider one might be repelled. We can immediately understand that whether this is so or not depends upon the psychology and experience of the individual. There are people who love spiders and hate chocolate. Vedana thus refers broadly to the reaction that we have to things that are significant to us, reactions that are based on our prior experience.

Samjna

A literal transliteration of this would give us co-consciousness. It refers to the kind of entrancement that comes over us that is triggered when we are in the grip of knowingness. When we think we know all about something already we are no longer paying much attention to the actual phenomenon before us. One often sees this with married couples. One starts to say something and the other already thinks that they know exactly what their partner means, even thinking that they know the partner better than he or she knows him or herself. Samjna is commonly translated as "perception" and it is certainly a way of perceiving, but clear perception is not samjna. Samjna is the kind of mesmerised perception that is coloured by supposed prior knowledge. It may put us in a state of rather less than full consciousness, a state of being on automatic pilot. We smell the coffee and move toward it with hardly a conscious thought arising. Samjna, therefore, is a kind of ephemeral trance. In the course of a day most ordinary people are in such trances much of the time, jogging along from one to another as different rupas come into view.

Samskara

D.T. Suzuki translates this as "confection". Other writers use "internal formation" or "mental formation". Confection is the most precise. We are talking here about the way that we go on working on our knowingness and auto-pilot patterns, deepening and elaborating them. This includes a lot of talking to ourselves and to others who share our predisposition in ways that cement our prejudice and develop it with stories and selective evidence. As this elaboration process proceeds it widens the scope of our attitude to encompass new elements associated with the ones that we already have fixed attitudes about.

Vijnaña

I have suggested that the best direct rendering of this would be to coin the neologism disconsciousness, in other words, the tendency to be conscious of things in a faulty manner. Commonly, the word is translated "consciousness", but this seems highly misleading. When we use the word consciousness on its own we generally imply a state of accurate awareness, but this seems to be exactly what vijnana excludes. Vijnana is a biased mentality. When one is suffering from this disconsciousness — and we all are in varying degrees in certain circumstances — one is relying upon samskaras rather than upon objectivity. Also, an outlook that is disconscious will be on the alert for existing rupas and will have a tendency to create new ones.

This analysis of the steps by which the mind becomes disconscious is useful. When I see a client for psychotherapy, typically she or he begins by telling a story that illustrates their problem or dilemma. This story is populated by the significant others in the client's life — mother, father, spouse, siblings, friends, colleagues and so on. These are the big rupas in the client's world. It is likely that the client will mention one of the most significant first. As soon as she does so, there is immediate evidence of vedana in the client's face and demeanour. In a trice the client enters into a samjna state and I hear or even see before me the habitual mental routine that infects the client whenever this particular rupa manifests in their mind space, whether by physical presence or in imagination. We all know this kind of thing. It occurs when we say, "I can't think of so-and-so without feeling such-and-such" or "...without thinking of the time when blah-blah happened." In other words, in relation to our significant rupas we are all programmed and readily enter corresponding trance states. The mind is conditioned by its object and by its prior knowledge.

All this is very useful in therapy, in daily life and in spirituality. In therapy it gives immediate indisputable evidence that helps one to diagnose what is going on. It also provides a variety of ways of thinking about possible interventions. One can, for instance, be distracted from one rupa by the salience of another; or, the rupa-ness of an object can change if the way that that object is construed changes; or, positive rupas may tend to drive out negative ones; and so on. Knowingness can sometimes be disrupted by evidence from new experience and samskaras can be dislodged by the juxtaposition of dissonant elements.

In daily life an understanding of skandha process can help one to observe one's own habits, tendencies and reactions. One can learn to be aware of the skandha cycle clicking round. At times of particular stress, one can see oneself "fuming by night and flaming by day" as the teacher says in the Anthill Sutra, and one can distinguish the stages and elements in such passion. This all enables one to have a bit more objectivity about oneself and, by extension, sympathy for others similarly afflicted.

In spiritual practice one may distinguish two levels. The less significant is that by identifying and analysing patterns of thought and behaviour, one may, sometimes, be able to modify them. This is really social training rather than true spirituality. The more significant is that by identifying and clearly seeing that this happens in oneself in one's own experience, one comes to have a tangible, irrefutable knowledge of bombu nature, and this understanding that, although we can change some things in ourselves, we can never sort out everything, makes us aware of the fathomlessness of samsara and may lead one to turn to what is beyond. It also, through fellow-feeling, provides the foundation for real compassion.

Dogen

Eihei Dogen (1200-1253) was the founder of the Soto Shu, a Japanese school of Zen based on a Chinese tradition. He was an important philosopher and his major work was called the Shobogenzo.

Dogen was an illegitimate son of a high official, Minamoto Michitomo. His mother died when he was seven years old.

He ordained as a Tendai monk. The Tendai Shu taught that all beings are intrinsically endowed with Buddha Nature. Dogen became preoccupied with the question, if this is so, why do Buddhas need to teach?

Not finding an answer, he went to study Rinzai Zen under the master Myozen who was the successor of Eisai, the founder of Rinzai Shu in Japan.

In 1223, Myozen and Dogen travelled together to China seeking further teachings. In those days this was a hazardous journey. Dogen went as Myozen's assistant.

He was in China five years or so. In 1225 he went to visit Master Ru-jing at Tian-tong temple. Thereafter he often referred to Ru-jing as "the Old Buddha".

Dogen had a great awakening through an encounter with Ru-jing in which the latter said, "Cast off body and mind (shinjin-datsuraku)."

Dogen returned to Japan in 1227 or 1228. His first distinctive completely original writing was Genjo Koan (Awakening Through Accepting One's Lot).

After several attempts to live and teach closer to the capital and running into conflicts with Tendai Shu, he accepted an invitation, from Hatano Yoshishige, lord of Izumo, in 1243, to move north into the more remote Echizen Province. Dogen and his supporters constructed a temple initially called Daibutsu-ji (Great Buddha Temple). Later it was renamed Eihei-ji and it remains the head temple of Soto Shu to this day.

While Daibutsu-ji was being built, Dogen fell into depression. This condition seems to have converted itself into anger and he wrote a strong critique of Rinzai Zen and then went on and on writing, in the next few years, pouring out texts that are regarded as some of the most challenging and stimulating in the whole of Japanese Buddhism.

Dogen advocated acceptance as the core of Buddhism, yet Dogen himself was a person of strong opinions. Opinions about practice, about such social issues as women's equality (which he favoured), about monastic discipline, and about doctrine, as, for instance, in his views about Buddha Nature, and about being and time. He was sharply critical of many of the other schools of Buddhism. While some would claim Dogen's writing as support for the idea that Dharma cannot be expressed in words, he was, in fact, an attentive scholar of the scriptures, especially the Lotus Sutra, and strongly criticised those who paid too little attention to them. He was a great stylist and his writings are often cryptic, poetic, paradoxical, highly suggestive and philosophically profound so that much controversy goes on over the precise meaning of his words.

By 1247, Dogen had found more favour with powerful people and was invited by Hojo Tokiyori, the regent shogun, to visit Kamakura and give him lay ordination. His stay in Kamakura, however, seems to have changed him. When he got home he wrote in a more fundamentalist style, affirming the basic teachings of Buddhism and asserting that the basis of Buddhism was the taking of refuge in Buddha, Dharma and Sangha.

In 1252 Dogen fell ill. The following year he travelled to the capital, Kyoto, seeking a remedy but died on arrival.

We might ask why did Dogen become depressed. Looking at it psychologically, we immediately focus upon the early death of his mother and the difficulties of being an illegitimate child, both in the sense that his parents were not married and also in that he had fallen out with both of his Buddhist "parents", Tendai Shu and Rinzai Shu. Until he went north he was fighting for a point of view that was being persecuted. Probably, with the protection of Hatano Yoshishige he may have felt safe for the first time. It is often at such a point that depression comes out. All the accumulated hardship and sense of injustice then came to the surface and, fortunately for us, he was able to sublimate that energy into his great writing endeavour.

His story leaves us with tantalising questions. Is it possible to be enlightened and depressed and/or angry? Can a person be, as, I think, Jack Kornfield asks in one of his writings, enlightened yet still in need of therapy? Is it, in fact, necessary to have some anger or burning animus in order to write works of genius? Is there a contradiction between Dogen's advocacy of quietism and his strident critiques? When Dogen suggests constant zazen, how does this relate to the practice of literally sitting in meditation? To what extent are Dogen's writings purely autobiographical — descriptive of his own spiritual struggle — and to what extent are they generalisable? Was Dogen right in being so critical of other schools of Buddhism? These and more questions have kept scholars and practitioners busy for many years and there is no sign of this activity diminishing. Dogen is nowadays perhaps more studied than ever before.

Dilemmas About Dogen or Dogen's Dilemmas

Dilemmas

Dogen Zenji is, perhaps, the most important historical figure in Zen in Japan. I am working on a translation of Dogen's seminal text Genjo Koan[*]. Genjo Koan is about enlightenment. It is written to a layperson. Later on Dogen writes other things that strongly suggest that he thought it is virtually impossible for a lay person to be enlightened. Did Dogen change his mind? If so, why?

Dogen is known for being a dedicated advocate of zazen. It has the highest value in his system and is presented as equivalent to enlightenment, yet in Genjo Koan, which is about enlightenment, he does not mention it. Why?

If you take Genjo Koan in isolation, if you knew nothing else about Dogen's writings, you would probably never guess that he regarded zazen as being so important. You would rather, I think, tend to think that what he is talking about could arise in a variety of ways.

---

[*] Published 2019 as The Dark Side of the Mirror, by Windhorse.

My own experience of spiritual practice would go along those lines. I have learnt important things from meditation, but also from other aspects of practice, from my relationships with different teachers, from adventitious circumstances of life, from devotion, chanting and prayer, from writing, and even from reading Dogen. Many of Dogen's own writings also suggest such diverse learning.

Dogen, however, makes a distinction between the kind of learning that is cumulative and the awakening that is satori. My own spiritual awakenings have certainly had some kind of contemplation as one important element, but that has not been the only trigger.

More Dilemmas

We can ask, 'Why did Dogen write?', given that he wrote a great deal. Some of the writings were initially delivered as spoken sermons. One can say that their purpose was to encourage people to do zazen, but such encouragement did not require such sophisticated prose, such wide ranging rehearsal of doctrines and stories, such poetry. Much of Dogen's writing revolves around koan cases — Zen stories of encounters between monks or between teacher and disciple, in which one at least generally arrives at some kind of enlightenment experience. It is therefore clear enough that Dogen also thought that enlightenment came via interaction and dialogue.

Zazen

Sometimes Dogen writes about zazen as sitting in a specific posture and managing the mind in a particular way. Sometimes he writes as though almost any activity can be zazen.

Dogen's text that most centrally focusses on zazen is called Fukanzazengi — Instructions for Zazen. Early in this text he reminds us of Shakyamuni training for six years and Bodhidharma for nine. This implies that enlightenment comes as a result after a period of time. However, later in the text, he says that training is enlightenment. These claims cannot both stand.

In any case, Shakyamuni, at least, clearly was not enlightened when he was "training" and what he was doing at that time was not zazen, and Bodhidharma we are led to believe was already enlightened before he started his legendary nine years facing a wall.

His Dilemmas

Were Dogen's writings as much a way of putting down his own dilemmas as of instructing others? Is what we are to learn here the way that a spiritual life, such as he exemplifies, is a continual series of dilemmas? Is he obliged to be consistent? Perhaps contradicting himself within the same essay is enlightened behaviour. Perhaps he was not sure about some of the answers. He probably wanted to think that lay people could be enlightened, but found in practice that they just gave him a lot of trouble. He probably wanted people to do zazen but realised that for many it was impractical. He probably wanted his message to be popular, but found that it wasn't.

He certainly did not have an easy time. His parents died when he was young. He became a monk. He went to the big Tendai monastery Enraku-ji at Hiei and then to the Rinzai Kennin-ji temple. When the abbot, Myozen, went to China Dogen went with him. However, on their arrival the Chinese did not accept that Dogen was a proper monk and treated him as a layperson, or at best as a bottom grade junior. Then Myozen died. When Dogen got back to Japan he probably expected his new understanding to be greeted with acclaim, but largely it was met with rejection. After ten years of trying to run his own monastery near to the capital he was forced to leave and move to a remote area. The school he founded was always teetering on the brink of being made illegal. He had to try hard to find persons of influence to speak up for him. He had some successes, but it was a difficult progression and he must have been near to despair on occasion.

Our Dilemma

So the moral of this is that the spiritual life is not easy or straight-forward, that it involves many struggles and often a good deal of lack of clarity. Our spiritual heroes are not people who sailed along from one great experience to another. Honen Shonin also went to Enraku-ji as an orphan, left, struggled, got exiled, and had many conflicts.

Our image of the spiritual life in modern times has been somewhat built upon the idea that it provides happiness and freedom from trouble. We asset strip it for techniques to use for personal growth but often miss the meaning of the body of practice that we have taken them from. We do not have a feel for enlightenment, we just want more immediate benefits for body and mind — exactly the things that Dogen learnt to let go of in China.

The lives of spiritual heroes are generally difficult. They do not get everything right. They do not have an easy time. Their practice does not yield a smooth ride. Their enlightenment gives them the energy to struggle, not a free pass. Shakyamuni said that a day without striving was a wasted day. My teacher Kennett Roshi said, on more than one occasion, that if enlightenment was just about happiness, then a dog asleep in the sun would be the ideal. There is more to it.

Here and There With Saigyo

Here is a poem by Saigyo (1118-1190), one of Japan's greatest poets, also reckoned a saint.

> Snow has fallen on
>
> field paths and mountain tracks
>
> burying them all,
>
> and I can't tell here from there:
>
> my journey in the midst of sky.

Saigyo was an independent Buddhist practitioner who spent much time travelling or in retreat, often at Mount Koya, the centre of Shingon Buddhism and later near to the Ise Shrine. He believed in honji-suijaku, the idea that the Shinto Gods were manifestations of celestial Buddhas, the supreme Goddess Amaterasu being a form of Vairochana Buddha, and so on. He came from a samurai family and initially trained as a warrior, but became disenchanted with court life with all its hypocrisy and double dealing. One thread running through his life was his inner struggle with the karma of his earlier life before he became a monk. Another was his observation of the steady degeneration of Japanese society into civil war during his lifetime. His exquisite poetry reveals sensitivity to people in all ranks of society, a fair amount of irony in his social comment, modest self-reflection, and a strong sense of the identity of Buddhism and nature.

In this poem, Saigyo is telling us literally about one of his many stays alone in the mountains, passing the winter in retreat in a hut, going out for walks in the snow. At the same time he is telling us about his inner struggle to know what is right and where to go, what to do with his life. The poem manages to suggest two completely different extremes all at once — a person directionless and lost and a person living the ideal life of complete nonattachment, as free as a cloud in the sky. We can imagine that Saigyo passed much of his life poised on this cusp.

Many people tend to think that when a person is enlightened, they have no more uncertainties, no more worries or loneliness, that they are happy all the time and have the answer to everything. When one is a Buddhist teacher one can be surprised to find that others are projecting such an image upon one. Saigyo, however, illustrates a rather different way of illumination — a path that is at once rigorous yet totally human.

We like predictability. It gives us a sense of security. We follow along well-worn tracks. Here, however, Saigyo talks of the situation when all the well-known tracks have disappeared. The heavens have opened and all is now a glittering, white sameness. There is a kind of melancholy, yet also of joy embodied in his words. The problem is also the liberation. This bittersweet quality that pervades so many of his works well reflects the emotional tone of the Dharma life of the true mystic.

Dogen and Saigyo

Saigyo and Dogen were both independent Buddhist monks. Saigyo was, perhaps, even more independent than Dogen in that he seems never to have been strongly identified with one sect or community, although he did have a great respect for Kukai and, therefore, a leaning toward Shingon. He spent a good deal of time in retreat on Mount Koya, but never actually became a Shingon monk.

Saigyo seems to have kept abreast of current affairs more intently than Dogen did. At least, we have little record that Dogen did so, but, then, the times of Saigyo were more dramatic with major civil war overrunning the country. Dogen may, in fact, have made more effort than Saigyo to curry favour with those who had power and influence, but such efforts were intermittent and brought scant fruit.

Saigyo had seen more of 'the world' than Dogen, in that he had been a samurai and part of the 'north facing guard' of the retired emperor before ordaining. He had clearly had a love life of some kind, but evidence is contradictory and details are lost. Many of his poems reveal him to be a sensitive man who sublimated his passions into a love of natural beauty. Nonetheless, he also spent much time engaged in rather challenging ascetic practices.

This mix of tenderness and harshness, appreciation of beauty and also of strict discipline, is characteristic of both men. Both came out of an aristocratic tradition, both rejected the worldly life and its hypocrisies, both sought to find an answer to the seemingly contradictory currents of grief and delight that flowed through them as a result of their personal experiences of the Buddhist truth of impermanence. Dogen eventually took his community to the mountains. Saigyo never had a community and went to the mountains alone. Both believed that this kind of yamabushi experience was, as we would say, 'good for the soul'.

Saigyo opened doors for Dogen, especially in the domain of permissible feelings. Where many believed that the proper course for a Buddhist monk was to renounce all passion in a rather self-repressive way, by the time Dogen came along, Saigyo had demonstrated that a Buddhist monk could record his loneliness, grief, longing, sense of desolation, fear of shame, embarrassment, sentimentality, and many other emotions, win poetry competitions, and still come to be regarded as a saint.

As we have seen, Saigyo was a follower of the idea of honji suijaku according to which Shinto deities were identified with celestial Buddhas. His sense of religion was, therefore, not at all narrow and could accommodate a wide range of influences, uniting them as much for their aesthetic qualities as for any doctrinal similarities. Dogen is generally portrayed as the founder of a sect, but this designation is rather misleading and, like Saigyo, he united within his approach to Dharma a much wider range of influences than many realise.

Saigyo and Dogen 'spoke the same language' and the wide extension and currency given to this 'language' by Saigyo certainly helped to pave the way for Dogen's masterpieces.

The Equivalence of Three Buddhist Principles[*]

In this teaching I would like to point out the equivalence between certain principles or concepts in Mahayana Buddhism that are normally taken to be very different and are generally associated with different styles and theories of practice. These three are bodhichitta, tathagatagarbha and nembutsu.

Bodhichitta is commonly associated with self-power practices. It is the mind of the bodhisattva, the "way-seeking mind", the pinnacle of altruism. The bodhisattva is willing to do anything and go anywhere in order to save sentient beings. However, when we examine this idea closely, we see that while the bodhisattva is irreversibly on the path to Buddhahood, he is not actually concerned about his own salvation. He simply takes it for granted that the path is its own reward.

Tathagatagarbha is the idea of a Buddha seed or embryo within the person. The concept is commonly closely associated with a certain idea of Buddha Nature and the principle of Original Enlightenment according to

---

[*] Transcribed from a talk at Oasis de Longue Vie

which all beings are, in principle, already enlightened and that what is necessary is that they wake up to this fact.

Nembutsu is the "thought of Buddha" that is expressed by calling the name of a Buddha, usually Amitabha, in complete trust that that Buddha will come and take the faithful to his Pure Land where enlightenment will one day inevitably follow. Followers of nembutsu do not generally believe in original enlightenment and do not think that they themselves are endowed with the abilities of Buddhas.

So, on the surface, these seem like three very different concepts designating quite different interpretations of what is going on in Mahayana Buddhist practice.

The core of Mahayana Buddhism is bodhichitta. The term bodhi refers to the enlightened vision that inspires us upon the path. Chitta is the perceiving mind, the heart that is touched by the vision. Bodhi is the essence of Buddhahood.

I think it is fairly easy to understand, therefore, that nembutsu and bodhichitta are really very similar. Nembutsu means mindfulness of Buddha. Buddha is Buddha inasmuch as he is identified with bodhi. Nen means mindfulness or heartfulness. Nembutsu is a matter of having Buddha in one's heart and mind. That is the core meaning of bodhichitta.

We should not, therefore, think that Pureland is one thing, centred on nembutsu, and Mahayana

Buddhism is something else centred on bodhichitta. We should, rather, understand that nembutsu and bodhichitta are two ways of saying the same thing.

They speak of great love, reverence and gratitude for the sublime vision that the Buddhas inspire and that somehow gets implanted, lodged within us. We can ponder how this happens.

Shantideva, speaking of bodhichitta, says:

> Just as, in a night all darkened by dense cloud
>
> a lightning flash may for an instant illumine the whole land,
>
> in this world, by the power of the Buddhas,
>
> a virtuous thought may fleetingly appear.
>
> (Shantideva 1.5)

Such a "virtuous thought" is the bodhichitta or nembutsu. The merit of such a thought is inestimable because it transports us beyond all calculation. It is simply unconditional love. As such it is something that we ourselves are not capable of. It does not arise as our own doing, but is, as it were, planted in us by the Buddhas.

In this sense we can say that it is no different from tathagatagarbha, the seed planted by Buddha. So we can say that all three ideas, bodhichitta, nembutsu and tathagatagarbha are simply different names for the same thing, each emphasising a slightly different aspect, but in essence, identical. Nembutsu is tathagatagarbha in that it is implanted in us by the action and grace of Amitabha.

This being so it is interesting for us to think about nembutsu from these different perspectives. Nembutsu as nembutsu is the Name or image of Amida Buddha. Nembutsu as bodhichitta is the inspiration flowing to us from all the Buddhas. Nembutsu as tathagatagarbha is the seed planted in us that grows into Buddhahood.

Whichever way we think about it, we feel ourselves to be caught up in a vast cosmic process that goes far far beyond our own little life. It is as if one were a leaf on a great tree or a pebble on a long beach. From one perspective one is insignificant, yet from another one is part of something much much bigger.

Nembutsu opens the heart to this bigger process. We receive the great merit and grace bestowed by the Buddhas and this then works secretly in our lives.

> Should bodhichitta come to be
>
> in the heart of a being caught in cyclic existence
>
> immediately that one becomes an heir of Buddhas
>
> object of worship to gods and men.
>
> (Shantideva 1.9)

In Less Than a Day

> The Pure Realm of Buddha, they say,
>
> lies in a land that is far, far away
>
> but if you are truly going that way
>
> you'll arrive at the gate in less than a day.

This little poem is based on a song by a wandering 'hijiri', or holy man, called Kuya (903-972) who travelled around Japan singing the praise of Amitabha Buddha and preaching. They were hard times and Kuya was often involved in helping to dig wells or mend roads or whatever else needed doing in the villages that he visited.

In the history of Japanese Buddhism there are quite a number of famous hijiri. Some of these people were fully ordained monks, but many were people who had taken on the life of the wandering bhikshu without any particular authorisation or initiation. Nowadays, of course, we have the opposite — people want the credentials, but never actually 'leave home'.

It is true that one can reach the gate of the Pure Land by having the right attitude, but if one does have the right attitude then it is going to have consequences for one's practical life. The hijiri trusted in providence. They accepted what came along and they practised kindness wherever they went. All this was inspired by the Buddhist vision.

Pausing in my writing, I just now opened the Lotus Sutra at random. It fell open at the chapter on the Appearance of the Treasure Stupa just at the point where the Buddha emits a light that enables the whole congregation to perceive billions of Buddha Lands in all directions. This is what Buddhas do. They have a light that enables us to see an inspiring vision, and when we see it we want to go there, and, even though it may seem far, far away, through the power of aspiration, you'll be there in less than a day.

What Is Samadhi For?

Many people would take the square one of Buddhism to be meditation, together with mindfulness and awareness which are then taken as being states of immediate attention, but do we really know what Buddha meant by these things? In many ways, we have invented a modern Buddhism that is some distance removed from the original. We can cut through this problem to some extent by asking what meditation is for.

Samadhi is one of the words that gets translated as meditation, though there is no associated verb in the Buddha's language. You can be in samadhi, but you cannot samadhi. Prototypically, in the texts, samadhi is sandwiched between sila and prajna. Sila is restraint and prajna is wisdom. Samadhi is a bridge between them. If we think of modern psychotherapy, we can say that sila is like cognitive behaviourism — it is the regulation of the conscious level of the mind and associated behaviour. Prajna is like analytical psychology — it is insight into the deeper mind. Samadhi, concentration, sits between these two. It is a bridge from one to the other. Long before Freud, Buddha realised that if we do not explore the deeper mind all our efforts to be good and do fine things are likely to come apart when assailed by the waves that rise from the depths, as anybody can know in a simple way just from their experience of trying to keep a New Year's resolution.

Finding Oneself Out

What meditation is for is to help us confront the reality about ourselves. When we start to see ourselves as we actually are and accept one another as we actually are, then we have a working basis. However, for many people today, meditation, mindfulness and awareness have ceased to perform this function. They have, instead, become medications— ways of escaping from what we actually are and abolishing the symptoms that are a natural consequence of what we are doing. To this extent — and it is a considerable one — what pass for meditation, mindfulness and awareness have come to function in quite the opposite manner to that originally intended. They have become a distraction from or tranquilisation of our everyday symptoms rather than a penetration into them. Were we to penetrate into them we would perceive how crazy our life is and we would seek liberation. Contemporary mindfulness, however, is largely intended to enable us to bear it longer.

This is so much the case that we may well have to devise other ways of bringing people to the real square one without which they do not have much of a working basis at all. This is one of the reasons that I now favour the use of nembutsu. So far, nembutsu has escaped from the clutches of the quasi-medics. Maybe if nembutsu practice starts to become more popular we shall get to the point where people are prescribing so many nembutsu per day as the appropriate cure for social lumbago or whatever. When that happens we shall again have to think of something new.

The Revelations of Foolishness

Whatever the method, the need is for us to start with reality and explore it more and more deeply, especially the reality of our own foolish nature, since this is what is so revealing. We need to become aware of it in an objective way. Beyond non-judgement, we need to arrive at the position of sallekha — of seeing that "this is not me, this is not mine, this is not myself." Of course, at first, this seems like a contradiction: I am to see how I really am and, in the process, realise that this is not me. That's right. This reality is just what is going on here.

The first step, if you like, is to see what is going on. The initial assumption is that this is "me". In a sense it is, but as we investigate, we discover that what one thinks of as oneself-going-on actually has no self in it. It is just-going-on, just as when we say "It is raining" the word "it" has no substantial meaning outside of that sentence. So seeing self and seeing non-self are two sides of one coin.

The Mud is Clay

To see these things is to enter into a great spaciousness. This is both an inner and an outer spaciousness. We could call the inner spaciousness the infinite unconscious. The infinite unconscious has no edges and is not under our control — which is why we call it the unconscious. Out of this infinity arise finite things — thoughts, images, feelings and so on. This arising is called samudaya. For the ordinary person, samudaya is like mud. It is dirty, sticky, messes things up, makes you slip up and make a fool of yourself, and it is hard to clean up. For the spiritual adept, on the other hand, it is like potter's clay. It is a malleable, creative medium from which beautiful and useful things can be shaped.

So we start at square one, which is really this muddy place where we are already. We have to see what we have got. This is how a teacher works with somebody, too. The teacher sees what is there. Perhaps what is there is a great fear or an intense anger or, again, lethargy or misery. Perhaps the person has a million ideas or perhaps does not think much at all. Perhaps they are endlessly and pointlessly busy or perhaps they are completely blind to what needs doing. Everybody has blind spots and sometimes it would be truer to say that there are only a few spots where they are not blind. The teacher notices these things and finds them wonderful, like finding a box of treasures. This is the energy, the fire, of the person, all bundled up in a particular way. This is the mud. So mud can be a treasure. With the mud we are going to make a jug or a cup or a sculpture or something like that.

We could change the metaphor and say it is like a piece of gnarled wood. The wood has grown through many experiences and is all twisted. With this unique grain we are going to make something beautiful.

Or it is like an herbalist going into a meadow. To the ordinary person it looks like a lot of weeds and he just wants to mow it all down, but to the herbalist there is here the material for a hundred meals and a thousand remedies.

The Working Basis

So the working basis is what is already there. It has its special energy and wonderfulness. Whatever it is we can begin by giving it a welcome. Recognising this square one is very important. We shall come back here often. Each time we shall find that something new has grown in the meadow, some new clay has appeared with some new quality. It is not that the practitioner already knows everything there is to know — each time it is a new creation — but with increasing faith and experience, life comes to seem richer and richer and that richness keeps appearing right here at square one.

Experiential Learning

So this is the original meaning and use of meditation. To stop and look. Really look. In the Satipatthana Sutta it says that the practitioner may sit down and attend to the breath. When he attends to the breath he notices whether it is long or short, rough or smooth. From this we have derived exercises in endlessly returning the attention to the breath as a means of dismissing from the mind whatever arises in it. I think this is a complete reversal of the original intention. The reason for attending to the quality of the breath is surely that it is revealing. If we attend to it while mindful of the teaching, we can look deeper and deeper. The breath reveals our inner state. It can be a first step in investigation. Buddha recommends investigation. What is one investigating? Mind. It shows immediately and indisputably in the body, and particularly in the breathing. When we are startled we catch our breath. When we are alarmed we may almost stop breathing altogether. When we weep we gasp for breath. The breath is a doorway to prajna — to seeing below the surface, seeing what is in us. If we then ignore the associations that naturally well up we are wasting exactly the opportunity that Buddha wants us to take advantage of.

Samadhi is concentration in order to investigate Dharma. Dharma is simple, yet fundamental, truth. What is fundamentally true in our life is what happens inside, not what we present on the surface and the "inside" is extremely deep. These investigations will lead us to the kind of understandings that Buddha was always teaching. They will take us to the Dharma experientially so that one knows for oneself.

Some Thoughts about Ambapali

In the time of the Buddha, Vesali was an important town. Northern India was divided into a number of states and political groupings. One of these was the Vajji Confederation and Vesali was its capital. We can imagine it as a rather colourful and lively city with several dominant clans competing, mostly in a good spirited way. They had to co-operate defensively because across on the other side of the Ganges was the ever ambitious kingdom of Maghada. The politics of Vesali were an on-going balancing act between the different leading families and between the different small states that were members of the alliance. This circumstance, however, made for creativity through the competition of ideas and styles. Each of the great families wore a characteristic colour, and had corresponding banners, so that you immediately knew which "team" people belonged to. The town was colourful in a quite literal way.

Soon after his illumination, Shakyamuni Buddha started to visit Vesali and attracted a following there. There were also followers of other philosophies in the town. It was one of those periods in history when many schools compete and there is a lively cultural and artistic life. In the realm of religion, as in other dimensions of culture, ideas and styles were in a creative dialectical ferment. We do not know for sure, but it is certainly conceivable that the development and elaboration of both Buddhist and Jain philosophies at least, owe much to this melting pot.

There are a number of stories about the Buddha's activities in Vesali and here I want to talk about the experience of one particular woman, Ambapali. The word Ambapali refers to the fact that she was a foundling. She had been abandoned by her mother, left under a mango tree (amba). It seems that she was brought up under the protection of the city. She will have been given a foster mother, but legally belonged to the city. She apparently grew into a stunningly beautiful young woman with large eyes, sensuous lips, a fine figure and long sleek black hair. In those days the status of women was subordinate and many men wanted to possess this alluring creature. It was soon realised that this was a potential source of trouble. Which family was going to get her? We can remember the Trojan War — conflicts over a woman can have disastrous consequences. How was this to be solved? These were different times from today. The city council decided that the only equitable solution was to keep her as public property.

Ambapali became a courtesan. She was given a rather fine house and servants and her work was to entertain gentlemen. Thus she made money for the city and received a steady flow of rich gifts from admirers for herself. She became famous. The reputation of Vesali for beautiful women and especially for the most beautiful of all, Ambapali, spread and added to the attraction of the city. The prosperity of the city depended substantially upon its position in the middle of one of the main trade routes in the Ganges valley. Merchants now had yet another good reason to include a stop in the city in their itinerary. Ambapali grew rich. She acquired enough surplus to buy the mango grove where she had been left as a child and thus became the protector of the mangoes that had protected her. She seems to have enjoyed her role, the luxury, the flattery, and the comfort of her position. However, she was also haunted by existential anxiety. She knew that all this indulgence depended upon her looks and looks do not last forever. As she matured she could, to a degree, substitute acquired charm and intelligence for sheer beauty, but, nonetheless, time takes its toll and time was inexorably slipping by.

Of course, she heard all the news and gossip and the talk of the town was the sudden emergence of a new guru, said to be a completely enlightened sage, who came from the Shakyan land to the West. It was said that he was virtuous and wise, that he had started a Sangha of dedicated spiritual practitioners, even converting some other well-established teachers and all their disciples by his magical powers. It was said that he had been an ascetic and mastered all the ascetic practices but then rejected them and now taught a so-called Middle Way, "lovely in its beginning, lovely in its development, lovely in its consummation". Finally, and most tellingly, she heard, his teaching seemed to be based upon a profound understanding of the matter of impermanence. Ambapali listened to these stories intently. They spoke to her condition.

The next time the Buddha came to Vesali, Ambapali offered him the use of her mango grove. Mango groves were good places for groups of wanderers to set up camp as the big spreading trees provide plenty of shade. The Buddha received the message and was happy to accept. When news came that the Buddha's Sangha were arriving, Ambapali got into her carriage early in the morning and went quickly to the grove to make sure that all was in order to receive her precious guests of whom she had great hopes. When she saw the Buddha she was deeply affected. He had a quiet dignity and, although he clearly carried great authority in his own community, he was approachable and seemed completely free of affectation. She was used to men viewing her as a sexual object but here was a man who seemed untouched by her sexual charm yet open and friendly nonetheless. He spoke to her of virtue, of the calming of the mind and of a wisdom that is deeper than mere appearance or cleverness.

Ambapali was delighted by her conversation with the sage and invited him to come with his Sangha to take a meal at her house later in the day and give teachings there. He accepted. Seeing that all was in order, she got back in her carriage and sped back into town to get everything organised for the reception of the Sangha later in the day.

As she was hurrying home along the road, there were, coming the other way, carriages of young men from the grand Vesali families pelting along in a race to be the first to get to the Buddha, each wanting to be the one that won the prestige of entertaining the famous sage at their house. They had not expected traffic coming the other way and there was a collision. We can imagine the pandemonium, raised voices, horses neighing, accusations, tears and confusion. In the course of the subsequent exchanges, the young nobles came to realise that they had been up-staged by a prostitute and that the Buddha had already accepted her invitation. Now the course of the dialogue changed with the young men offering all kinds of inducements to get Ambapali to relinquish her claim on the Buddha. They realised that she would be a hard bargainer but could not believe that she could not be persuaded if enough money were forthcoming, but Ambapali would not budge. She said that even if they gave her half the city she would not relinquish her privilege of having the Buddha eat and teach at her house.

And so it was. The Buddha came with his friars and all sat down on the prepared seats and Ambapali's servants served the monks food and she herself served the sage and after a silent and dignified meal all the lay people and monks present settled to hear the Buddha speak. He gave a profound discourse on impermanence. It was exactly what Ambapali needed to hear. He told how peace of heart was not to be found by relying upon ephemeral things but by taking refuge in eternal ones and how such a secure refuge is naturally expressed in a virtuous life, a pure heart and a practical wisdom grounded in fundamental truth. Then he administered the five precepts appropriate for lay followers of the Dharma. Ambapali was again completely satisfied and uplifted. She said that the Sangha could have free usage of the mango grove whenever they were in Vesali and this thus became another centre for Buddhist activity in the region.

After the Buddha had left and gone on his way to another city, Ambapali treasured and pondered upon his teaching and her experience of her encounter with him. There was something very special about this man that transcended normal experience. She felt, as so many others did, that she had been in a presence that, while deeply human, was also somehow super-human. This transmission she cherished and kept in her heart. The more she reflected upon it the more right the path of the Buddhadharma seemed and the more shallow her life of luxury. She felt very bashful of making such a radical change, but one day, following a strong inner compulsion, she made her way to visit the Buddha again and begged to be admitted to the Buddhist Order as a nun. She gave all her finery back to the city that had nurtured and protected her and set out into the homeless life.

In the text the Therigata, which records the words of the nuns, is recorded the verses that she spoke in old age: "Once my hair was beautiful, now it has fallen out; once my skin was smooth, now it is covered in wrinkles, once my feet were dainty, now they are cracked and shrivelled, once my teeth were fine, now they are yellow and broken, the words of the truth-speaker are eternally valid."

Ambapali lived a vibrant life despite initial adversity and, when inspired by the Tathagata, valiantly followed her heart, disregarding material advantage. The mixture of being driven by an existential koan and inspired by a glowing example is the template of so many stories of spiritual enlightenment. In our liturgies we call her, "Ambapali, foremost in understanding impermanence". Having just come out of hospital myself* following an experience demonstrative of human mortality, I can well appreciate this classic story.

---

* In 2016, following a pulmonary embolism

Vijnana and Ayatana

Vijnana and ayatana are words that occur with great frequency in early Buddhist texts. Ayatana is generally taken as referring to the senses and vijnana to consciousness. However, the basic meaning of ayatana is "that which is out of control" and the word for consciousness is jnana, so vijnana actually seems to refer to the unconscious, or, to be very precise, as suggested earlier, we might use the word disconsciousness.

Watching the Cat Flap

These two words occur in many many places in the Buddhist texts. In many passages it seems not unreasonable to construe ayatana as referring to the senses. However, if one is clear about the basic meaning of the word, then having the senses so designated gives a much fuller meaning to the teaching. If the point is that the senses are outside of personal control then one gets a distinctive picture of the kind of mind model that the Buddha is working with. He is really talking about the senses as being like pet cats. Cats are only semi-domesticated. They go out hunting and you never know what they are going to bring home. When Buddha talks about guarding the sense doors, he has this kind of idea. The sense door is like the cat flap. Perhaps sweet pussy is just about to bring in a rat and dump it in the hall. In the same way, the senses serve us well in many ways, but they are only semi-domesticated and seem to have minds and intentions of their own which sometimes means that they bring in things that we did not intend.

Stocking the Unconscious

Vijnana is the last of the skandhas. The skandhas can be construed as giving a model of how we internalise experience, and where does that experience end up? In the creation of a mentality that may be deluded or enlightened, and is mostly held unconsciously. The point is that the senses bring material into us and it is not always what we would have wanted and is not always the sort of thing that has a beneficial effect. Buddhism talks about the mind having a kind of store or cellar where things that have been brought in remain. It matters what one's cellar is full of. This is part of the original meaning of mindfulness: what one's mind is full of.

In fact, the whole skandha teaching can be seen as a model of how the cellar of the mind can get packed with stuff that can be a spiritual liability. This is why Thich Nhat Hanh, for instance, makes much of the idea of mental diet. Furthermore, this is not just an individual matter. Large numbers of people watch the same TV programmes, are exposed to the same greed-provoking advertising, the same hate-provoking propaganda, the same delusion-provoking cultural myths. What we pay attention to lays down structures in the unconscious and these structures shape one's mentality and character.

As many of these structures are shared with other people, they provide the basis of a culture, most of which we tend to take for granted. This becomes the matrix of our mental life. Within this matrix, conscious mental activity finds its channels, but, like flowing water, it tends to follow the lines of least resistance. We might think that we are making free choices and "being oneself", but mostly we are flowing along lines created by material that was originally brought into us by our unruly senses over which we had little or no control.

Spiritual training, therefore, is not just a matter of going with the flow nor of just seeing what feels right to oneself because these types of choices may simply be reinforcing existing delusion. It is not even just a matter of awareness and conscious intention, since it is even more important what goes on at a less conscious level. This is why liberation is not simply a matter of making a conscious decision. We need liberation from what we think of as ourselves.

The unconscious can also be stocked with good stuff and this is what Buddhist mindfulness is really about. If one is constantly aware of Buddha, then the cellar of the mind is all the time receiving Dharma and so filling up with good and wholesome influences. The mind that is full of good helpful things will naturally generate wisdom and compassion without conscious contrivance.

Roaming in the Depths

Ayatana is also an element in many compounds, including some not directly relating to the senses. The two terms, ayatana and vijnana, come together, for instance, in the seventh dhyana. This is the penultimate dhyana called, in Pali, viññanāñcāyatana which is vijnana-añca-ayatana. Ñanamoli and Bodhi translate this as "infinite consciousness". However, the words taken individually and then put together would appear to mean something like the "intense arousal of the uncontrolled disconscious". This could certainly be a rapture (dhyana), but in a way that is hardly conveyed by the cool sounding term "infinite consciousness". The conventional translation implies mental mastery, whereas the words actually suggest exploring the wayward nature of mind by allowing it to roam in its own deep dark depths. This all makes one think of analytical psychology, such as that of Freud or Jung. Could it be that the so called higher dhyanas are actually intended to be deeper psychological investigations? Sorting out what is disconscious could be a good description of deep analytical psychotherapy.

All of this gives a rather different feel to what the Buddha was up to. It makes his enterprise much closer to psychoanalysis. In modern psychotherapy we have many schools and they represent different levels. There is behaviourism. Below that we have cognitive theory. Below that we have the attitudinal therapies that are called humanistic. Deeper still we have the analytical. Buddhism has all of these in a single system. Buddha perceives many layers. He says that an observer would see the superficial, the good behaviour, the personal restraint. A more perceptive person would see the mind training, the management of consciousness, but the most observant person would see below the surface altogether (prajna) into the vijnana where ayatana makes añca. Añca refers to excitation — the kind that makes one's hair stand up. So the Buddha wanted us to explore the depths as well as to regulate the surface. Unless we explore what the disconscious is it is unlikely that any resolution that we make at a conscious level is going to endure very long.

Sigmund Gotama

I, therefore, have a suspicion that Buddha was a lot more like Freud than we realise and that he was telling us about the uncontrolled senses that feed passions that move below the surface. He encouraged us to explore them, but not mistake them for any kind of personal true nature. All the phenomena of the uncontrolled disconscious are actually dependently conditioned. This is what Buddha understood. Everything that arises from a cause or condition is subject to change and does not last forever.

This helps us to understand the distinctive nature of Buddhist liberation. It is not simply the freedom to do whatever one feels like doing because it involves a recognition that a lot of what one feels like is grounded in things that came into us without our full consent. If we think again of the senses as like six pet cats, we can see that the presents that they bring us are not always quite what we might have ideally chosen. So liberation is also liberation from ourselves, from the accumulation in our cellar. This does not necessarily mean cleaning it out completely — the cats are still at work — but it does mean changing our attitude toward it and this can be a function of understanding how it works.

There has been a tendency to equate meditation with enlightenment. Meditation is exploration, and the most useful explorations are those that reveal human nature to us. This will not reveal any kind of pristine goodness. It will show us the waywardness — what Freud called the "polymorphous perversity" — of the human condition. This is enormously useful knowledge and experience. It saves us from arrogance and it is the foundation of compassion.

It also helps us to understand how it was that the Buddha recommended dhyana exploration yet also said that even the deepest, most thorough penetration of this kind did not constitute enlightenment. Therapy can be a great aid, but the true test is real life, and the ultimate secret to living a good life is not really how sorted out one is, but what is most important in one's heart. However much disconsciousness we might have, or however much we might have cleared up, we also have a capacity for mindfulness. Or, to put the same thing differently, no matter how bombu we might be, we still have a capacity to keep Buddha in our heart. It is intrinsically beneficial to investigate and sort out some of our mess, but since the senses are ayatana it is like clearing drifts while the snow is still falling. It is impossible to get to the end of the job. Nonetheless, high above, the sunlight is shining and making the snow beautiful.

So it is an intrinsically valuable activity (and Buddhism recommends it) to investigate the reality of mind as we experience it and uncover the disconscious activity that goes on there, even though doing so is an interminable task. Yet, at the same time, Buddhism also points out something else, something even more important and valuable, which is real liberation, a sudden change of heart and awakening of faith that results in everything being seen in a new light. These two aspects of Buddhism complement each other. The liberated person will investigate more readily because of having abandoned the common resistance to doing so. The investigator, through observing how disconscious he or she is, will get to know the reality of inexhaustible bombu nature and so seek liberation.

Conclusion

Understanding vijnana as disconsciousness or delusion gives us a much better understanding of Buddhism than translating it as consciouness. Realising that the term that gets translated as the senses literally means the uncontrollables also gives us a useful insight into what Buddha meant. Taken together with other Buddhist teachings this helps us to have a sense of what it is realistic to try to change and what must simply be accepted. It changes one's sense of what one does and does not have responsibility for. It also gives us a sense of what being liberated from self implies.

Self Psychology East and West

It is not necessary to create a 'self' before you abandon it.

The attempt to square Western psychology with Buddhist psychology sometimes yields useful ideas, but it also often leads to confusion. The respective attitudes to the notion of 'self' is one of the key dividing lines between the two systems.

Most Western psychology is concerned with enhancing the self just as Western philosophy is much concerned with self-knowledge and keen to assert that self-consciousness is the factor that distinguishes human beings from other beasts. Buddhist psychology, on the other hand, has a completely different view of the matter. Regarding self-consciousness, it is apparent to any pet owner that cats and dogs have self-consciousness and, for instance, are, at least briefly, quite capable of manifesting such phenomena as a guilty conscience or shame. Regarding self-knowledge, from a Buddhist point of view, the purpose of it is to eliminate obstacles to compassion and cultivate humility through an awareness of our failings. It is not seen as a way of enhancing some special quality that qualifies humans as super beings. In Buddhist psychology, self is mostly an obstacle. It is the fact that the little light of self is so much right in front of our eyes that makes us unable to see the greater light of truth that pervades the universe.

In order to attempt to reconcile these two disparate systems some people came up with the idea that one has to develop a self before you can give it up. This was a skilful and somewhat deceptive manoeuvre. It made Buddhism into the senior partner in the arrangement while completely emasculating it in effect. It was the senior partner in that giving up self was thus made into the 'higher' achievement. However, at the same time, the implication was that we are almost all of us at the earlier stage of still needing to build up our selves, so we are not yet ready for Buddhism and should concentrate on Western psychology.

This is not how Buddhism sees it. From the Buddhist point of view we have an excessive attachment to self at birth due to past karma. There is nothing so capable of exhibiting self-centredness as an infant. For sure the infant also wants to love and be loved, but that does not change the matter. As we grow up the process of psychological maturation is almost entirely made up of learning to set self aside, at least for brief periods. The mature person knows how, sometimes, to put others first; how to, occasionally, be objective, even in his or her own case; to rise above a situation and not give way to the first selfish impulse that comes along. At the simplest level, growing up is about getting self under a modicum of control.

However — and this is where psychology comes in — a good deal of what actually happens is not that self is given up but rather that it is concealed and/or trained into more circumspect or devious ways of getting what it wants. Since almost everybody is playing the same game, adult society becomes a rather convoluted affair in which we all half know what we are doing and collude with one another, but still go around in a substantial degree of blindness.

It requires quite a high level of sophistication to play the social game well and effectively and this can be the stuff of novels, including some of the best of them, which often give more insight into the matter than many psychology texts. Inevitably there are those among us — and not a few — who develop a variety of malfunctions as a result. Western psychology seems primarily concerned to help people to play the self game more effectively whereas Buddhist psychology has the avowed aim of getting us out of the game, or, at least, getting us to take it less seriously.

Letting It Go

Some years ago I read a Dharma teaching in which the teacher used the slogan: "Where there is hurt, there is self." The teacher said that this was one of the most useful "rules of thumb" that he had come across in all his spiritual training. I know what he means.

In fact, spiritual training depends upon us being willing to look at our self, not as a precious thing to be defended, but as the probable source of most of our own troubles. Of course, mostly we are unaware of it doing so. In modern parlance, we say that there are unconscious motivations. However, these subterranean rumblings have symptoms on the surface and near the surface, a bit in the same way as magma below throws up volcanoes above. Volcanoes can remain dormant for periods of time and then erupt periodically. We are much the same.

The symptoms that break the surface are apparent to others, whether they are visible to ourselves or not. We export our hurt. We dump it onto others like clouds of descending volcanic gas. Because we are all at least half-civilised, the other person probably does not tell us that we have just disgraced ourselves, but, all too often does tell all our friends.

The symptoms that are a little below the surface are therefore rather useful both at the level of saving face socially and at the more profound level of spiritual training — investigating what is deeper still, and extinguishing the flames. The level immediately below the surface is usually a feeling of hurt. The ordinary person usually responds to noticing their own hurt feelings by withdrawing or retaliating. The spiritual person learns to use such feelings as a clue, a first step in an investigation.

The investigation does not need to be massive. There is always the opposite danger of taking oneself too seriously and becoming self-obsessed in one's quest for perfect self-understanding. Usually, all that is needed is a willingness to see that one might have been in error. One might have over-stepped the mark, talked too much, seemed overly self-assured, assumed an authority that one did not in fact have any right to, or something of the kind.

If we investigate a little further, we may find that we are caught up in an unnecessary power struggle or are defending a territory that no longer exists, or feeding a resentment, or just exercising an old habit that used once to work well but is now thoroughly anachronistic.

The other day, for instance, over dinner a topic of conversation came up and I made a witticism and was told by the listener that they had already heard that joke a hundred times. Ouch! But it was right. I was being a bore. It was not necessary and also there was the slightest tinge of aggression in it. What was that all about? So, I found one or two things worth looking at a bit more. Then let it go.

The purpose of investigation on the spiritual path is to let it go. Even Freud said that when a neurosis is cured it is forgotten. Zen Master Dogen said the same thing.

There are pitfalls on both sides. On one side we defend the self and on the other side we become obsessed with investigating and curing it. These two extremes are equally forms of self-idolatry. So, the last word is, let it go.

Samadhi Soup

Concentration

Samadhi means concentration — like Heinz concentrated soup. One way to understand Dharma is to concentrate your soup. In your soup there are many ingredients — not just wholesome vegetables like leek and potato. There are also spices called greed, hate and delusion of many kinds. Some like it hot. This concentrated mass of goo is the homeless home, the ever seething cauldron of real life.

False Holiness

Mostly people are trying to dilute, bury or unsoup their soup. Diluting means trying to become pure water. There are lots of wet people wandering around in spiritual centres competing in the race to have the thinnest soup. Yet adding water does not remove the goo — it just spreads it out and makes it thinner so that it ends up making everywhere sticky. This stickiness is false holiness.

Unsouping

Then there is the therapy world. That's where you try to unsoup your soup — trace it back to the original ingredients, put the carrots back in the ground. That might not be a bad idea if you have a particularly bitter soup, but generally the best way to improve a soup is to put something else in rather than try to take something out. Taking stuff out of one's soup is the idea of trying to get back to a pure, uncontaminated self. Fortunately or unfortunately there is no such thing. Life is life-in-a-world. The world is not contamination, it is essential substance. More life requires more world concentrate, not less.

Buried Soup

Outside of the spiritual and therapy factories, burying the soup is more popular, but that does not work either — that's what we call hypocrisy. Buried soup still has to be dug up every so often and it then tastes awful. We see a lot of this in the political world. In recent history a particularly nasty murder was carried out by the agents of a powerful nation. When he heard about it, the leader of another powerful nation said that the killers had done a terrible job at covering up what they had done. This was an unusually frank remark. So much of politics is a matter of keeping nasty reality out of view.

Thick Cream Soup

Real practice is to concentrate life; that is the way. Life should not be milk and water, it should be thick cream.

People talk about samadhi and think that it is some kind of technique or, even worse, a treatment. They think that Buddhism is meditation and meditation is medication — a cure for the stress disease, or something like that — this is all wrong. In fact, Buddhism will cure neuroses, but not the way you think.

Samadhi is undiluted life. Samadhi is not something you do. When it is taken as a mental get fit programme, it just becomes a hobby. Samadhi is not a process, it is the thick soup of your life, or, if you prefer, it is clotted cream, not skimmed milk. If it is any kind of action then it is like tasting. It takes faith to put a spoonful into your mouth.

Enjoy Your Soup

Samadhi has no particular home because it makes home wherever it is. It is not just one perfect mind state. It does not really matter which bit of the soup ends up on your spoon. It is all essentially the same soup. There might be a bit more carrot in this spoonful and a bit more pepper in that one, but that kind of difference is really neither here nor there. Buddhas enjoy their soup.

Fo Tao Li: The Ideal Life

A Chinese Slogan

Fo Tao Li are three Chinese words, none of which have exact equivalents in standard English, except that we have now imported the word Tao itself, and, from Sanskrit, 'Buddha' for Fo.

Li is a key term in Confucianism, meaning correct conduct, propriety, or humane naturalness. These three qualities do not exactly correspond in English, but they did for Confucius — you can sense the general meaning.

The expression Fo Tao Li, therefore, signifies the union of the three religions of China: Confucianism, Taoism and Buddhism. By extension it can indicate a spirit of fundamental ecumenism.

Religions are human attempts to understand and live in accordance with the great mystery that is the meaning as well as the alpha and omega of existence. No religion is perfect, but they incorporate millennia of wisdom and experience, and often, as in the Chinese case, they complement one another. To be religious is to believe in the deeper meaningfulness and entrust oneself to it, all the time recognising that all human formulations of it will fall short. They fall short, yet a formula like Fo

Tao Li is a good indicator, "a finger pointing at the moon" as we say.

Qualities for the Good Life

Fo means Buddha, which signifies the most perfect sage who dedicates life to the wellbeing of all. The Tao is the mysterious way of things. The word is sometimes translated as 'Way' but the English word is only a very approximate rendering. The Tao encompasses the ceaseless churning of Yin and Yang. Li signifies to live in a natural yet wise and humane manner that is deeply respectful both of the gods and of human society.

In respect of the gods, Buddha is "the teacher of gods and humans", the Tao is their origin and also that which sets their parameters, and Li is respect for the rites that sustain them.

Consummately Human

So what is a person of Fo Tao Li like? Such a person is a consummate human being. He or she has few wants or desires, yet is able to enjoy what comes along heartily, is deeply respectful of serious things yet knows how to have fun, is genuinely modest and humble, yet also knows how to wield authority when necessary, is spontaneous, yet knows how to be formal when appropriate. Such a person can conduct a good ritual in the temple, derive from it the deep meaning, and apply that sense in everyday life, extensively, beyond, according to the myriad different circumstances that may arise.

Such a person is an artist of life. He or she has a full palette of colours, has not discarded any emotion or faculty, but has brought these energies to a fine development. They are respectful of others, of history, of tradition, of religion, of nature, yet not in a stilted way and not so narrowly that they cannot also invent, adapt, or bend with the wind when necessary. They have a certain deep dignity yet have no objection to rolling up their sleeves and doing the most mundane work, finding spiritual treasure therein.

Such a person, while being refined, is also liberated, while being free, is also at home in whatever formal setting they find themselves in, as at home in a cave as a palace and vice versa. Such a person is happy and well knows how to laugh at the ironies of life, yet also lives in continual wonderment at how things unfold.

Fo Tao Li are three complementary dimensions. Each benefits and expands the others.

Unpredictable Relationship

Individual Practice versus Relational Practice

Buddhism is often presented in a rather individualistic manner in the sense that it is described as a practice for the individual to do on their own. Each must walk the path. This type of idea is not wrong, but it carries considerable danger of misrepresenting the balance and scope of Buddhist teaching.

In fact, the great majority of Buddhist scriptures describe interactions between people. What is profoundly interesting is the Buddha's compassion for different people who come to see him. Then the koans of Zen are also mostly descriptions of interactions between masters or masters and disciples. Again, the famous stories of Tibetan Buddhism describe the interactions between Milarepa and Marpa or Tilopa and Naropa, or Guru Rinpoche and the people he met. It is mostly about how illumined beings interacted with others and the whole tradition descends through such interactions and derives from those original encounters that people had with Shakyamuni.

It is, therefore, just as true to say, or even more true to say, that Buddhism is a style of relating, as to say that it is an individual practice. What is the difference?

When we think of an individual practice, we tend to think of something with a fixed protocol. When people talk about 'my practice' they mean that they have a ritual of some kind that they do that they believe has a good effect upon them, hopefully leading to their own illumination. Meditation is just as much a ritual as lighting a candle if what we mean by it is a fixed form of practice done regularly. In fact, meditation may be even more strongly 'ritualised' than lighting a candle, since each candle is slightly different.

When we think of interactions, however, each one is unique. One cannot be in control. It is like a dance: just as much depends upon the other as upon oneself and then there is the influence of the circumstances within which the interaction takes place. So if we take only these three things — self, other and circumstance, it is apparent that the self-element is in the minority. This, therefore, calls for flexibility and a certain wisdom.

If we go back to the example of lighting a candle, one should be able to see that one could do it as an individual practice, in which case the candle is merely a utility, or one could do it with some degree of relationship to the candle as the 'other'. In the latter case, each instance of lighting a candle is going to be more distinct and unique than if one does it as an individual practice. So there is an important difference of attitude here and the relational attitude is much closer to the essence of Buddhism.

Unpredictability

Buddhism is a wisdom religion and much of this wisdom is the practical wisdom of knowing how to relate to others and of skill in relating to them when they do or say something unexpected. As we have just seen with the candle, 'others' do not always have to be animate. When things become 'others' in this sense, they 'teach' us, and so become Buddhas and Dharmas. When everything becomes so then we live in the midst of the 'myiad Dharmas' and 'myriad Buddhas'.

When Shakyamuni went to see Angulimala, the brigand, he did not know what was going to happen. He was learning as well as teaching. We can immediately see that a characteristic of the Buddha was a kind of courage or fearlessness in meeting others, no matter who they were. If we think of this as being one of the main hallmarks of Buddhism we start to get an important sense of what Buddhism is all about. We can also see that somebody who lives in such a bold way learns a lot and learns fast. Thus, they are continually growing and changing.

For many people the attraction of having a practice lies in the security of predictability. This, however, is definitely not what Buddhism is about. Buddhism seeks security in taking refuge in Buddha, Dharma and Sangha, not in any technique or self-controlled practice. So here there lies a pitfall. If one has a practice, then the aim of that practice should be to get one beyond dependence upon the practice, not leave one immersed in attachment to it. One has to penetrate to the deep meaning of the practice, which is always taking refuge, no matter what form of practice one is using.

Then there is a second kind of pitfall which is that the partial security provided by the predictability of practice can itself function as a delaying tactic, enabling the practitioner to avoid really letting go.

Clapping

Refuge is itself a relationship practice. It is to entrust oneself to the Buddhas without knowing what they will do with you. When one lets go of self, one puts oneself in a position where the mission that the Buddhas have for you can become apparent. This can seriously disrupt one's taken for granted life.

Relationships are not predictable. One has to play one's part. To play one's part is to be 'one hand clapping' — as in the children's game where two people clap hands together, but the other hand is not under one's control, so to make the two to meet is never quite the same from one instance to the next.

So Buddhism is like that — a relationship practice. The art of making two hands come together in a clap, only one of which is one's own, requires something more than just individual practice. Like practising tennis, one needs at least a wall that will bounce the ball back and each time it comes at you it requires something slightly new.

Facility in response does come with practice, but it is practice that is interactional.

The relational attitude thus makes a big difference. Buddhism is transmitted by encounter because the right kind of encounter is Buddhism.

Can a Tile Be a Mirror?

Nangaku and Baso

There is a story about two monks, Nangaku and Baso. Baso has been practising meditation for ten years. Nangaku comes along.

> Nangaku: What is the use of meditation?
>
> Baso: To make a Buddha!
>
> Nangaku picks up a tile. He starts to rub the tile.
>
> Baso: What are you doing?
>
> Nangaku: Making a mirror.
>
> Baso: You can't make a mirror by polishing a tile.
>
> Nangaku: You can't make a Buddha by meditating.
>
> Baso is enlightened.

This is a very important story and it was dear to Dogen.

The story tells us that gradual study (polishing, meditating) is endless. It has no natural limit, like polishing a tile. You will never get to the point where it turns into a mirror. A tile cannot become a mirror.

However, in Dogen's sense, the tile is a mirror, since it showed Baso to Baso. Therefore, the tile was a mirror already. The mirror is a mirror before it is polished and it is a mirror after it has been polished. The polishing is also a mirror. The polishing is a mirror when the tile turns into a mirror and also when the tile does not turn into a mirror. When the tile does not turn into a mirror, it mirrors not turning into a Buddha. Mirroring in this way it turns Baso into a Buddha. When Nangaku and Baso are both Buddhas they are the same. They are the same qua mirrors, but there is nothing the same about these two mirrors. Baso becomes Baso. When Baso becomes Baso he forgets he is Baso. Forgetting he is Baso he becomes a mirror. This mirror, however, is still just a tile. Baso is still the same old Baso. Therefore, there is no need to polish the tile. On the other hand, the mirror can become a tile when Baso is enlightened. When Baso is enlightened, not only the tile, but rivers, mountains and trees all become Buddhas and Buddhas become rivers, mountains and trees.

Realising Anger

A Fierce Flame

Anger is hate energy. It is like an acetylene flame. You can use an acetylene flame to cut through steel or to weld things together or to start a fire that will burn your house down. Life too is full of possibilities.

Generally we get frightened when anger appears. Anger is very infectious. It shows up in one person and soon everybody is feeling it. Fear and anger are like an alternating current switching back and forth — now rage, now fear, now rage, now fear, now... When it is strong it can bring out a sweat.

It is a rather acute energy — short and sharp. It can disappear as quickly as it appears, but in that short time it can do an awful lot of damage if you are not careful. When you have an acetylene torch, you need to know how to use it, or you can get badly hurt.

Of course, this is true of most tools. If you use them badly you can hurt yourself. The torch is just another tool. On the one hand, it pays not to be foolhardy, waving it about randomly as if it were nothing. On the other hand, you don't need to be afraid of it if you have a steady hand and a clear purpose.

There is a story about a samurai warrior wandering into a Buddhist temple. He sees the monk and challenges him. He says, "What use are you priests? And what is all this rubbish about heaven and hell that you confuse people with?" The monk looks at him and, with some animation, says, "You? You call yourself a soldier! Huh. You are a disorderly wimp, that's what you are." The samurai's hand goes to the hilt of his sword and he is just starting to draw it. The monk changes his manner completely and with great calm and kindness says, "Here open the gates of hell." The samurai, sensing the monks more friendly manner and lack of fear, relaxes. The sword drops back into its scabbard. "And here open the gates of heaven," says the monk. "Now that we have met one another, can I offer you some refreshment?"

Clear Purpose

Clear purpose means knowing what your life is dedicated to. The human lifespan is not that long so it pays to make the most of it. Choose a path that is not going to leave you full of regret in later years. Do something with your life that is intrinsically worthwhile. You may have to try a few things in order to refine your choice. In my own life I have progressed through being an accountant to working for a charity to becoming a social worker to being a therapist to being a priest. Yet all the time, my inspiration was the truly wise sages — the Buddhas of all times. I had a spiritual vision from my earliest years — the challenge has been both to find how to apply it and then to have the courage to just go for it.

Anger Fever

How do you get a steady hand? Practice and experience. Handling anger is very intense experience. Sometimes you feel as though you are going to explode into a million pieces. You don't, of course, but blood pressure and body temperature may well rise. You can use physical symptoms like that to gauge what is happening.

Maybe somebody is taunting you, needling the things you value, running down your reputation, threatening, or actually damaging things you love and need for your purpose. You can feel your body getting hot. Fever. Pressure. Physically your organism is getting ready for fight or flight.

Restraint

Now because we are half-way civilised, we have learnt various strategies for not just doing the thing that nature has prepared us for which might be homicide or running away as fast as legs can carry one. However, it is important to respect these gifts of nature, even if we have learnt prudence and restraint in using them. If we start from a position of thinking that the natural instinct is "bad" or "evil" we are condemning the very stuff that we are made of.

Offering

This might mean having a conscious awareness of feeling violent — that's powerful — or it might not have any cognitive content, just feeling the feeling. Really what is needed at this point is not personal mastery. What is needed is a truly spiritual act — something deep — which is to make oneself into an offering. It is like turning to the Buddhas and saying "This is what I've got. It's just arrived and it's burning hot. I hope you like it." That is a kind of prayer and you might say it but actually there is no need to say anything — it is the act of turning and offering that matters, that and being willing to accept what comes.

This requires faith. It may seem crazy but Buddha can bless even the most searing rage and in that blessing there is nothing but pure love. When you feel it, the fire of hell becomes the light that illuminates heaven.

More on Anger

Eliminate

In some branches of Buddhism, anger is seen as something that should be absolutely eliminated. These kinds of teachings are very important and beautiful. They represent the Hinayana point of view. Why not just enjoy being good? Simple really — or maybe not always. There are some further things to be said.

The suggestion is that when one is completely illuminated spiritually one never becomes angry. It is probably true that anger in such a person is rare and occurs in a different way for different reasons.

Divert

There is, of course, a difference between what we feel and what we do. It is possible to train oneself not to express anger even if one feels it. Is that a good thing? Sometimes it is a matter of good manners. The English are, perhaps, particularly good at expressing anger in oblique ways, such as damning with faint praise or using irony. At least this can have an element of humour in it, but it can still cut or burn.

Probably, the best one can do sometimes is to divert the energy into a different channel. We can see this kind of sublimation at work in many people who support social or political causes. Behind their altruism is a rage about something. This is, however, not always so very far from the surface and much social action can be a matter of condemning and deploring this or that action by others, or, worse, attacking those persons.

What Would Buddha Do?

It does appear that the Buddha expressed himself rather fiercely on some occasions. In the Snake Simile Sutta poor Arittha gets a thorough dressing down for misrepresenting the Buddha's teaching, for instance. The Buddha's position on angry expression, if you like to call it that, is that it is only appropriate when it actually does some good. This means, really, that the enlightened person does not get angry just out of feelings of personal hurt. This is right because enlightenment is that state in which one is not caught up in conceit. That characteristic sensation that we call "feeling hurt" is a pretty accurate marker of the presence of ego investment.

However, we can probably all think of times when somebody else's anger has brought us to our senses about something, or made us desist from doing something foolish. These times are not common, but they certainly occur. The problem here is that it takes the wisdom of Solomon to know in advance what the outcome will be. Anger is an emergency reaction and/or an expression of extreme displeasure — just as the Buddha was displeased with Arittha — and, for most of us, these are not times when one is most considered in one's actions. In fact, it is probably substantially because, at such a moment, one feels the impact of something that is not anticipated that makes the encounter powerful. So the injunction to only get angry when you judge that it is wise to do so is a tall order. There probably is a split second in which such a judgement might occur, but no more.

So it is not much use having an injunction that demands that one make a judgement before getting angry — things don't work that way. What is needed, and I think this is what Buddha means, is that by being beyond conceit one then only gets angry on those occasions where something of much wider than merely personal interest is at stake and these are the occasions when it might do some good.

Nonetheless, overall, I think that what is really important is that what happens between people is authentic and real. In the longer run, that is what "does good". Trying to assess goodness of outcome on some utilitarian basis is really spiritual materialism and not going to work.

The Flame of Life

As for those who still are, in varying degrees, caught in the web of conceit — and which of us is not? — one should recognise that the anger they express — or the other passions, whatever they may be — is their life energy. It is the sign that they are alive and it is exactly the same energy as will make them/us into an enlightened person.

Anger is one of the first emotions to appear in the baby. The baby knows how to cry and scream and this is how it stays alive. It is the only power it has. When it is hungry, or needs something, its only way of getting it is to scream. The good parent says, "My! He's got a good voice." The baby we were is still alive and well inside us too, and although one can organise one's life so that it is not roused too often, I doubt that there are many of us who do not feel that infantile rage mounting from time to time.

The Reviler Story

If we think of the story of the Reviler who comes and abuses the Buddha, we remember that when he has stopped insulting the Buddha, the Buddha then asks him if he sometimes has guests come to his house and the Reviler says he does and the Buddha asks if, when guests come he offers them food and a resting place and the Reviler says that he does, and the Buddha then asks "But if, Brahmin, your visitors do not accept what you offer, to whom does it then belong?" The Reviler says, "Well, if they do not accept them, they stay with me," and the Buddha then says, "It is just so in this case. You revile and scold us who do not do so back. So we do not accept what you offer, so it stays with you, it belongs to you, Brahmin."

Now the moral of this story is clear and useful, but if one thinks about and imagines the incident, we actually have here a rather reasonable Brahmin who is willing to listen to what the Buddha is saying and, if this incident actually occurred, then the Buddha must have sensed that speaking in this way would, in this case, do some good. If so, then this is a rare case. Normally, if one spoke as the Buddha did to an angry person one would get a response something like: "You think you're so clever, don't you? Look at you, all full of your own cleverness. Proud! That's what you are. Proud, and too clever for your own good." The abuse would not stop, but be amplified.

There is a story about a person coming to a talk by another Dharma master and heckling and abusing him for some time until the master stood up, looked at him fiercely and said with his full power voice "Get out of here. Right now. Go!" and the man left. The next day, the master met the man in another situation and was perfectly friendly to him as if nothing had happened. This was certainly a real incident and something real happened between the two men.

These stories tell us that there is not just one way to be that fits every situation. Dealing with a reasonable person is not the same as dealing with an unreasonable one. Responding to words that are chosen and intended is not the same as responding to ones that are rash and loose. There are as many situations as permutations of personalities.

Feel the Fever

I could say that in my life I have learnt to control my anger, but it is not really a strictly accurate thing to say. It would be truer to say that I get angry only much more rarely than I did and that even on those rare occasions, I tend not to lose my objectivity about what is happening. I feel the feeling welling up and I also see the situation. It is good to feel energy welling up. That is life. I feel wonder at it. I say to myself "You know, I am really angry about this," as I feel my blood hot and my body tense. I wonder where the anger is going to take me. So I have both feelings simultaneously — the anger and the wonderment. Perhaps I lose some sleep. Of course, the anger does not go on and on for ever, but if I respect it, it usually yields some insight. It shows its colours, we might say, and, in the end, I am wiser for that. Perhaps it turns into another feeling, or perhaps it reveals a connection with something important in my life or perhaps it tells me that there is something that does require decisive action, or whatever.

So, yes, overcome hatred by love, but not just naively and superficially and not in a formulaic way that is liable to escalate rather than really defuse the tension.

The Big Scene

The same is true at the level of international politics. Right now in the world what is required is more understanding. We in the West need to understand why the Russians feel so paranoid about NATO bringing its lethal weaponry closer and closer to their borders and why so many Arab people distrust us. Because we think that our way of life is best, we see nothing wrong in spreading it, but other people, who do not think it is best, experience this as invasive. So we tend not to see what they see and they do not see what we see. What is needed is not so much that we all stop being angry with each other — though that might be a natural outcome — we need rather to stop being so conceited, to stop thinking our way is best. That was the essential teaching of Buddha. It is conceit that is the root of the problem, not the existence of emotional energy. The latter, when stirred up by the former is a problem, but the problem is solved by overcoming the former — the conceit — not by suppressing the latter — the emotional energy.

Confidence in Love and Understanding

The baby is not to be despised. For sure it is good to grow up and I am all for spiritual maturity, but I respect the child too. The child has the raw energy that the adult needs. As we grow up we learn to turn a lot of that energy against itself which produces a kind of inner exhaustion. If our lives are to bloom, we need to liberate that energy and we will not do so by repression, only by the growth of confidence in love and understanding and by seeing through our own conceit.

Decay of the Body

One of the classic forms of Buddhist meditation is contemplation of the decay of the body. To perform this meditation monks would go to the charnel grounds where dead bodies were burned or were sometimes simply left to be eaten by vultures. One could observe every stage of decay and these stages are recorded in detail in the Buddhist texts — how the body gets eaten by maggots, how flesh falls away, how bones disassemble, how eventually there is just dust.

One of the 'benefits' of modern hygiene is that there are no longer such places where one can go and see it all in process. However, a compensating 'benefit' of modern medicine is that one can now contemplate the decay of the body by observing one's own condition. Nowadays we live with a great variety of ailments that in the old days would have carried one off. Thus, as one gets older the number of such gradually gets greater and, broadly speaking, they tend to get worse rather than better. Getting old generally means putting up with an ever increasing degree of bodily decay.

In my own case, to the casual observer I remain a healthy looking specimen. Making a list of my current ailments, I came up with twenty items ranging in severity from 'trigger finger syndrome' through psoriasis and migraines to abdominal aortic aneurysm and pulmonary embolisms. There are actually few areas of my body not evidently affected one way or another and one can reasonably assume, I think, that the few areas that are showing no symptoms are, nonetheless, suffering wear and tear much like the rest. After all, they have been around just as long and been through the same degree of roughness of life.

I reflect that I am relatively fortunate that all my different components seem to be decaying at much the same rate. Some poor souls have one bit fall to pieces at an early stage while everything else is still in fair working order which seems like rather a waste.

The whole point of the Buddhist meditation on these matters is to bring one to a degree of objectivity about the whole matter and, thereby, to eliminate one's fantasy that one is a special case, different from all the rest of the universe — a fond delusion that generalises to all manner of other kinds of lunacy — and thereby restore a measure of sanity.

Praying for All Lineages

This morning in our service we chanted our "Prayer of All Lineages"*. Buddhism started from Buddha Shakyamuni and then spread throughout Asia and now is coming to Western countries as well. Buddha was a wonderful teacher who seems to have been able to bring out the best in people as well as help them overcome their blindnesses and become more wise and compassionate. However, each person is different and his leading disciples likewise. Each had a special talent. Shariputra was wise. Mogalana was good at meditation and yoga. Asaji was good at keeping the discipline. Ananda was kind, and so on. When new younger students came to be disciples, Buddha would allocate them to one or other of his chief disciples according to their need or talent. Thus, from the very beginning there were different schools of Buddhism, even while the sage was still alive.

As the Dharma spread far and wide this diversity continued. Although there are a variety of lineages, after Shakyamuni himself there was never really a Buddhist supreme prelate, like the pope. The nearest thing is the

---

* page 4, Nien Fo Book: The service book of Amida Shu, Amida Shu, 2018

Dalai Lama but he is only officially the head of Tibetan Buddhism. Different schools all developed in their different ways.

In many schools of Buddhism there exist "lineage prayers" that celebrate the lineage of main teachers in that particular tradition. When I was a Zen monk, we used to recite every morning the list of eighty-five teachers from Shakyamuni down to our own present day teacher. These lineage traditions have been used to help establish the legitimacy of particular groups at various times in history, although modern scholarship has revealed various lacunae in them.

As Buddhism comes to the West it comes into a different culture with a different religious history. Here we are also used to having different denominations, but they did not mostly originate in an attempt to cater for natural human diversity so much as from conflict and disagreement. In Buddhism it is not unnatural for a person to study more than one school. In the West, however, there is a greater possessiveness about congregations and rivalry between sects. It would be a shame if this sectarian disease got too established in the new-to-the-west Buddhist religion. In our own Sangha, therefore, we do not have a separate prayer, we have a "prayer of all lineages" to celebrate the great diversity of ways in which the Dharma has been transmitted to the present day.

Reciting the prayer also gives one an appetite to study the lives and teachings of all — or at least some — of this vast collection of great Dharma ancestors.

Shariputra and His Brother Enter the Way

Shariputra and his brother Maudgalyayana were two of the greatest disciples of Buddha. Shariputra was renowned for his wisdom and Maudgalyayana for his ability to enter into transcendental states.

This is how it all started.

One day Shariputra was out walking and he met a monk called Ashvajit. Shariputra was impressed by the demeanour of the monk and asked him who his teacher was.

Ashvajit said that he was a disciple of Prince Siddhartha who had renounced the world of birth and death, had left home to practise and had attained supreme enlightenment.

Shariputra asked Ashvajit what was the teaching of this great sage.

Ashvajit said that he was only newly embarked upon the path and asked how could he possibly express the supreme wisdom of Shakyamuni?

Shariputra, therefore, begged Ashvajit to just tell him some essential point in simplified form so that he could get the flavour of the teaching.

Ashvajit said, "All phenomena arise in dependence upon conditions. He expounds the causes and conditions and the way beyond them. This is how he teaches."

At this, Shariputra had a great awakening, attaining what is called 'stream entry'. He went back to where he was staying and Maudgalyayana came out to meet him. Immediately seeing that Shariputra was in a state of alacrity he asked him to share what had brought on his good mood. Shariputra told him all about his encounter with Ashvajit and Maudgalyayana was similarly inspired and also became a 'stream enterer'.

There are a number of important points about this story.

1. The spiritual awakenings in the story come from inter-personal encounter. In these encounters there is communication of information and teaching, but there is also communication of a radiance. Ashvajit gave Shariputra not just teaching but also his demeanour. There was thus subliminal communication that was every bit as important as the conscious content.

2. Both instances of spiritual awakening in the story happened as a result of the receipt of second hand information. Shariputra and Maudgalyayana received the Buddha Dharma without meeting the Buddha. The Dharma thus ripples out.

3. Shariputra and his brother were clearly 'ripe' for spiritual awakening. In fact, they were looking for teaching. They were spiritual seekers. Ashvajit was the trigger that tipped them into a new spirit.

4. Part of what Ashvajit manifested was modesty. He does not claim to be wise. He starts by demurring.

Shariputra has to press him in order to get the teaching. Therefore this story also illustrates the principle of not teaching an unwilling audience. Only when Shariputra has demonstrated that he does really want to know does Ashvajit proclaim the Dharma.

5. The actual content of what Ashvajit shares is a version of the Four Truths. Worldly phenomena are dependent upon conditions, but it is possible to go beyond this. This is the liberative message that Shariputra was looking for.

In due course, the two brothers go to see the Buddha, take refuge and become disciples.

Buddha's Last Words

Almost at the end of his life, Shakyamuni said:

> Atta-dīpā
>
> viharatha
>
> atta-saraṇā
>
> anañña-saraṇā,
>
> dhamma-dīpā
>
> viharatha
>
> dhamma-saraṇā
>
> anañña-saraṇā.

Common Renderings

This has been variously translated, as

> Be islands unto yourselves, refuges unto yourselves, seeking no external refuge; with the Dhamma as your island, the Dhamma as your refuge, seeking no other refuge

or

> You are the light, abide in this, rely on yourself, rely on no one else, the Dharma is the light, abide in this, rely on the Dharma, rely on nothing else.

I would like to comment on some of the translation difficulties and offer an alternative.

What is Dīpā?

Firstly, there is no consensus about whether dīpā means "light" or "island". "Light" seems more likely to me and the majority of commentators seem to agree although this was not always so. Early renderings tended towards "island". In some ways it makes little difference to the sense whichever way you translate the rest as I shall explain below. It is also possible that the word has both meanings.

What is the Punchline?

The crucial points are where you put the emphasis and how you render the term atta. Many commentators have taken the emphasis as being self-reliance and have taken the general drift as being "Rely only on yourself and use the Dharma as support for doing so." I think this is wrong. It seems to me pretty clear that the punch line is dhamma-saraṇā. Dhamma-saraṇā is what Buddha taught throughout his ministry. It was the teaching he gave to the first two people ever to become Buddhists whom he met on the road when travelling after his enlightenment, before even he gave the Setting in Motion of the Wheel of the Dharma discourse, and that discourse is also a commentary on how to take refuge in Dharma. All along, Buddha teaches, "Take refuge in Dharma," so it is totally consistent that this should be the teaching that he wants to leave people with. So this is not a teaching about self-reliance, as many Westerners and self-power Buddhists would like to make it. It is a teaching about taking refuge.

What About Atta?

Atta means self. The controversy about the term atta (Sanskrit atma) has generally revolved around whether it implies something about the Hindu idea of a soul (atma) or, at least, about an enduring self, and what this says about other non-self teachings by Buddha. However, I think this misses the point. Here atta is a reflexive pronoun. The word atta means self and, as in English, it can become a noun, as in "the meaning of the self is a problem in philosophy", but it is more commonly used as a reflexive pronoun or adjective meaning roughly the same as auto — as in self-sufficient, self-contained, self-starting, self-generated, self-confident and so on. I think this is how it is used here and this means that the term atta-dīpā is a term of this kind, indicating a light that does not rely upon anything else, an unconditional light that needs no fuel. This is not a statement about the atma, it is a statement about the Dharma. The Dharma is the only atta-dīpā — the only light that is eternally shining, that relies on nothing else, that is not impermanent. Such a light could be also described as an island, unconnected to other land.

I therefore suggest that this passage is a single whole in which all the lines give different perspectives upon the one vital theme which is take refuge in Dharma. It is not a combination of two statements, one about "the self" and the other about "the Dharma" with no apparent connection between them — even a hint of a contradiction. If you take it in the way most commentators do, there remains a difficult problem of explaining how the first four lines connect with the second four. It is quite common in Western Buddhist books for only the first four to be mentioned. We are told that Buddha's last words were that you should rely upon yourself. I think this is a gross distortion, trying to make Buddhism into Westernism.

The Dharma is "self-lighting". Atta-dīpā is the Dharma. Dharma is spontaneous truth, uncontrived, independent, unconditional. Therefore it is atta-dīpā.

Some Other Small Points

Viharatha means to dwell or abide. However, it is worth pausing over the word for a minute. The term vihara came to mean a small Buddhist monastery, but it seems to have originally meant a park. In the time of Buddha many towns had parks and it would be in such a park that ascetics would gather, stay and give teachings. In due course, the Buddhist Sangha was given some lands which were generally parks, groves or orchards and they put up huts there and this was the origin of monasticism. However these base camps were mostly only used in the rainy season retreat when one needed some shelter from the monsoon. A few monks would remain through the year to look after the place, but the main basis of Buddhist life was wandering. This is why the term "monk" is not really quite right. Buddhist bhikkhus were friars. Anyway, the relevant point here is that at the time of Buddha's demise viharatha probably still had the implication of "dwell in the open" and therefore had a sense of not getting enmeshed in the household life, the life of conditions, an implication of freedom. This implication is wholly consistent with the point that the Dharma is an unconditional light or unattached island.

Anañña-saraṇā means take no other as refuge. Saranā means refuge taken. Añña occurs in the Abhidhamma term añña-maññā (the 7th paccaya in the section on Conditional relations) meaning interdependence or co-dependence — the illustration given is the legs of a tripod that cannot stand without each other. Given modern usage co-dependence might be the better translation. So if añña means co-dependency, anañña means freedom from co-dependency. Relying upon the Dharma frees one from co-dependency. We are inclined to seek refuge from dukkha in various forms of co-dependency and Dharma is the remedy.

Viharatha and anañña-saraṇā, therefore, both have implications of steering clear of worldly involvement represented by the household life and enmeshed relationships. The whole passage tells us that the way to avoid such enmeshment is to rely upon the Dharma which is the natural, spontaneous radiance.

Final Words

My preferred translation, therefore, runs as follows...

> Spontaneous light
> Abide therein

Spontaneous refuge
Seek no other
Dharma light
Abide therein
Dharma refuge
Seek no other

Two Famous Koans

If you are familiar with the koans of Zen you will know at least these two. The first is "What is the sound of one hand clapping?" and the other is called Joshu's Mu. The second is based on the story that when the Buddhist Master Joshu was asked whether a dog has Buddha Nature, he said "Mu" which usually means "No." Zen has a characteristic kind of dialogue in which spiritual truths are expressed in a kind of symbolical dialectic. Thinking about these two koans might get you into it.

So what is the sound of one hand clapping? It is that one does what is best unilaterally. If the other hand comes to meet you, that is wonderful, but if it does not, no matter, one still does one's part. A community is like this. Each person does their best and there is then a surplus of goodwill sufficient to absorb setbacks. When one hand is clapping, the other is encouraged to join in. This is the perfect situation. Each person is completely absorbed in his or her faith and practice and so is a perfect example to everyone around them. People who come to visit them feel good about it, get caught up in the atmosphere and want to come again. Those who reside feel joy in each other's company. Those who go away feel that they have something solid behind them. They feel able to go forth and be one hand clapping.

Usually when one goes to the temple at the appointed time everybody is there ready to join in the ceremony together. Even if one had been sluggish or reluctant to go, when one arrives and joins in one feels good. Sometimes one goes to the hall at the appointed time and nobody else shows up. One thinks, that's fine, they must all have good things that they need to do. One lights a candle and get on on one's own. That is one hand clapping. Sometimes the others show up later. Sometimes they don't. Sitting in the divine presence one feels happy either way — one way for the solitude and the other way for the company. Sometimes it is oneself who does not show up, sometimes for a good reason, sometimes not. In any case, one knows that one is still loved and whatever vicissitude of reason or emotion one is going through, one knows that there is here a fund of love and goodwill and all will be well. This is the sound of one hand clapping.

Why Did Joshu say Mu? When one hand claps, it enters emptiness. When Joshu was asked if a dog had Buddha Nature he said "Wu" (Mu in Japanese) which means "No" or "Empty" or "Without". To which the hearer may say, "But I thought it was Buddhist doctrine that all sentient beings have Buddha Nature." This response, however, betrays an intention to cling to formulas. We should ask ourselves who or what is the dog? Just as we need to know who or what is the one hand that claps. When we have found the dog, we can find out if it is empty or not. Perhaps we will discover that true Buddhist faith and practice is a matter of emptying the dog again and again. Or perhaps we shall find that the dog was empty from the very beginning. Or perhaps the old dog just likes lying in the sun, in which case, we must ask: who or what is the true sun? And when the dog is lying in the sun, does it get full or does it stay empty? Is Buddha Nature something that comes and goes? When it is coming and going, what is it up to? Is one hand clapping the same as one dog barking? Is the old dog barking the same as Joshu saying, "Wu"?

Buddha Nature is not a personal asset, it is something that appears when one hand claps. When an old dog is empty he does not think about one hand clapping, but it claps all the same.

Why Is It So Hard to Be Natural?

Unnatural Existence

Neurosis — unnecessary worry — is an aspect of living in an unnatural way. Why is it so difficult to be natural, to be straight-forward, to be in tune with one's instincts? Why do we worry unnecessarily and then, when we worry appropriately, think that there is something wrong with us? Why do we preserve a secret self that we dare not show to the world? When we consider the question in this last form, it becomes apparent that the answer does not lie entirely within oneself. In modern life, we live a thoroughly unnatural existence. We were not really evolved for this. Yet, even in terms of what we were evolved for, which was probably to live in small relatively isolated family groups, perhaps in the savannah or forest margins or perhaps on the coast, gathering, hunting and fishing, it is still not that easy to live naturally. People in less economically developed lands do tend to be happier and more carefree and have less of the hang-ups and neuroses characteristic of our civilisation, but they still have complicated lives that are a good deal less than enlightened. Life can still be "nasty, brutish and short".

It is often the case nowadays that people are more interested in finding ways to eliminate the symptoms of living an unnatural life than they are in eliminating the cause of those symptoms by living more naturally. Buddhism has got caught up in this in the fashion for using meditation or mindfulness as a cure for stress in such a way that it is not really a cure at all, but simply a way of reducing the symptoms on a short term basis. In fact, training oneself to turn one's attention to the here and now is, in most cases, really a form of distraction. It briefly takes one's mind away from the causes of tension and this induces some degree of welcome relaxation, but as soon as one stops doing the exercise, the "to do list" or the in-tray reasserts its demands and the stress generating situation is found to be unchanged. Rather than change our lives, we would rather find ways to avoid the symptoms. This is not enough, but I wonder if the deeper message of Buddhism will ever get through.

To Stop Trying is Not So Easy

Really, to be natural and to be enlightened are much the same thing. We say: when Shakyamuni is, was and will be enlightened, he realised no birth. What does this mean? One thing that it means is that you are what you are, you were what you were and you will be what you will be and this is not something that you should be ashamed of. There is a basic paradox. We will make things happen when we stop trying to make things happen. We shall be more how we should be when we stop trying to make ourselves be the way we think we should be. This applies whatever it is that we think we should be — more of a saint, a more effective gangster, a better parent, the most cynical person on the planet, whatever. We shall be perfect when we stop trying to be perfect at whatever it is. At a subtle level we are caught in a problem of control. The problem of life is caused by will displacing willingness.

People commonly think that one needs to become conscious in order to bring about change. However, the person who becomes aware he is alcoholic generally does not stop drinking. The person who knows she is fat may go on a diet, but a year later she probably weighs the same as before, or even more. Simply being conscious does not change ingrained habit. The person became alcoholic for a reason. It was, we could say, a form of self-medication. Perhaps there were things he did not want to feel or think about. That intention to avoid led to the drinking habit and simply being aware that he is drinking will not change the underlying urge to try to avoid life.

Guilt

Perhaps we think we have to heal the past, but the past is past and, anyway, is not exactly how we remember it to have been. Perhaps we feel we have to guarantee the future, but the future will not be what we expect. Perhaps we feel that there is something wrong in the present time, but the present time is what it is. Perhaps we think there should not be so much suffering in the world. A noble thought and, in itself, quite natural. However, even while I write these words somewhere some animal has probably just been ripped to pieces by another one for its dinner. I did not do anything to cause nor to prevent it. Am I, therefore, guilty? In one sense yes and in one sense no. No in the obvious sense. Yes in the sense that I willingly and wilfully participate in this life in which suffering is an intrinsic dimension. This latter kind of guilt is built in. One has to take it on without being crippled by it and without running away from it. Much of our supposed self-improving is actually just the working out of deep existential guilt and a wish to try to avoid life as it is.

Knowing Deeply

The life of Shakyamuni is instructive in that he only arrived after swinging from one extreme to the other. Mostly, we try to reduce our swings or hide them, but he really went for it. He swung as far as one can go in the direction of self-indulgence and then in the direction of self-punishment. He gave them both a good try. This must mean that, thereafter, he knew them and knew them in a way that most people do not. We could say that he had tested self-power to its limit and found it lacking.

There is a world of difference between knowing in one's bones and knowing in one's head. So it was quite natural for him to not fall into extremes later, not because he had a theory about the middle path, and not because he was constantly monitoring himself for tendencies toward error, but because he knew it in the same way as a person who has been burnt does not put their hand in the fire again. He did have such a theory and he did monitor himself effectively, but these were only means to implement what he felt deeply from experience. When we have the theory and/or the technique we are liable to think that that is what matters, but they are not much use without the deeper knowledge.

Avidya

So some of the reason that we live unnatural lives is that we continue to be ignorant of what this artificiality is doing to us and we are party to that ignorance — we have a range of strategies to perpetuate it. This wilful ignorance is called avidya. This is one reason why a large part of Dharma training is unlearning rather than learning. A second reason is that learning is one of our strategies.

The modern educated person has a tendency to confuse knowing and knowing about. Knowing about something is not the same as knowing it. I know a certain amount about China but I have never been there. Actually, I probably know more about China than I do about Korea, but I have been to Korea several times. I know Korea in a quite different way to the way I know China. There are many people who know Dharma in the way that I know China.

So, in a funny kind of way, we can say that in the modern circumstance it is quite natural to be unnatural. You would be, wouldn't you? In fact, being natural in this kind of world is rather unnatural, in a certain way. Such is the paradox of modern life. Enlightened people are likely to be seen as odd.

Such Faith is Rare

However, as I said earlier, this is not just a problem of modern society. Much about modern society exacerbates it, but there are also universal human factors. Relationships are always complicated, even if you live in a cave, and they put pressure on the individual to betray his or her deeper instincts, yet we cannot live without them. This is a challenge to develop relationships of a kind that are supportive of liberation — what we call Sangha. To do so requires a faith that transcends ephemeral circumstance, and even long lasting circumstantial conditions, and such faith seems to be rare.

Crazyana

Thank You, Rinpoche

The term crazy wisdom is generally associated with Chogyam Trungpa Rinpoche[*], a remarkable teacher who was the first person to give me a real taste of what the Dharma is all about.

Rinpoche had been born and educated in Tibet as the 11th Trungpa tulku. A tulku is an incarnation of a famous teacher. Tulkus are educated within the monastic system in a strict, but caring manner. As a young tulku, Trungpa had several important gurus and learnt many practices and traditions. However, when he was driven out of Tibet by the Chinese invasion and some of his teachers had disappeared into Chinese prisons, never to be seen again, he decided that what mattered was not so much the forms of tradition, but the actual lived life of the Dharma.

Perhaps the inspiration for this attitude came particularly from one of those lost teachers of his, Jamgon Kongtrul of Sechen. When Trungpa had asked the Sechen lama what enlightenment was, Kongtrul said, "There is no

---

[*] pronounced rim-po-shay

such thing; but this is it!" Trungpa had learnt early that there were some gurus who were better at conveying the form and others who were better at living the spirit. When he came to the West where the traditional forms were either unknown or, too often, treated as exotic curiosities, he decided that he had to start from scratch.

When I First Found Buddhism

When I first found Buddhism, which was soon after Rinpoche had come to the UK, there was not a lot of form to be had. There were few established Buddhist groups at that time and what there were were more academic than practising. To study Buddhism meant to study about it, not to do it. Trungpa was... well, I was going to write the cliché, 'like a breath of fresh air', but in fact he was more of a whirlwind, all energy on the outside and dead calm in the middle.

So Trungpa Rinpoche started from scratch and took to heart that Dharma is investigation of real life. And real life is pretty crazy. Wisdom, in Buddhism, is prajna. Prajna means to look below the surface. So, take real life and look below the surface, and you see plenty of craziness. The traditional form of religion is to shape people into the model of moral people, but underneath that outer shape they can be just as crazy as ever. In fact, the circumstance of being fitted into a shape can make you even crazier.

You've Got What You've Got

I'm not saying there is anything wrong with being moral — I'm just saying that there is something to be said for authenticity. When the Sechen lama said "this is it'" I don't think he was making a clever remark about living in the present moment, he was talking about the fact that you have got what you've got. However, whatever you've got — which may well be a bundle of really crazy stuff — the Buddhas still throw a light on it, still smile at it like a benign parent, still enjoy the life spirit that it evidences. When you live in that smile, then you know that you've got what you've got, but you also know it is a whole lot more than you thought. However, having a whole lot more does not mean that you have got rid of the rest. The term yana in Sanskrit means a "vehicle". The crazy yana is what we are going along in.

Hinayana

Could Buddhism, which started in the West in the days of let-it-all-hang-out Hippydom, be now in danger of becoming a kind of rather straight-buttoned, killjoy puritanism, in which the self-perfection project leads people into adopting a spiritual manner on the outside, but does not really touch the cauldron of self-righteousness, self-pity, self-entitlement and self-silliness on the inside? That does not even look at it in fact, but just goes on and on with the hubris of polishing an appearance of righteousness? Buddhism is not just about living on lentils and carrying out a procedure that one calls "my practice". That is hinayana. Hinayana is not really a school of Buddhism, it is an attitude toward Buddhism. It is the attitude that seeks personal rightness, personal benefit and no-sign-of-craziness. It is Buddhism in a small bottle.

Mahayana

Nor is the apparent converse really an answer. Turning from self-perfection to altruism, which is the avowed principle of Mahayana, very easily becomes just another form of self-aggrandisement. There is nothing much grander than the ambition to save all sentient beings and it is interesting that in that approach the notion of inherent Buddha nature has become so very popular. Surely this is just self-perfection in another guise, one in which all problems that arise from the intractableness of human nature are quickly kicked into touch by the strategy of saying that all will be well when one's inherently perfect nature comes into its own. The obvious retort of asking what one should do in the meantime tends to be brushed aside with either "Try harder" (Zen) or "Be patient — it takes many lifetimes" (Tibetan). Surely a more direct confrontation with common perversity is warranted and, indeed, desperately needed. It cannot be that nothing useful can be done this side of complete enlightenment.

Crazyana and Sillyana

Crazyana is different. Crazyana is what happens when we abandon Buddhism-in-order-to-get-something-for-me, which Rinpoche called 'spiritual materialism', and start looking at life 'just as you are' with all the self-silliness still happening. After all, that is how the Buddhas see us. They are not taken in by pretending. They see straight into the heart. They see how really silly we are. If it is painful to one to realise that the Buddha sees right into one's heart, then is it because one is ashamed of what he sees there. Well, that shame is part of the silliness, too. One could start right there. Investigate. Wow! Real human nature with no clothes on! What he sees there may be dukkha, but dukkha is a noble truth, a real foundation, which makes a much better ground for spiritual life than the shifting sands of self-idealism.

The Root of Compassion

I now practise, more or less, in the Pureland style of Buddhism. One of the things that I like about Pureland is its realism about the human condition. We are all 'bombu' which means, roughly, 'foolish beings of wayward passion'. However, even here, it is difficult to really get away from the question: "Yes, but how can I get to be a better class of bombu?" Which, of course, is to miss the point completely, but is a wonderful example of human silliness. It makes me think of the infamous Madame Mao who followed her husband's injunction that all revolutionaries should wear boiler suits so as to identify with the working masses, and so sent to Paris to have some very chic boiler suits tailor-made. We are like that, right? We mouth a doctrine of ordinariness while convinced deep down that oneself is something different

— both better and worse — or just plain too frightened to put our money where our mouth is. The point of pointing this out, however, is not so as to say: so straighten up there and perform better — it is, rather, to help us see that being human is like that. If one can really digest that truth, then one is somewhere near to compassion.

Dormice

Buddhism is not about me being better, nor worse for that matter; it is about compassion and wisdom and wisdom is really crazyana. Of course, if one is abandoned to compassion and wisdom, third parties might say that one is a good person, or they might just be shocked and disapproving that one is not performing according to their image of what a good person is supposed to look like, but the point is that the goal is not to arrive at a position where others have such-and-such an opinion of one or, indeed, that one has such an opinion of oneself. Self isn't in it. It is self that is crazy and that up-welling craving to be something — that is really crazy — but it is studying just that, just as it is, just as one is, that is the wisdom that feeds compassion. Compassion is fellow feeling for other people who are as crazy as oneself. Otherwise, like the dormouse at the Mad Hatter's Tea Party, we are really just sleeping through our life rather than fully participating in it. The dormouse needs to wake up.

Dealing With Emotion: The Fixless Fix

A Common Question

People ask how to deal with emotions. It is bad enough having things from outside oneself to deal with, without having to cope with what wells up inside.

When we say "dealing with" we often mean fixing. We are thinking: How can I fix my emotions? This means: how can I just have the ones that I want to have and never have the ones that I don't like?

What Comes Up

In Buddhist terminology emotion is samudaya. This is a long Sanskrit word meaning that they come up. Ud means up. Udaya means they come up. The "sam" bit means that they come up with something. With what? Dukkha. It's dukkha that's to blame. What is dukkha? You are. I am. We all are.

Dukkha is sometimes rendered into English as suffering, or affliction or dissatisfaction — in fact nobody has found a perfect translation. Dukkha is what comes and tells you: you are still alive. Most people don't like that too much.

Disturbance

We could say that dukkha is disturbance... Dukkha is disturbance. Dukkha is also non-disturbance. When we are not disturbed we fear boredom. We start to go flat. We don't like that. When they put people into flotation tanks of pleasantly warm water, which goes on feeling very nice for about twenty minutes, and paid them real money to stay there for as long as they liked, most people were soon begging to be let out. Doing nothing is a pain. So we don't like non-disturbance. But we don't like disturbance either because it tells us that we are not in control of what's happening.

Rather Be a Rock?

Not only are we not in control, but we are also still alive. Being out of control would not be so bad if one were a rock — right? Then there would not be any emotions. So the most fundamental thing about emotions is they tell us that we are still alive. One is still a human being.

There are forms of "spirituality" around that aim to make people become like rocks. That is one of the reasons that people take up meditation. However, that is not what Buddha intended meditation to be. Maybe that is why there was originally a taboo on making Buddha statues. The original representation of Buddha was a space — an empty seat, say, or footprints. A space has possibilities. A rock is... well, a rock.

The Spock Fallacy

So fixing one's emotions might mean no longer being what you are. That would be good wouldn't it? Wouldn't it? Perhaps if one was a space alien one would be happy all the time. Actually one does not need to go to Planet Vulcan. There are some drugs that can do that for you. And then you die.

Actually, a real Vulcan, if there were one, would be alive and so would have emotions. Disturbances and non-disturbances on Vulcan might be a bit different, but not much different. Life is dukkha and after dukkha, samudaya. It's just the same for sheep, cockroaches, birds, and no doubt was for dinosaurs —that's life.

As Much Life as You Have

So what is really required? What is needed is not less life. What is needed is more life. Actually you can't have more life than you have got, but you can stop trying to have less. One can open the window and let the air of life into the room where one is hiding.

Perhaps if you open the window you think that a tiger is going to jump in and eat you or a tsunami is going to break over you and drown you. It might happen. But at least you will have had one moment of real, undiluted life before you get eaten. More likely what will come through the window is a whole swatch of different stuff, good, bad and neutral.

Damn the Dam

You see, searching for happiness is a mug's game. Happiness is an occasional by-product of more life. The very word "hap-piness" means that it is something that just hap-pens. Searching for it means trying to put a break on the river of life. For sure you can put a dam across the river of life, but you cannot hold the water back forever.

The reason we are afraid of the internal tsunami is because we know that we have already dammed too much up. If we had just let it flow like an ordinary river there would never have been the possibility of this wall of water that we fear. The reason that many people fear to say "no" sometimes is that they fear the pressure of the part of themselves that wants to say a lot more than just "no". It is the murderous rage inside that threatens to overwhelm. Consequently, they put on a false smile and say polite little things that they don't really mean and the dam gets higher and higher. Beware such people — but this is difficult to do since there are so many. And one might be one oneself.

Dharma Enquiry

So what does Buddhism recommend? Study. Enquire. Don't think you already know. Go on exploring. You never know what is round the corner. Remember the teachings and study reality. Remember that the Buddhas accept you just as you are — they really are that crazy! Study what you are and what comes before you in life. The world of the Buddhas contains much more than we imagine. Be willing to be surprised. That's all. Investigate. Find out about reality. Yes, that's ALL — I don't mean investigate in order to change. I don't mean find out in order to cover up. I mean see what is really there. Forget the self-perfection project or searching for your "real self" and take life just as it is.

Maybe you find a lot of greed or compulsive habits or that one seems to be desperate in various ways. Probably one finds quite a bit of fear. Whatever. It is. It is what it is. It is life. It is being a human being. Being a being is better than not.

Don't Stop

When one has investigated, investigate some more. All this takes faith, of course. Remember that all the time you are investigating the Buddhas are watching and laughing their heads off. But it is a friendly laughter. They are laughing because you are coming a little closer to them.

A Buddha is nothing special. That's what is special about them. They are alive. Perhaps one is sad because mother is dying. What else do you think you should be? Perhaps one is frightened because one's economic position is threatened. That's normal. What if the worst happens? Then one will deal with the situation. Dealing with the situation is quite different from trying to fix the emotions.

Fix by Not Fixing

There are extreme situations where the emotion is so strong that one is paralysed. That happens sometimes. Not often, but it is possible at the limit. If one is paralysed, one is paralysed. There is nothing to be ashamed of. It will pass. And remember, every feeling has something to teach and it is not just what you are expecting. So investigate and go on investigating. Whatever, keep learning. Studying oneself is learning about everybody else. When you really know yourself you won't be so bothered about yourself - but life will still go on teaching.

So, investigate real life. And when you find something, make that the basis for more investigation. The way to fix emotions is by not fixing them. When life comes knocking on your door, don't tell it: Aliens not wanted here. Say, come in and teach me — I need some lessons.

Punyayashas: Buddha Child on Golden Ground

A Serious Boy

According to the stories, Punyayashas came from a Brahmin family from Saketa, or perhaps from Pataliputra. He was a quiet, serious boy who became interested in the Buddhist religion and became a follower of the Sarvastivada, a school of Buddhism that no longer exists, but which has had substantial influence on some of the great figures of Buddhist history, both in what they agreed with and what they argued against. Getting involved in religion brought him out of himself and he joined a troop of travelling Buddhist minstrels. Thus he became involved in the bhakti style of Buddhist practice.

Buddha-Bhakti

Bhakti was never a school of Buddhism but it was a widespread and popular style. It did not propose a philosophical system or particular interpretation of the sutras, but was a way of expressing one's self-surrender. Bhakti is devotion. It is a yoga of total dedication and self-overcoming through song, dance, ritual and entrancement. Bhakti practice often involves chanting a mantra, or calling the name of a deity, and doing so with a fullness of love, emotion and reverence. It is to be in love with the divine. Such practice may lead to trance, rapture and ecstatic states.

Nowadays we tend to translate the term dhyana as meditation which has a rather cool, intellectual or disciplined and puritan feel, but the word may be better translated as rapture, referring to states of absorption rather than awareness. Bhakti, then, is a highly emotional approach to religion in which one immerses oneself in divine love and adoration. In India, Bhakti was eventually largely taken over by Hinduism, perhaps because more puritan forms became powerful in Buddhism. Some Westerners will have seen Hari Krishna devotees walking in the streets chanting and playing drums or other percussion instruments. This style of religion was formerly Buddhist and Punyayashas was a wandering practitioner of it.

We can tell from these stories that the tenor of Buddhism in those days may have been much more open than it has tended to become. We may remember that when Buddhism was becoming popular in the 1960s and 1970s it was associated with beatnik poets, happenings, and the alternative society. It was a religion of liberation in many senses of the word. Since then it has tended to attract people of a more straight-laced temperament. No doubt this is a pendulum that swings.

Practising Buddha-Bhakti, Punyayashas travelled about with the group of minstrels, young men and women who sang in the bazaars songs of ecstatic devotion, or sad melodies about the vanity of life.

The Encounter

One day Punyayashas met the Buddhist Master Parsva.

> Parsva asked: From where have you come?
>
> Punyayashas: My heart does not travel.
>
> Parsva: So where do you live?
>
> Punyayashas: My heart is not attached to a place.
>
> Parsva: So you are unattached?
>
> Punyayashas: Like all the Buddhas.
>
> Parsva: You are not all the Buddhas.

Punyayashas was taken aback and went away. After twenty one days he returned and said: "As for all the Buddhas... then you are not the master either," and they laughed together.

The Meaning

Punyayashas was a bit of a saint from very early in his life, but he became somewhat over serious about his religion to the point where people were alarmed by him. It is said that before his meeting with Parsva, wherever he went the ground turned golden. This is an ironic way of saying that he was too holy.

Parsva brought him down a notch and he took it to heart and let go of his attachment to Buddhahood. Then he and the master were able to laugh together. Being a Buddha and being a master are empty designations, even though they do mean something.

Parsva teased Punyayashas with a gatha:

> I knew a sage would come
>
> for the ground changed to gold.
>
> He will sit under the Bodhi tree
>
> and the flower of awakening will bloom.

Punyayashas replied more modestly than before with another gatha:

> It is the master who sits on golden ground
>
> forever teaching true realisation.
>
> By turning his light upon me
>
> I was allowed to enter samadhi.

Parsva then ordained Punyayashas saying: "The Treasury of the Tathagata's Great Dharma Eye I now hand over to you to guard and cherish."

A Buddha Child

Each person has their own form of koan. Being too holy is one. As a young man he took his religion very seriously. I remember that during the period of "flower power" one sometimes met people who called themselves "Jesus children." Everybody was into getting high in one way or another, and these people were high on Jesus. Perhaps the young Punyayashas was a bit like that.

Well, religion is a serious matter, but when a person takes it too seriously, it is usually themselves that they are taking too seriously. When we think we have got hold of the ultimate meaning of the universe, we can implicitly start to assume that we are something pretty special. So a koan also involves some kind of ego inflation. As we get established in life we each start to rely upon something.

Stepping Up is Stepping Down

In a certain way, every koan is a false refuge and every awakening is a matter of finding a better one. However, as we are self-invested in our chosen attachment, pride stands in the way of change. In order to let go one has to take a step down. Because Punyayashas trusted Parsva he was able to take the latter's rebuff, go away and think about it seriously, and come back in a good spirit. Then they were about to meet on a more equal footing with all artificial roles dropped away. However, because they were able to meet in this way and Punyayashas was able to see that Parsva was not self-invested in being the master either, Punyayashas respected him the more and treated him as master thereafter.

Soon afterwards, Parsva died. Punyayashas continued his travels and in due course met Ashvaghosha who wanted to know what Buddha is, but that is another story.

Three Aspects of Delusion and Enlightenment[*]

I was reading a passage of Dogen Zenji, the great Zen master. It says when you are enlightened, you are getting more enlightened all the time. When you are in the midst of delusion, you are getting more deluded all the time. It is very interesting because you can take this, both at an individual level and at a collective level, and perhaps also at a one to one level. When you consider these three ways, it says something about how Buddhism — transmission of the Dharma — works.

On an individual level is probably how people understand it when they first read it. At an individual level, when you are enlightened, then everything you encounter enlightens you more. In this sense we can see that being enlightened — having satori — is, among other things, a facility in learning. A good teacher is somebody who is good at learning, always curious, always interested, always investigating. When a good teacher finds that he has made a mistake, he or she is very pleased: "Oh good! I learned something new!" When an

---

[*] Transcribed from a teaching given at Oasis de Longue Vie

ordinary person finds that he has made a mistake: trouble, confusion, shame, hiding and so on. While the enlightened person is only interested in learning, ordinary people are interested in their own reputation, their presentation for the sake of their image. The enlightened person just learns, they just have an interest: "What are those birds saying?" The difference between being enlightened and not being enlightened is that in not being enlightened, the self gets in the way. In a certain way, enlightened people are always alone, because they are not concerned with the social presentation. Enlightened people are alone with the birds, or alone with the trees, and the same in their attitude to other people. Things are just as they are. This is at the level of the individual.

But then when we think about it more collectively — the illusion is not only mine, it is everyone's. We feed each other's delusion. You give me your illusion. I give you my delusion. We live in a soup of delusion. We delude each other. So this is why Sangha is important. We might say: well it all comes from within, but this is not entirely true. When you look at Buddhism, you see that Buddhism is very much concerned with creating the right environment. Here we have a special room. We are surrounded by (pictures of) teachers, great beings. We have a particular atmosphere. We have put the Buddha where we can bow and so on. So we create an environment and even deluded persons coming into a beautiful temple garden — a nice little flowing river, a Japanese bridge, and so on — they feel something. When you are amongst people who are peaceful and happy, it has an effect. You still have your own troubles and your delusions, but you are touched, you are affected. So in the middle of delusion we are not only in our own delusion, but in the midst of social and collective delusion. Some of our work as Buddhists is to create a wonderful environment. Maybe we cannot create Pure Lands exactly, but still something. When you have refuge in the Pure Land in your heart, then naturally you create Pure Lands in your environment. This is not just for yourself. Maybe it starts for yourself, like a mirror, but then it is for everybody else. Sangha means we help each other. It doesn't mean necessarily help like a social worker — sometimes perhaps — but just by our way of being, our ordinary kindness, well, just our 'ordinariness', by not making unnecessary fuss, we create a clean environment so there is not so much self, not so much contamination. So this is refuge in the Sangha, collectively being in the middle of illumination, instead of in the middle of delusion. "What should we do?" Buddha says: "Keep good company, be among good people." "Good" here in the West, tends to be taken in the sense of doing good, quite active, but in Buddhism, good is more in the sense of "pure", "uncontaminated". It's more just having this clean space where there is no aggravation, where no new karma is created. So, keep good company!

So let us then look at the third level: the level of one to one. Good company is very important. It is very important in a relationship. We are being good for one another and of course the epitome of this is the disciple and the teacher or the practitioner and Buddha. There is transmission.

So how should we think of transmission? You may think the teacher gives you something. But in a way, he takes something away. Transmission is giving something or taking something away because what is transmitted is peace. What is transmitted is that cleanliness, purity. I try out my delusions on him, but he does not respond. I push forward, but there is nobody pushing back. So experience of working with a teacher is often like that. You push with your delusion, and you just fall over. There is no push back. So Buddha is good, kind and wise. Buddha is not caught up in my games and yet he is still there, he still loves me. At first you think, "He is not going to play my game", and you can be upset, if the other person doesn't play your game. But when you discover that the other person does not play your game, but still loves you, some new possibility arises in life. You see something is possible you didn't think was possible before, because you only played your game because you thought you had to, but you don't have to. Ego is just made up of these games and these heaps of stories that we tell ourselves that make us keep playing artificial games. We don't have to keep playing. So, one to one, there is this kind of very special friend. Ordinary friends often support our delusion. We have trouble – the ordinary friend says: "Have a drink! Three glasses of whisky and you will feel much better!" But this makes matters worse. The following morning, you have the same problem and you've got a headache as well. So we say, kalyana mitra — skilful friend, special friend. We think we are receiving, but actually it is a two-way street, we help each other. The disciple helps the teacher and the teacher helps the disciple.

So this is what Dogen is talking about. When you are in the middle of delusion, either collectively, one to one, or on your own, you just make more and more. Everything you take, you take as food for your delusion. But when you are in the milieu of enlightenment, illumination, awakening, then you just have more and more. There is a new exciting discovery. This it true in yourself, in your relationship and in your community.

Buddha's Ambivalence About Meditation

Buddha Taught Dhyana

The Buddha taught "meditation" in a number of ways. I have put the word in quotes because there are several Sanskrit words that get translated as "meditation" and none of them fully corresponds with the English word, either in its traditional or its modern sense. One of these words is dhyana. Dhyana is the word from which the word Zen is derived. However, mostly Zen teaches only one form, called shikantaza, a form of "just sitting with no deliberate thought," and this bears only a distant relationship to what Shakyamuni taught under this heading. The Buddha generally taught four or eight dhyanas, the first of which is definitely a form of deliberate thought. From here on I am talking about dhyana as taught by Shakyamuni and as described in the Pali texts.

Generally speaking, the dhyanas are states of rapture rather than open awareness. They start with a focus and this focus is only left when they move into trance-like states. This is rather different from what is mostly taught these days.

Conditions for Dhyana

There is no verb "to dhyana" so the equivalence with "to meditate" is loose. Dhyanas are states that one might enter into and explore rather than procedures or things to do. Their occurrence is dependent upon certain conditions.

The basic conditions are as follows.

1. Desire for and delight in the Dharma (MN64,11).

2. Seclusion: dhyana occurs when a person is alone and enjoying being so.

3. Sobriety: the practitioner is not engaged in the pursuit of sensual pleasures. This implies being clean of drugs, not indulging overly in food, and being generally adapted to a basically ethical lifestyle.

4. An initial wholesome focus. There are many suitable subjects. The most suitable are the objects of refuge — Buddha, Dharma and Sangha.

I shall not go into the details of the eight different dhyanas here except to say that the first involves applied and sustained thought, the second, third and fourth constitute a progression from rapture to equanimity, the four higher dhyanas are open to different interpretations. For the purpose of this present teaching, a general sense of the dhyanas as being about states of rapture and equanimity, spaciousness and the deeper mind, experienced when one is alone, will suffice.

The Purpose of Dhyana

The Buddha says that the purpose of entering these states is to overcome the "five fetters". The five fetters are:

1. obsession with one's own body
2. perplexity
3. attachment to conventions
4. obsession with sense pleasures
5. ill-will

The Paradox

So the dhyanas are valuable for this purpose and in sutta 64 (MN) it says that they lead to the Deathless. However, we might ask how this comes about and the answer turns out to be somewhat paradoxical. In sutta 52 (MN) we learn that the reason that the practitioner turns to the Deathless is that he realises that these very dhyanas themselves are conditioned and volitional and since everything that is volitional and conditioned is impermanent, they do not constitute a suitable goal. It is by realising the insufficiency of the dhyanas that the practitioner is induced to turn to the Deathless.

So, exploring one or more of these dhyana states may have two possible outcomes. The first is that, because of one's devotion to the Dharma one will become one who after death is going to be reborn in a Pure Land and will attain nirvana there without returning to this life. It is clear in the Pali texts that this is seen as the less good outcome. The best outcome is that the practitioner realises through this experience that no state that comes about through volition and conditions — in other words, through self-power — can lead to nirvana and if the practitioner becomes steady in this realisation then he or she will "turn to the Deathless" and, by doing so, enter nirvana.

So there is an interesting paradox here. Dhyana can lead one to nirvana by bringing one to the realisation that dhyana cannot get one to nirvana. In other words, in order to get to nirvana one has to know that nothing else does the trick and the only way to know that is to try those other things that seem most likely to do the trick and find out that they don't.

This is not Sallekha

The other possibility also exists, namely that turning to the Deathless, or being so devoted to the Dharma that one is later reborn in a Pure Land, could both occur without one ever attempting the dhyanas. So there can be salvation with dhyana and salvation without dhyana.

This ambivalence about the dhyanas is brought out even more clearly in the Sallekha Sutta (MN8) which is sometimes considered to be one of the most important suttas. The sutta as a whole is about sallekha, which means the attitude of "this is not me, this is not mine, this is not myself" by which a person is freed from wrong view. Here again the Buddha describes the eight dhyanas in exactly the same formulaic way as in many other suttas, but at the end of his description of each of them, he says, "A person practising thus may think that by doing so they are practising sallekha, but this is not what the Buddhas call sallekha." He then says that the first four dhynas are merely pleasant abidings and the four higher ones are merely peaceful abidings.

A Mixed Message

It rather appears, therefore, that the Buddha faced a situation not so different from that which pertains today in which large numbers of people think that meditation is a method by which they can reach some kind of final spiritual goal and that that is the essence of what Buddhism is about. The Buddha himself, however, seems to say that the best you can achieve by dedicating yourself to meditation is that the dedication may be rewarded even if the meditation isn't, or that, it could be that through realising that the meditation does not achieve what one thought that it did one might, at that point, "turn to the Deathless" rather as he himself had done when he found that asceticism did not work.

All of this leaves us with a mixed message. According to Buddha, meditation of the dhyana type can help us overcome the "lower fetters," it is a pleasant or peaceful abiding, and we may learn things from the experience. However, it is not, in itself, the cause of spiritual awakening except in the same indirect sense that anything can be at the point where we give it up. Furthermore, dhyana meditation is, in any case, somewhat different from contemporary meditation and it is questionable whether there is any basis in the teaching of Shakyamuni for such methods as "choiceless awareness" such as are very popular these days. One imagines, however, that the Buddha would have had a similar attitude to contemporary methods as he did to those of his own day. So the verdict is that meditation is fine, good and useful but not essential and not everything that it is often cracked up to be.

The Fundamental Point

Perhaps the most crucial and fundamental point, whether you meditate or not, and whether you ever enter a dhyana state of not, is that all states and methods that are "conditioned and volitional" are impermanent and are therefore not the Deathless and are therefore not nirvana and not the goal of Buddhism as Shakyamuni taught it. Volitional means deriving from self-power. The Deathless refers to Other Power. So at the very core of what was taught by Shakyamuni Buddha is the key observation that it is when they discover that self-power does not do the trick that people make the vital shift and find true faith.

QUESTION: Didn't the Buddha pass through the dhyanas when he was dying before entering final parinirvana?

ANSWER: Yes, according to the text that is so. The Buddha taught and practised entering the dhyanas and clearly thought that it was a wholesome, but not essential, thing for a spiritual practitioner to do.

QUESTION: Are dhyanas always and necessarily conditioned and volitional?
ANSWER: A very good question. No. Dhyana states of peace, equanimity and so on can arise naturally and spontaneously. One may fall into a dhyana state rather

than contrive it. We are then talking about what may be called a state of grace.

QUESTION: Were the dhyanas that Shakyamuni entered the result of deliberate practice or of grace?

ANSWER: I think the answer must be both. It is clear that he learnt the practice of entering into dhyanas and also taught it as technique, but he must also have experienced natural dhyanas. Buddha enjoyed peaceful abiding when there was nothing more pressing needing to be done.

QUESTION: So does this mean that a person who has found faith in other power might still do self-power practices?

ANSWER: Yes, but that person will regard what he or she is doing in a new way. Thus a person who has faith in self-power does a practice in order to achieve a state whereas a person who relies upon other power may do it as a celebration. Relying upon other power as salvation does not mean that one ceases to be a volitional being — one is still human and still living in the world of conditions. One still does things and reaps the relative consequences of them for good or for ill.

Effacement

The Salekha Sutta

The eighth sutra in the Majjhima Nikaya is called the Salekha Sutta, which means the sutra on Effacement.

The sutra is basically in four parts which seem mildly in contradiction of one another, so it is possible that a degree of irony is intended. I am inclined to think that the Buddha was rather a master of irony, but it was sometimes lost on his more pious followers. However, it is evident that the sutra is about good character.

The scene is a conversation between the Buddha and an enquirer called Cunda. Cunda wants to talk about doctrines about the self and the world and he asks if those who are beginners can possibly understand these teachings. It is a reasonable surmise that by beginners, Cunda means those who have not attained high proficiency in meditation.

A Modern Question

Cunda, therefore, is not unlike many modern people who come to Buddhism. He is primarily interested in meditation and in abstruse doctrines and thinks that the height of attainment is to be proficient in meditation and to understand the nature of the self or the non-self doctrine and the nature of the world or reality. Many contemporary books on Buddhism are preoccupied with these topics. The implication of Cunda's question is that those who do not do so cannot understand the important matter.

This is Not Me

The Buddha's reply is to say that in order to have the right view of the world or of the self one needs to see what one is talking about in a certain way. What is that way? It is: This is not mine, this is not me, this is not myself. The Buddha says that when a person sees things in this way then they understand all that they need to (whether they are a beginner or not). "This is not mine, this is not me, this is not myself" constitutes effacement.

Dhyana is Peace and Pleasure Here and Now

The Buddha then rubs the point in by going through a description of all of the degrees of dhyana (meditation), starting from the first dhyana:

"It is possible that, secluded from sensual distraction and unwholesome states, a bhikkhu enters into and abides in the first dhynana, which is accompanied by applied and sustained thought, rapture and pleasure, born of seclusion. He might think 'I am abiding in effacement' but this is not what is called effacement in the discipline of noble ones; this is called, rather, a pleasant abiding here and now."

The Buddha then goes on to the second dhyana in similar fashion, and then the third. If this is the first time that you have read the sutra, you probably tend to assume that effacement is going to be the final and highest dhyana. However, when the Buddha gets to the eighth and highest dhyana he says, "But this is not what is called effacement in the discipline of noble ones; this is called, rather, a peaceful abiding." He calls the first four dhyanas pleasant and the second four peaceful, but neither set, not even the highest, constitutes effacement.

Good Character and Patience

So what is effacement? The Buddha goes on to list 44 items. Now it is quite possible, likely even, that the list has grown with the telling, so as to include as many items of Buddhist teaching as possible, or maybe the Buddha really did repeat 44 items three times as recorded in the sutra, but we can readily grasp the message from a small sample.

"Now, Cunda, here effacement should be practised by you. Though others be cruel, we shall not be cruel. Effacement should be practised like this. Though others kill, we shall not go killing. Effacement should be practised like this. Though others take what is not given, we shall not behave like that. Effacement should be practised like this... though other be envious... avaricious... fraudulent...deceitful... though others adhere tenaciously to their own opinions, we shall not behave like that. Effacement should be practised thus."

The Buddha says that by practising effacement, one rescues oneself from all unwholesome states and only one who does so can rescue others.

He then concludes by saying that he has thus taught effacement and thereby done his duty as a teacher and ends by telling Cunda that he can now go and meditate.

Actions Reveal Attitude

There appear to be a number of subtleties and ironies in the sutra.

1. Buddha demonstrates his consummate understanding of meditation practise yet says that that is not where it's at. Yet, nonetheless, at the end, sends Cunda away to meditate.

2. The Buddha does not affirm Cunda's implication that only those who have reached an advanced state can understand. He reiterates the teaching that he gave in his second sermon to the five ascetics. This implies that Buddhism is simple in concept.

3. Buddha defines effacement in terms of noble behaviour and attitude, thus subtly undermining Cunda's belief that what matters is a clear understanding of doctrine.

So the Buddha is saying that actions speak louder than words, but also that underlying doctrine there is perspective and perspective is a matter of how we regard things, especially how we regard the things that come and go. How we regard things shows in behaviour. In terms of

Buddhist theory this means not identifying with the skandhas. This, therefore, is a teaching on non-self but in an entirely practical, non-doctrinal form. Buddha is interested in people living the holy life. Theory is there to support that, not to substitute for it.

Not Taking Credit Builds Long Term Benefit

So what is effacement? Effacement is a combination of noble action and refusal to take the credit. When Buddha says that meditation is a pleasant abiding here and now he is saying something similar to the words of Jesus when he says, "They have their reward already." We generally translate dhyana as meditation, but this probably gives a too intellectual turn to what Buddha is saying. What he is talking about might be better rendered by the word rapture. The holy life yields all kinds of immediate benefits as well as longer term ones. Modern taste takes this as suggesting that one should grasp the immediate and ignore the other, but the Buddha's meaning is almost certainly the converse. Rapture brings an immediate satisfaction that is equally immediately exhausted whereas effacement brings long term benefit to self and other.

Of course, this is an over-statement because meditative disciplines can help in the process of training oneself in effacement, but there is a contrast intended in the sutra.

The Buddha is describing noble behaviour. A noble person is one who does his duty and then retires. It is what is expressed when somebody says, "It was nothing. Don't think of it." The true bodhisattva is often not conscious that he or she has done anything good. They just do what needs doing. Afterwards, if somebody comments, they are likely to say something like, "What? No, anybody would have done the same." This might not be literally true, but the noble person has a good opinion of everybody, so it is sincere and genuine for them.

Clashing with Contemporary Values

In the contemporary world, values of this kind have been in retreat. We are nowadays expected to advertise ourselves to a much greater degree than used to be considered proper. A value system of helping oneself and speaking for oneself has grown up. I remember that when I was younger gestalt psychology was much in vogue and it preached an extreme form of self-responsibility. The slogan was that nobody could make one feel anything — one was to be completely responsible for one's own feelings. However, Buddha says to regard one's feelings with the attitude, "This is not mine, this is not me, this is not myself." The gestalt idea was intended to counter-act the tendency to blame others. So far so good. Buddha is not advocating blaming others, nor denying the facticity of feelings, but he is advising us to acknowledge that many of these things are out of our control, but nonetheless one can still act in a noble way. A popular speaker, Susan Jeffers, used to be known for the saying, "Feel the fear and do it anyway." This is closer to the

Buddha's prescription. Effacement means to do what is good, generous and noble no matter what feelings one might have.

Effacement is also a matter of equanimity. It is about the patience to not be swept away by short term considerations, nor by concern for one's own fame and gain. This is the real meaning of non-self in practice.

I think we see clearly in this sutra what the Buddha is aiming for, and, while not easy, it is not something that is out of the reach of ordinary people.

Bencho: Successor of Honen

Bencho (1161-1238) was the successor to Honen as the leading teacher in the Jodo School. The role of great successor is very important. Would we have Christianity without St Paul and St Peter? Would Dogen Zenji be remembered without Keizan Zenji?

When Bencho was 14 he went to study Tendai Buddhism on Mount Hiei and in 1183, age 22, he entered the great Enraku-ji temple. He had two teachers there, first Kwan-ei and later Shoshin. In 1190, age 29, he returned to his home province and became head of Yusan temple. The age of 29 is a turning point in the lives of many people. In 1194 he had a spiritual awakening and entered upon a new period of spiritual search, renouncing ambition and acquisitiveness and seeking higher truth.

In 1197, age 36, he visited the 65 year old Honen Shonin who was now living in his hermitage at Yoshimizu. At this time, Bencho was still rather proud of his own learning and knowledge and his search had become one of putting difficult and clever questions to people to see if they could answer them.

Bencho arrived at Honen's place a bit before 2pm. Honen welcomed him and Bencho was soon putting his questions. Honen weighed up the younger man quite quickly and said, "As you are a real scholar, I think I should explain to you three kinds of nembutsu: the one described in the Mohochiquan, that of the Ojoyoshu and that proposed by Shan Tao..." Honen then went into a detailed exposition and was still talking at midnight. Bencho was completely fascinated and thereafter took Honen as his teacher, spending as much time in his presence as he possibly could, always learning.

The following spring, 1198, Honen gave him a copy of Senchakushu. At this time Senchakushu was an unpublished semi-secret work that Honen had written at the behest of a former Regent of Japan, Tsuki-nowa. This was Honen's way of giving 'transmission' to his most favoured disciples. Later that year Honen sent Bencho to Iyo province to preach the nembutsu for half a year. Bencho proved to be quite a successful missionary. He then returned and assisted at Honen's hermitage until 1204.

During this time most of the studies centred on Shan Tao's Commentary on the Contemplation Sutra. A key element in this work is Shan Tao's description of the 'Three Minds'. Bencho understood the Three Minds as follows:

1. The sincere mind: a mind of simple confidence that the Pure Land awaits one.

2. Profound mind: a deep appreciation of how unworthy, lacking in self-power for salvation, and 'bombu' one is, coupled with confidence that it is precisely for such as ourselves that Amida attends.

3. The longing mind that yearns for the Pure Land for oneself and all others.

He maintained that when one has settled faith then the Three Minds arise naturally within one.

In 1204, Bencho returned to his native province of Chinzei and continued his missionary work with even more success than before. At this time there arose a question whether the practice of nembutsu was a 'final' teaching, or merely 'introductory' and, correspondingly, whether it led on to the esoteric teachings of Tendai as a consummation, or not. Bencho sent a disciple of his with a letter of enquiry to Honen who wrote in his own hand that it was not and never had been his teaching that nembutsu was merely introductory. This signed statement in his own hand has played an important part in the development of Jodo teaching.

In 1212 (or 1211, depending which calendar one uses) Honen died. Bencho continued to propagate his teachings. In 1228 he held a nembutsu retreat of 48 days at Ojo-in temple and there launched a booklet bringing together his own understanding of what he had received from his teacher. This was called "Nembutsu Teaching for Future Generations as Certified and Sealed by my Own Hand." When he had completed this work, a vision of Honen appeared before Bencho, reducing him to floods of tears. This greatly increased Bencho's confidence in his own teaching mission.

In those days there was a famous holy site at Mount Kora. Bencho determined to do a 1000 day nembutsu retreat there and organised a party of devotees to practise together. Around the 800th day, they heard news that priests from another temple on the mountain were planning to come and drive them away. The retreat group were unsure what to do and were generally in favour of leaving the site. However, Bencho prevailed upon them to stay put. The following morning the priests from the other temple arrived, but, instead of being hostile, they came bearing offerings. Apparently, during the night, they had all had a similar dream of a great light shining from the west and a voice saying that the Buddha light was shining because of the priest saying the nembutsu. Thus peace and friendship were restored and after that the holy site at Mount Kora flourished for many years.

Bencho was a very devoted practitioner, saying nembutsu morning, noon and night. He once said, "People say that Kokawa Temple or Mount Koya are good places for retreat, but as far as I am concerned there is no better place than the bed from which I arise every morning." He also said, "Always be thinking of death and of the Buddhas. Who knows? — death may come after any breath, so keep saying 'Amida Buddha please help!'"

Toward the end of 1237 he became ill and early the next year he passed away while reciting "The Buddha Light illumines all sentient beings throughout the ten quarters."

Getting Out of Prison

Dhyana and Chains

Buddha says that dhyana releases one from "five fetters" — fetters are chains, as in prison. We are prisoners and dhyana is a kind of freedom. The five are

1. obsession with one's own body
2. perplexity
3. dependence upon a conventional or ritualised way of being
4. obsession with sense pleasures
5. ill-will

The Medical Analogy

So we could say,

1. hypochondria
2. anxiety
3. obsessive compulsive disorder
4. borderline personality disorder
5. paranoia

and then treat meditation as a kind of medicament. This is certainly what some people are trying to do. This is also one way of smuggling Buddhism into a materialistic culture. I don't mind them doing this, so long as they smuggle Buddhism into the culture and don't smuggle the culture into Buddhism.

The biggest problem for people coming from such a culture into Buddhism is that they bring such a fix-it-and-dispose-of-it attitude with them. It is so pervasive that a whole Sangha can easily become subverted in this way and become a kind of mental hospital — a place for fixing the mind — in which there are no real physicians, but the patients are all treating each other. When the lunatics take over the asylum, real Buddhism is not to be found.

The Mind is Already Fixed

The mind does not need fixing. The mind is fine. It works. There is no problem in the mechanism. The problem is in the application. A perfectly good mind can be employed for all kinds of purposes from the most altruistic to the most diabolical. Even if the mind were faulty in some way, the same would be true.

The Prison Analogy

So why does Buddha say that dhyana will release one from these things? Firstly, it probably does help us to think in terms of "being released" rather than "being cured". They are both good metaphors, but we are not really talking about diseases that are to be got rid of, we are talking about opening a door onto a much bigger and less confining space. The little cell does not need changing, but when we realise that the door is open we can walk out. When we look back we can see how that little room fits into the whole architecture. We do not need to demolish it.

This analogy, maybe, gives us some idea of what dhyana is. Dhyana is spacious. There is room within it for many things. Dhyana gets translated as "meditation" and one then wants to know how to do it, but dhyana is not a verb. Dhyana is a noun. It designates mind space, heart space, vast space.

Things You Can Do

Being Alone: For sure, there are things you can do. For instance, you can spend some time on your own. Aloneness is a good way in, because when you are alone it is more difficult to blame everybody else. The reason that, in Zen, everybody sits facing the wall is so that one is more alone at that time. My teacher used to say, "When you meditate, there is just you and the wall... and there is nothing wrong with the wall." Spending time alone gives one another dimension.

When one is alone one discovers one's own rhythm. One also sees one's own habits and preoccupations. Being alone may be a kind of hell sometimes, but it is a real space in which one is oneself in a more total way. This is one aspect of dhyana.

Settling: Another aspect is settling. When one is first alone one may feel as if all the dust in one's life has been swept up by a whirlwind and is swirling around one. After a time, however, the dust settles. Let the dust of your life settle. Initially, perhaps, one thinks that one needs to get rid of it, but flailing one's arms in an effort to clear a space in the dust storm just raises more dust. It will settle of its own accord if allowed to. So this is another aspect of dhyana.

Aloneness need not always be literal. Simply taking on complete responsibility is a kind of aloneness. Doing what you really think rather than what you think will make other people think what you want them to think about you is aloneness. This is called ekagata. That is also dhyana.

Rapture: Dhyana is also engagement. When we do something wholeheartedly, even if it is sitting in the sun, that is a kind of dhyana. Dhyana is rapture. This is why, in Buddhist training, one sometimes says to do one thing at a time and give it full attention. This is not so much to develop skill in attention or consciousness — though that is handy — it is to give one an experience of a pure space.

Great Spaciousness

So dhyana is great space. It is leaving one's little cell and going out into the big hall, or even into the garden, or the hillside beyond. There is nothing to be destroyed or got rid of. You might do it sitting down cross legged on the floor, but not necessarily. Dhyana is not a protocol nor a treatment, it is a mental space and that space can be found anywhere.

So why do we build ourselves a little cell? Essentially out of fear and fear comes from feeling unloved and unsafe. Angulimala gave up killing people when the Buddha offered to protect him. The Buddha protected him by putting him in a monk's robe. Buddhist practitioners are often referred to in the texts as "sons and daughters of a good family". Buddhism is the family of Buddha — it is a good family and people in it do not need to be afraid and huddled in little self-manufactured mental cells because in this good family one is loved just as one is. When one starts to trust that love one experiences dhyana, one's nervous obsessions fade in proportion, one's perplexity no longer obscures everything, the sun comes out from the clouds. The clouds now decorate the sky instead of hiding the sun. This is not because one has perfected a method, nor is it even that one's bits of fear and confusion have disappeared; they are just a lot less important, a much smaller element in the scheme of things. The space has got bigger because one feels as one loved rather than as one abandoned, as one released rather than as one imprisoned, as one in one's own country rather than lost in the desert. The gods protect and the Buddha smiles.

Anshin: Part One ~ It's Alright

The term anshin is Japanese. It is commonly translated as 'settled faith'. As such it is one of several forms or aspects of 'faith'. Other aspects are shinjin, bodaishin, and another for which I do not know the Japanese term, but which — in the language of India — is called abhilasa. Each of these is worth a teaching in its own right, but we can briefly define them as follows.

Dawning Trust

Shinjin is the dawning of trust, the opening of the heart. It involves a 'turning around' or change of heart, often springing from contrition or inspiration or a juxtaposition of the two. We can think of Shakyamuni seeing the 'Four Sights'. In such an awakening one is seized by new light, or, driven by a sense of having gone astray, seeing new possibility and feeling new verve. In a sense, and sometimes actually, shinjin precedes anshin and can be its foundation. Then we can say that anshin is the maturing of shinjin.

Faith in Action

Abhilasa and bodaishin can be thought of as flowing from anshin and so as being subsequent, at least in a logical sense. Abhilasa is something like 'willingness', the willingness to do whatever is for the general good. Bodaishin is really the mind of enlightenment, or, at least the condition of heart that conduces to it, sometimes called 'the Way-seeking mind', a great compassion toward all sentient beings. So we can understand anshin as nested within these wonderful spiritual qualities. When we call out toward what is sacred to us, that calling is truly spiritual if and when it is touched by such qualities. These are what we worship and aspire toward, hoping that they will be granted to us, will bless us and hold us. This is what we pray for.

Although I have described them somewhat as a sequence in the last paragraph, all these dimensions of 'faith' really function together. They are its modes or moods. Insofar as one's life is grounded in faith, at any one time one or other of these aspects will be showing.

Trust in the Heart

'Faith' in Buddhism is perhaps not identical to faith in other religions, since here there is more emphasis upon a state of 'heart' or 'mind' and less on belief or assertion. Buddhism is not so much adherence to a creed and more a journey of exploration and grace, so that faith, here, is the willingness to wholeheartedly entrust oneself to that journey irrespective of where it may take one. The obstacle is attachment. Faith is like letting go of the rail on the side of the swimming pool whereas attachment is like adding more and more rails. Soon the rails, though each initially seemed so necessary and fine, have become the bars of the cage in which one has one's limited existence. Inside one's cage one may read about the wonderful life of liberation, but it lies beyond one's reach.

Entering upon the Path

Even if we manage to leave our cage, squeezing out between the bars and slipping away, we may still be bringing some attachment with us. We may think that we are going to develop these qualities as personal characteristics, we are going to get and possess them, and (we secretly hope to) be admired for them. They are going to displace the characteristics that have been given to us by our immemorial karmic history, most of which are nothing like so noble, and we shall then be more perfected beings. Such is the pride we carry into our spiritual life.

However, what we gradually or suddenly learn or realise is that it does not work quite like that. It is not really that any part of what we are is to be given up, but it all comes to be bathed in a new light. That light may be thought of in many ways — the light of the Buddhas, the Divine Light, the Light of Truth, whatever. This thing we call 'faith' that brings peace to us like a miracle, is not something we manufacture, nor own, but is a kind of grace that alights when we start to take ourselves less seriously.

To Know the Self Is to Forget the Self

This diminishing seriousness is a function of familiarity. As we come to know ourselves better, to see ourselves more clearly, we perhaps start to realise that we are not actually as special as we always wanted to think we were. We find in ourselves much the same characteristics — good and bad — in varying degrees as we find in everybody else. Their joys and sorrows, pride and shame, anxiety and relief, peace and panic, are all rather similar to our own, and our own to theirs. As this obvious truth becomes real to us, much of the mesmerising fascination of our own story fades. It is not that it vanishes, but it becomes less compelling, less central to the meaning of life.

Bedrock

When I recognise common humanity more authentically, something deep relaxes. It is as if a cosmic grandmother had soothingly said, "It's alright." That is faith. I am never going to be self-sufficiently perfect or self-justifying, whether in rightness, saintliness, victimhood, vengeful heroism, or whatever other role might offer itself. I rely upon something vaster, pervasive, and beyond grasp. This "realisation of alrightness" is shinjin. When it is established in an enduring deep way, that is anshin. When it expresses itself in action, that is abhilasa. When it transforms one's perception of the world, that is bodaishin.

Such anshin faith provides a kind of bedrock in one's life that is independent of condition or circumstance, which is why it is called "settled". Although the vicissitudes of conditional existence in a world of impermanence continue, when one's heart has been touched in this way one can face whatever may come and not lose faith.

Anshin: Part Two ~ Domestic Bliss?

Anshin is a Japanese word, often translated as 'settled faith', as I explained in the previous section. It is a particularly important term in Pureland Buddhism. However, the theme is of universal implication and relevance.

Bringing Peace to the Heart

The term 'an' means peace and 'shin' means mind or heart. The Chinese character for shin is, in fact, derived from a drawing of a heart. So if we were to write anshin in modern emoticons, it could be:

This, perhaps, gives us a feel for what anshin means: something that tenderly brings peace to the heart. In this simple idea lies one of the main themes of spiritual practice that transcends differences of creed or community.

Love is Both Culprit and Cure

This wish for peace of heart finds a rather mundane, utilitarian expression in the current craze for a certain kind of 'mindfulness'. People want 'relief from stress', stress being disturbance of the heart, and in our modern way we look for a technique. However, such heart stress cannot really be cured by a distractive technique that only gives temporary respite, welcome as such respite may be. It behoves us to look at our lives in a more fundamental way if we wish to eliminate the roots of the problem rather than simply abate the symptoms for a while.

Of course, we all know instinctively — and it is apparent to us as soon as we look at the emoticons — that this all has something to do with love. It is love that can both stress and soothe the heart. In this sense, we are talking about the yoga of the heart chakra. Anshin, therefore, is about soothing the heart and mending broken ones. It is love that can most disrupt our lives and it is also love that brings great bliss. However, there are many varieties of love, many objects of love and many ways in which love can be expressed or hidden.

Symbols of Innocence

The dove symbolises innocence and simplicity so the peace that it brings is unsullied by hidden corruptions. Doves have symbolised peace in cultures as diverse as ancient Egypt and classical China, and in the Bible the dove represents the Holy Spirit that descended upon Jesus at his baptism by John in the River Jordan. Also, earlier in the Bible, at the end of the flood, a dove brings an olive branch to Noah signalling that the waters are going down and there is land. The troubles are coming to an end. So this is a rather universal symbol of the restoration of calm.

The Chinese character for 'an', however, is not a picture of a dove, it is a picture of a woman in a house. This was a very practical matter. In ancient China where these symbols originated there was often local warfare and at such times the women and children would take to the hills and hide. When peace came they returned to the villages and homes. So when the women were in their houses, there was peace.

Peace Beneath One's Own Roof

This brings home to us the fact that while the issue of war and peace is of immense importance, the peace that matters most frequently to most people is the one that they try to achieve under their own roof. Peace, therefore, in most cultures, is also closely linked with domesticity. In some religions, however — Buddhism, for example — while this association exists, the greatest peace is said to lie in going forth out of domesticity into the 'homeless life'.

Peace of mind, therefore, has a macro and a micro level socially. The little wars that we fight with our nearest and dearest can be just as bitter and taxing as the big wars that go on between nations and ideologies, and there is a good deal of parallelism between the two. Warfare only occurs in a few species such as humans and ants, but domestic squabbling is evident in every sparrow nest in our barn and the bird flying home with some titbit in his/her beak in an effort to restore calm is by no means a species specific gesture.

The Romantic Ideal

In fact, probably most people think that the way to establish peace of heart and mind is to find the right partner and establish the right kind of relationship — whatever that may be. The fact that the key to success in a popular novel is so often that it depicts such a conclusion following after difficulties illustrates the fact that this is a common archetype. It is surely the basis of the 'serial monogamy' that is increasingly the pattern in our contemporary society, as people reiteratively seek happiness by what they believe is the only promise available.

The Complementarity of Inner and Outer

The spiritual paths, however, tend to suggest that the path to bliss is not through finding the right other, but through changing the self in some crucial way so that one can or could be at peace with a diversity of others — ultimately that one can be a bringer of peace to the whole world. Perhaps the ideal relationship is actually one in which those partnered together are held so by common commitment to such a noble ideal.

Nonetheless, even in those paths that take such a view, it is generally through a crucially important relationship that such a personal change takes place. It is in the encounter with a significant other who disturbs our conceit that we can find liberation from it. We thus come full circle. Release from addiction to seeking the right other comes as a result of an encounter with the right other. However, the 'right' other may not be the one we expect. Furthermore, such an encounter disturbs the foundations.

The term anshin implies trust. For us to benefit from either type of relationship there has to be a lot of trust and for that trust to work it really has to transcend the relationship itself. So here is the contrary cycle: arriving at the right quality in oneself depends upon the right relationship, but forming the right relationship depends upon a right quality already established in ourselves.

So we go round these circles, now this way, now that, seeking peace, fleeing it, receiving it, bringing it, disturbing it, losing it, finding it, bestowing and redeeming it, and if our faith can endure through all of this, well, that is anshin.

Anshin: Part Three ~ Symbolism of My Island Home

In the previous teaching we looked at the emoticon image for peace, being a dove with an olive sprig in its beak. In ancient Greek mythology, the dove and the olive branch were attributes of Eirene the goddess of peace. The olive was also associated with Athena who had given the olive tree as a gift to the city of Athens, though in her case the bird holding the branch was an owl. Because of the generosity of this gift, the gods made Athena the patroness of the city and that is how it acquired its name. Just as Athena's gift brought prosperity to Athens, so Eirene gives birth to Plautos the god of prosperity. Peace should allow us to prosper. The olive is a very ancient symbol of peace, probably going back to pre-Grecian times.

When I was a child, I lived in Cyprus. Cyprus is one of only two countries in the world to have olive branches on its national flag (the other is Eritrea). The olive also appears on the country's shield seal.

I remember that there were olive trees all over the island. Like many of the most beautiful places in the world, Cyprus has seen many conflicts and the island is currently divided into the half that is part of the European Union and the half that is occupied by Turkey. In history it has been occupied by a great many political powers — Phoenicia, Greece, Rome, Venice, the Byzantines, the Crusaders, and so on. When I was there, there was a struggle going on for independence from Britain.

So Cyprus can be a place of beauty and peace and also one of war and conflict. Even more strongly than its connection with Eirene, the island is associated with Aphrodite, goddess of love. This seems apt. Love is also associated with both beauty and peace on the one hand and struggle and conflict on the other.

I think that if we are to be truly "impassioned for peace" as it says in the Buddha's teachings on 'right speech' then we also have to be realistic in our appreciation of the importance of war in human history and psychology. People do not go to war out of insanity nor mindlessly. They do so for reasons that seem powerful at the time and war does achieve some things. If we are to have true, deeply established and lasting peace in our communities, it will not be by simply suppressing conflict and ignoring these realities. It will be because we shall have found other less violent ways to achieve what war accomplishes.

One of the most obvious things that a war does is that in many respects it wipes the slate clean and permits a new start. The longer 'peace' continues, normally, the more rule-bound, timid and stultified society becomes. It is like the clutter that can accumulate in a house. Every so often one needs a spring clean and a ruthless throwing out session.

Another thing that war achieves is that it creates an arena for heroism in which people take great risks and stretch themselves to their limit. Long periods of 'peace' very commonly lead to a society becoming effete and 'safe' in a way that takes away most opportunity for anybody to stretch their spirit to its limit and find out what they are really capable of. History is full of examples of societies that became 'soft' and were then overrun by ruder barbarians from beyond the frontier whose more primitive society had more vigour.

What can we learn from this? That our peacefulness should not be mere quietism, nor should it be a disqualification of risk and adventure; that we need periodic opportunities to go back to basics and restart our lives from principle, rather than from the messy accumulation of comforts and conventions that have grown up over the years.

The Buddha was stridently opposed to 'accumulation' seeing it as a barrier to freedom. The ancient Greeks believed in adventure, struggle and heroism and their societies incorporated conflict and debate.

The spiritual life should be as demanding as warfare. We should be at least as vigorous in our commitment to peace as we are to the cause when war breaks out. Only then will war become redundant. The trouble is that we tend only to stir ourselves when things have reached a bad state. Were we more alive earlier things would go differently.

I am much concerned with promoting peaceful community. This is not just a matter of being peaceful individuals. It is also a matter of creating scope for people to be fully alive and vibrant and to interact in ways that deploy their whole being. We can avoid destructive conflict, not by suppressing it, but by cultivating a sense of realism about life and human nature.

I do miss my island home. My memories of being there, for all that I lived through a period of violent insurgency, are sweet ones. The reason for this is that I was surrounded by love. The presence of Aphrodite was real for me then and I was formed by it. The presence of Eirene and Aphrodite and the other goddesses continue to be important realities for me to this day. People may find it difficult to understand the attraction of the pagan gods, but the fact is that they are much closer to us than the totally idealised figures that religion often presents us with.

The memory goes with me and inspires my efforts to make a little heaven. I hope you will join me, or make some similar effort in a domain of your own so that when we meet we can share our stories and experiences, and make a libation to the gods together.

Anshin: Part Four ~ The Judgement of the Oracle

I asked the I Ching to tell me the way to end war and achieve peace. The answer came as hexagram 25. There were no moving lines, so this was a quite definite and timeless response from the oracle.

Hexagram 25 is Wu Wang which means Innocence. It consists of the trigrams ch'ien above and chen below. Ch'ien is 'heaven' and 'chen' is action. So innocence is when action is under the direction of heaven. Then one is innocent.

The oracle presents this as a supremely important virtue — supreme success! Great good fortune comes from persevering in it. To act innocently means to have no ulterior mercenary or selfish interest, but simply to do what is right for its own sake. Innocence and the way of heaven — these are things we can have settled faith in. In fact, they are virtually synonymous with such faith. Innocence is the secret of the peaceful heart.

Sometimes, people ask how they can know what the right thing is, but this is slightly to miss the point. It is not that there is just one thing that is the most right thing of all. There are always many right things. Everything that we do that conduces to the creation of good conditions is a right thing. Such actions are in accord with Wu Wang. They are under the protection of Heaven.

What kind of conditions are good? Ones that make it more possible for people to live innocently. In this world it is impossible to be completely innocent in the sense of never doing harm or never being implicated. The world is not made that way. So the innocence intended here is really purity of heart. Even the person with the purest heart will be implicated in some of the harm that happens in the world. There is no escape from that. However, in the person of pure heart, this circumstance is a foundation for compassion. We are all in this boat together.

Nonetheless, it is possible to advance conditions in the direction of support for innocence. When there is trust and goodwill between people, they naturally revert to a more innocent state. This is not to say that the fundamental nature of people is all good, but rather that it can go either way — many ways — according to conditions. By establishing trustworthy conditions we not only act well, we also help others to do so.

When we establish a spiritual community this is what we are doing. We are trying to make it possible for people to live closer to this ideal of wu wang. If we have a settled faith in doing so, then we shall ourselves be following the Way of Heaven.

Here, at my hermitage in France, we have a bit of a head start in this matter. It is surrounded by natural beauty. Not only that, but it is well off the beaten track. We saw in the last teaching that places of great beauty can sometimes be the scenes of the most terrible conflict. It is best, therefore, not to boast too much about this good fortune. Take delight in being unregarded. All the great sages have pointed out the danger of attracting envy. This is a good example of the matter we are talking about. If one provokes envy in others, that is not setting up conditions for innocence.

So we can rejoice in our good fortune and also in the good fortunes of others, but do so discretely. Anshin is like that. It is not showy. It does not proclaim itself. It just gets on, completes simple duties, and acts naturally.

D.T. Suzuki tells the story of the conversation between a vinaya master and a zen master. The former asks the latter how he disciplines himself in daily life. The zen master says that when he is hungry he eats and when he is tired he sleeps. The other comments that that is no different from anybody else, but the zen master does not agree. He points out that most people's heads are full of all kinds of turmoil so that they never just eat or just sleep. They do not do so innocently because their heart is not settled. I think that this story gives a good sense of anshin.

Hexagram 25 implies action. Innocence is not just passivity. Faith makes action possible. Most people under-achieve. This is because they dither. They dither because they lack faith and are full of uncertainty, at least, and often also of guilt and fear. The innocent person, however, can just get on and do whatever it is that needs doing at the time.

It strikes me as demonstrative that the oracle produced a reply with no moving lines. It is an innocent reply with neither doubt nor dithering. It is not going anywhere. Innocence is a peaceful heart, settled, an end to strife and a foundation of peace, and in delivering it in this way the oracle not only pronounces it, it also demonstrates it. How fortunate we are!

Anshin: Part Five ~ Four Sukhas

We might ask, how is faith to be protected? Another way to ask the same question is to ask, what does faith want? If we want something to be big and strong, we should feed it the right food. The right food for anshin is what are called the Four Sukhas. The word sukha means bliss. We have already looked at how faith is connected with innocence and simplicity. The Four Sukhas carry this idea further. The word sukha also occurs in the word Sukhavati which is the Indian word for the Pure Land of Buddha — the sukha land.

Four Sukhas

The first sukha is renunciation. This is something that faith wants. Faith is, in many respects, the opposite of compulsiveness. When we do not have faith we cling to things. It might be some addictive behaviour or it might be possessions or status or other things that feed the ego. Either we feed faith or we feed the ego. Dogen, in one of his talks, says that practitioners of the way do not treasure possessions or rank or sensual indulgence, they just treasure time. That is a profound observation. When we are caught in compulsivity, time starts to blur. The spiritual practitioner "does not waste time" as it says in the Most Excellent Mirror Samadhi*. So renunciation is clearing a space where our time can be totally experienced and we do not miss a moment of our life.

The second sukha is seclusion. Faith likes solitude. When there is opportunity the practitioner likes to retreat. This does not mean that he or she does necessarily spend a lot of time alone — she might or might not — but she or he is not clinging to people. The spiritual teacher is able to give disciples a lot of space because he has no particular interest in controlling them. Each has their own life. The teacher helps, but much of that help consists in helping the person to find their own space. So faith frees one from co-dependency. This also means that the person of faith can be decisive. This is another face of innocence. When one's motive is in accordance with Heaven there is nothing to fear.

The third sukha is peace. Faith loves peace. Faith means not being at war, neither with oneself nor with others. A person of faith does not stir up trouble, does not add energy to conflict. This does not mean, however, that he or she is a wimp. Peace requires active care. As was said in an earlier teaching in this series, we should work at peace with the same commitment and energy as people work at war. My mother would say that the war years were the best years of her life. She meant that it was a time when people naturally and willingly co-operated and

---

* page 16, Nien Fo Book: The service book of Amida Shu, Amida Shu, 2018

supported one another, there was great goodwill and friendliness, and people were united. Of course, it was for a destructive purpose. The ideal is to have those same qualities for a constructive one.

The fourth sukha is bodhi — awakening. Faith loves to be awakened, loves to discover. The idea that faith is a dogmatic attachment to fixed beliefs and a refusal to look at evidence is not at all what is meant by faith in Buddhism. Actually it takes faith to be open enough to look at ideas that challenge one's pre-established position. It takes faith to doubt. Dogmatism and clinging to fixed positions is more a symptom of fear than of real faith. The person of settled faith takes things in their stride. Discovering that one has been wrong about something is always helpful — how else can one learn, grow and improve? When once we are awakened to faith, we go on being awakened by all the miscellaneous circumstances of life that we then run into. The person of faith has the faith to be willing to take risks with their life. It is for this reason that they do not fear finding things out that shatter their previous world. They have confidence that the newly emerging world will also be fine.

Back to the Forest

The Buddha wanted that we renounce the things that tie us down. However, we no longer live in a society in which one can simply go to the forest and live off the fruit of the land. Society has become immensely more complex and there is no free space left. Therefore, we have to create little pure lands where such a life can be lived.

I am fortunate to live in a forest retreat. When I was young and grown-ups asked me what I wanted to be when I grew up I would tell them that I wanted to be an eccentric and live in a wood. This would make them laugh. However, my dream has come true.

One is only safe in company if one is completely content being alone.

One can only safely say yes, if one would be completely happy to say no.

One can only live fully if one would be quite content to die.

One can only handle being in authority when one knows how to serve.

Contentment means to be without hankering. Loneliness, for instance, is a hankering for company, whereas a person who is free is happy in solitude. A person who has no hankering for possessions can be trusted with things. A person who has no hankering for position can be trusted with authority. A person who has no hankering for particular states can be at peace in his mind.

Anshin: Part Six ~ Faith in Therapy

Faith evidently plays a significant part in psychotherapy. Whatever school one follows, the "therapeutic alliance" is important. In some forms of therapy it is virtually the be-all-and-end-all of the work. Such an alliance rests upon the faith that the client has in the therapist and this reflects the faith that the therapist has in the client. In fact, therapy substantially consists in a relationship in which the therapist has faith in the client, often in ways and to a degree that the client himself does not have.

When we say "has faith in the client" we are referring to the client in his life. A person is always situated. All the ordinary aspects of life are conditional. In practice, therefore, this means that the faith that the therapist has in the client is a faith that the client can cope with the circumstances that are arising for him, no matter how extreme or grievous they may be. This is what is sometimes called 'unconditional positive regard'. In order for this faith to have credibility, the therapist must enter into the life of the client to such an extent that she has an easy familiarity with and feeling for the 'world' of the client. In effect, therefore, the work is quite object related. The therapist 'stands alongside the client' as the client goes forth into his life.

However, from a spiritual point of view it is worth distinguishing between ordinary circumstance and eternal things. When we talk of anshin we are not just talking about ordinary confidence. We are talking about a faith that transcends the ordinary. Only such a faith can really be 'unconditional'. In practice, ordinary human beings such as ourselves are not totally unconditional. However, if we live a spiritual life, we do have confidence in something beyond, something that, perhaps, remains mysterious to us, but, nonetheless, we regard as ultimately, not merely circumstantially, reliable. This is what is called taking refuge.

It is because the therapist takes refuge that she is able to provide unconditional support. This does not mean that she will be perfect in every response or accomplish some amazing ideal. It means, rather, that there is something deep within the meeting that cannot be explained in ordinary terms that carries the encounter forward in benign yet unexpected ways.

These two levels refer to what in Buddhism is sometimes called "the two truths" which are "relative truth" and "absolute truth". This is not really a philosophical notion, it is more an experience. The two levels do interact. It is her faith in the transcendent refuge that enables the therapist to let go to a sufficient degree and really enter into the client's "relative world" and it is because she can and does do so that the client subliminally picks up that there is something more than just ordinary 'relative' confidence operating here. In the best case this results in the client also finding a refuge that transcends ordinary life circumstance. When this happens, therapy and spirituality merge. In lesser cases, the therapist's faith in the holding power of refuge is sufficient to give the client ordinary confidence so that he goes through whatever life trial it may be in a way that brings him to growth and constructive change rather than defeat.

In either case, the client emerges with more faith than he had before. He might or might not have words for this, might or might not have a spiritual practice of his own. If he does, then he will have a vocabulary for talking about such things. However, even if he does not, still the increase in faith operating in his life will be an asset that will benefit him in many ways, not just in the matter discussed in therapy, but in all dimensions of life.

Anshin: Part Seven ~ Practical Application

Now a lot of guests have arrived and my period of solitude has come to an end. During the times of being here on my own or with just one other person for company, I have been doing a lot of physical work. The doctor recommended that I keep active in order to improve my blood circulation. However, throughout all this time, my primary motivation is always to try to make this place more welcoming and more serviceable for the guests who come. Some of these things are very practical. The two most substantial developments are the creation of a new eating area and the flooring of part of the barn to give extra storage thus permitting a much freer use of living space in the main house. These are all practical applications of my faith in the Buddha, the Dharma and the Sangha and the working out of the grace of the deities. When one has such a faith one finds that one's capacity to get things done is vastly enhanced because, as was said in the earlier I Ching teaching, when one is in accord with the Way of Heaven there is no obstacle.

So whether one is in the midst of many people or one is completely alone or whatever the circumstance might be, the important thing is to have a connection, a refuge, that carries one through. Today has been a day of historic change with the British decision to leave the European Union[*] — a decision that I personally think to be most unwise. Seeing the news I felt shocked. However, such vicissitudes happen. Many things are part of processes too big for the individual to have much influence. Things happen and we have to respond and live through it. I am very grateful to have the security of a faith that gives me confidence that I shall go on doing what seems like the right and constructive things whether the conditions are supportive or adverse. Faith is not just going with the flow. Sometimes it is a matter of standing against the current. I shall continue to support internationalism on the wider scene and, in my own little patch, to make good conditions for my visitors. This is by the power given by faith.

---

[*] The Brexit referendum on 23rd June 2016

Eightfold What?

Buddha Tao

The Fourth Truth is called Marga, the Eightfold Path, but in Chinese, it comes out as the Eightfold Tao. I like it. Tao has a different feel from "path". Path feels narrow. Tao feels all-encompassing. The Tao is our benefactor — the mysterious promise of life, always functioning in a beneficent way. Tao is always everywhere.

The best way to live is in accord with the Tao, but given that the Tao is completely mysterious, how is one to do that? The answer to that question would give you the nature of the Eightfold Tao... or the Onefold Tao, or the Millionfold Tao, or the Tao to the root of minus one, or the Tao of motorcycle maintenance, or whatever, and they would all be the same Tao.

Not Unproblematic

Maybe you read about Buddhism, and you read the Four Truths in the conventional way and you learn that the Eightfold Path is the method to get enlightened and you think it is unproblematic to understand, just difficult to do, yes? But actually, the Eightfold Tao is THE great mystery. Shakyamuni Buddha did not even discover it until he was completely enlightened. What is "right" view? "Right" thought? "Right" samadhi? Thinking that because one has a string of terms one has got "something" is delusion. All you have got is another distraction.

Nembutsu is the Third not the Fourth Truth

Sometimes people ask why it was that Honen substituted nembutsu and other power for the self power way of the Eightfold Tao. I have a little book called "Jodo Shu: A Daily Reference" in which this very question is discussed. I have a lot of sympathy with and affinity to Jodo Shu, but in my understanding, this is the wrong question. Honen did not substitute nembutsu for the fourth truth, he offered it as the deep meaning of the third truth. This is quite different.

Dukkha leads to samudaya. In the person with no nembutsu (of whatever form), samudaya just leads to more dukkha and that is samsara. If you are not familiar with the Buddhist terminology: affliction brings stuff up and if you have no deeper way of dealing with that stuff, then the things you are liable to do with it just create more affliction and trouble.

To get off the hamster wheel requires a sideways jump, which is an act of faith — shinjin — because it is free fall after that. That is nirodha. Nirodha is taking your life in your hands and giving it away to the best thing you can imagine. Nirodha generates marga quite naturally, without you even needing to know what all the words mean or even know that it is happening.

Not Until You Are Buddha

Thinking that the fourth truth is easy to understand is a mistake and thinking that it is the means is also a mistake. The fourth truth is the Tao, is enlightenment, is IT. You won't understand it, let alone be able to do it, until you are a Buddha. And the third truth is how that happens. Which is faith. Faith, here, is to have Buddha in mind and trust. Entrust to the mystery. So long as you have a hazy notion of Buddha Tao, that is enough. Your soul knows what your mind never dreamt of.

Nembutsu means to have Buddha in mind, or, we should really say, to have Buddha in your heart. That means to be a Buddhist. A Buddhist is somebody who has Buddha in his/her heart. This is not a sectarian matter. All Buddhists have Buddha in mind while they are still deluded beings. The more they really have Buddha in mind the less deluded they get because Buddha works secret magic inside the heart. It is not really that Pureland is the school that does nembutsu instead of what other schools do, it is that Pureland understands what all Buddhists do as being nembutsu... or it is not Buddhist practice. If it is done in relation to Buddha it is Buddhism.

The Root and the Flower

If you take the Eightfold Tao as a syllabus, then you can go on learning an endless amount about it. There are acres of teachings on right behaviour and even more on right speech, understandably. Right livelihood is a challenge for many and right effort is obviously a key to much else. Lots to study. However, this is not a Lego set. You cannot put awakening together from construction pieces. In fact, you cannot put it together at all. We treat the Eightfold Whatever-it-is as the root when actually it is the flower and the flower grows and opens naturally when the root is in good shape.

The root is underground. It is hidden. It is not in the realm of consciousness. When we have faith it is going on, growing in the dark. Faith is just the willingness to take in the Light, which, in this analogy, means having the Buddha in mind.

Best Friend

This is why sudden awakening and gradual cultivation come together. There are tipping points. We tend to think that the cultivation comes first and gets us to the tipping point, like adding sand grains to a scale until it tips. Actually it's the opposite. When we face life just as it is, something tips. Gradual cultivation is then the resulting downhill slide.

It is not just a matter of degree. Either you have faith or you don't. Either Buddha is your best friend or something else is. Either one is facing life honestly or one isn't. Either you rely upon the birthless truth or you rely upon ephemera. And when you do the Tao is all over the place, everywhere you look, and when you don't it is working secretly behind your back, because, Buddha always was your best friend, even when you didn't realise it.

Love and Destiny: The Way of Ashvaghosha

Mysterious Man of Letters

Ashvaghosha was born into a Brahmin family in Saketa in Northern India. He is counted as one of the early masters of Buddhism, teacher of Kapimala who, in turn, was teacher of the famous Nagarjuna. In his own right, Ashvaghosha became one of the greatest poets in Indian history and was also a playwright of note. He became a great populariser of Buddhism, especially of that approach in which faith (shraddhā) and devotion (bhakti) are central. However, we know very little about his personal life. The Buddha taught effacement and Ashvaghosha practised it.

The Vital Encounter

According to traditional stories, he initially became a wandering Hindu ascetic. At that time it was common to hold debates between religious practitioners or philosophers. The loser would become the disciple of the winner. Ashvaghosha often challenged Buddhists, but none would debate with him because of his formidable reputation as a debater. Eventually, however, he met his match in an encounter with Punyayashas.

Ashvaghosha asked Punyashas, "What is Buddha?"

Punyashas said, "You want to know that? The Buddha himself does not know."

This expression has a double meaning. At first sight it suggests that Ashvaghosha is Buddha even though he does not know it. However, it also means that a Buddha does not know what he is. In fact, a Buddha is endlessly finding out what it is to be what he is. A Buddha is constantly learning.

Buddhacarita

Later, Ashvaghosha became a famous poet. He wrote in classical Sanskrit and is acknowledged even by non-Buddhists as one of the finest poets in the early history of India. Some of his works survive to this day, notably his Buddhacarita (Life of the Buddha) and his poem Handsome Nanda. We can see from his Life of the Buddha that he thought of the Buddha as destined from birth for his role as Tathagata, yet also describes him as a hero struggling with obstacles. These two dimensions are only compatible if we assume that although the Buddha was destined, he himself did not know it, so that he was continually in a process of finding out what he is supposed to be.

Religious Consciousness

This tells us something important about the spiritual life. It is a process of finding out, of investigating Dharma (dhamma vicaya), as Shakyamuni himself said. In order to do so one must keep in mind the Buddha's sense of that term as a religious consciousness, a mindfulness of one's relationship with the divine — with the eternal Buddha, the Tao, Heaven, however one conceives it — and then encounter each situation in life letting it be problematised by that mindfulness.

Ashvaghosha meets Punyayashas and asks, "What is Buddha?" So here are the three elements: self, other and Buddha. Awareness of Buddha is religious consciousness. If it was just an encounter between the two men it would be a purely humanistic situation, but if it is an encounter in which both have Buddha (or God, or the transcendental) in mind, then it becomes a koan.

Both men are, in that moment, enquiring about Buddha. Punyayashas sees Buddha in Ashvaghosha. Punyayashas, being spiritually awakened, is always discovering Buddha. In this instance, he discovers Buddha in his encounter with Ashvaghosha. By discovering Buddha in the other he discovers how to be himself and, therefore, we, as outside observers, can say, he is discovering how to be Buddha. Buddha is not a stereotyped role, it is to be genuinely alive in the fullness of one's situation, which, to say it another way, is to fulfil one's destiny.

To Know Each Other Completely

So, to completely fulfil one's destiny is to be Buddha in one way or another. Most people never do. So we can ask what it is that enables a person to do so. This is why Ashvaghosha is asking "How can I be Buddha?" Yet, a Buddha is somebody who is all the time finding out the answer to exactly that question. So in that moment, Ashvaghosha is Buddha discovering Buddha, and he discovers Buddha in the mirror that is Punyayashas.

Punyayashas, similarly, is finding out his destiny. So at this moment, these two are standing in one line. They know each other completely. Each is contributing to the destiny of the other. This is love.

Destiny does not mean the same as predestination. In predestination, what is fore-ordained must happen, whereas in destiny there is something on offer, but what is meant to happen does not always transpire. What Ashvaghosha really responds to in Punyayashas is the latter's love and it is this love, this deep knowing, that creates a destiny for Ashvaghosha that he, in turn, discovers through this encounter. In this manner, it is said that the old Ashvaghosha is chopped down, as a tree is felled, and a new Ashvaghosha appears, but the new Ashvaghosha is the one who is fulfilling his destiny.

Horses Wept

We do not know what Ashvaghosha's name was originally. The name Ashvaghosha means "crying horses". It seems that he was such an eloquent preacher that when he declared the Dharma even horses wept. His writing expresses a strong poetic tension between sensuality and asceticism. It seems to say that sensual pleasure is exquisite, yet renunciation is even better. He writes as somebody who seems to know what he is talking about so we can assume that this had been an important theme for him himself, yet we know nothing about his love life, nor about why he left home to become an ascetic. In fact, we know hardly any biographical details at all.

To Fulfil One's Destiny

Ashvaghosha's sense of the Dharma was connected with an idea of destiny. How are we to understand this? Shakyamuni is commonly presented in Buddhist texts as the successor to a long line of Buddhas going back in cosmic time. Ashvaghosha's writing does not include this element. Instead it sees him as the culmination of Indian religious and cultural tradition as a whole, not just Buddhist.

So there is here the sense that each person has something that they are to do, a destiny to fulfil. They may or might not do it. This destiny is shaped by the conditions that impose and the love that is available. The Buddhas are those who love copiously and so create great destinies for many other beings. These are like invitations. The Buddha predicted enlightenment for people when he saw that they had received and accepted such an invitation. To be awakened, therefore, is to set aside one's personal ideas and ambitions about oneself and become willing to receive and accept what the universe has planned for one, and, in doing so, one becomes a devotee and, incidentally, also becomes a maker of destinies for others. This is all by the power of love.

The Merit of a Fan

This morning in our Sunday service, I gave a talk about the meaning of the fan that is often carried by a Buddhist teacher. I had with me a fan that my mother purchased in Cyprus in 1952 or thereabouts. Today is the anniversary of my mother's death so there is great sentimental value in this object. I can imagine her choosing it on a stall. Life in Cyprus moves at a slow pace so there would probably have been conversation with the woman behind the stall who may well also have been the maker of the fan. Mummy would have been wearing a white frock with a flower pattern on it. I remember the wide skirt. I particularly remember it because I was a shy child and when Mummy wanted to introduce me to one of her friends I would catch a corner of her skirt and twizzle round so as to disappear into the fold of the cloth not to be seen.

The fan has a similar purpose. When the teacher imparts something — gives the precepts, for instance — he may cover his face with the fan. This is a way of becoming invisible. It is not the teacher that is being transmitted, it is the Dharma. The teacher is a medium. This is similar to the point about things being done by the robe.

In order for the Dharma to be transmitted, the teacher must disappear. The Dharma is bright and the teacher becomes dark, hidden. This is what in China, especially in Taoism, was called the dark wisdom. It did not mean dark in the sense of malevolent, but dark in the sense of modesty, of yin rather than yang, and of naturalness. In his essay Genjo Koan, Master Dogen talks of the importance of becoming dark. When water is dark it becomes a mirror. The mirror mind is a Buddhist ideal.

So the good teacher is not trying to be anything more than just what he or she is. When one is completely natural, one is, in this sense, not there. There is much talk these days about the importance of 'presence', but the best presence, from the point of view of Buddhism and Taoism, is one that displays emptiness. Absence is wiser.

So the fan can symbolise effacement, the letting go of self and the willingess to perform whatever task or duty is needed. It is also a protection. The light of the Dharma is brilliant, like the sun. You cannot look at it directly. The appearance of the dharmakaya will burn your eyes. Thus we always actually encounter the Dharma in some slightly less intense or 'sambhogakaya' form, a form in which we can enjoy it. As long as there is the least self-consciousness left, the Dharma will scorch us. This is very like myself as a little child hiding in Mother's skirt. Self-consciousness is actually horribly unbearable.

So the priest, performing the holy work of the Dharma, may occlude his face — may resort to the 'face before birth' — in order that there simply be the transmitting of Dharma which is other than self.

Grandmotherly Mind

In Japan, it is said that the person who heads a spiritual community should have 'grandmotherly mind'. Here we are not referring to any particular grandmother, but rather to an archetype. This grandmother carries certain dignity and so can be imposing when necessary, but most of the time is kindly and considerate of everybody in the community. She brings calm and balance to the situation and makes everybody feel loved — because they are.

A spiritual community is not like a commercial enterprise, nor is it like the army. There is a hierarchy of responsibility and authority, but it is the duty of those in higher positions to have a gentle care for those in lower. In particular, it is vitally important that the spiritual guide not use his or her authority for the purpose of advancing his own interests. Perhaps the abbot would like a certain trainee to stay and look after him, but if it is in the interest of that person's spiritual training that they go elsewhere, then so it shall be.

Again, when somebody has stepped out of line or done something stupid, the leader has to do something about it, but it is imperative that at such a time deep compassion for the person who is in error predominates. One needs to be the grandmother, not the dictator.

As leader of the community, I have to think very hard about the right way to tackle this type of situation. The spiritual progress of the trainee is far more important than the efficient running of the temple, yet simply allowing such a matter to pass and the lesson not be learnt may not be wise.

Of course, there are many things that one does simply let pass, because it is much better that a person find out for himself. When somebody new comes to the temple one generally gives them plenty of rope, as it were, so as to see what they are capable of and what level of concern they have for others, how conscientious, how able to see what needs doing, how ready to join in with others and so on.

Actually, the better the trainee is doing and the better the relationship that you have with them, the more direct one can be. However, in every case there is a considerable art to giving directions without an overflow of ire or irritation. The trainee will generally sense whether there is a fund of goodwill behind the corrective remark or not, but this is not automatically the case, and the instructor should only go so far as will actually help the person.

In order to do this one has to put one's own wants and agendas aside. With a bit of self-reflection, one can generally feel whether one's ire is active — it is evident from the temperature of one's body and the tone of one's muscles. One needs to have as a higher priority the wellbeing of all the members of the community, so, sometimes, one needs to take a little time to reflect before acting. In our order we have precepts not to punish, not to blame, and to have a tender care for others, 'especially when one believes them to be at fault or mistaken'.

These precepts are immensely important, but, of course, rather challenging to adhere to all the time. People are bound sooner or later to do things that get under one's skin. What is one to do? My teacher Kennett Roshi used to say, "Firstly, consider your own training." Sometimes it is better to sleep on an issue than to try to tackle it while one is hot. On the other hand, if one is cool, then tackling it immediately may sometimes be best. All of this means that one has to develop a sensitivity to one's own state as well as that of the other person. Love and trust are always tested.

At the same time, it is important that one be natural. Grandmother is naturally kind, naturally concerned for the grandchildren, naturally understanding, yet with a down-to-earth wisdom borne of long experience and deeper perspective. Although codes and precepts are valuable, the real essence of Buddhism lies in having the right-heartedness from which such behaviour arises, rather than from adherence to a code.

Does the Dharma Need Updating?

In my view, there is a widespread tendency at work in the process of introducing Buddhism to the West that is systematically distorting the Dharma message of Buddha.

This is occurring as well-meaning Westerners import into Buddhism ideas that they believe in that are no part of the original Buddhist message.

Sometimes this is done unwittingly. People believe that idea X is good. They also believe that Buddhism is good. They then assume that idea X must, therefore, be part of Buddhism. At other times, it is done knowingly. The person knows that idea Y is not part of Buddhism but believes that Buddhism therefore needs bringing up to date or "Westernising" and therefore thinks that they are improving upon the Buddha's message by introducing their favourite ideas. In my opinion, the former is an innocent yet unfortunate mistake and the latter usually occurs in circumstances in which the person concerned has failed to deeply understand the Dharma message and, equipped with a shallow understanding, has found the Dharma lacking in some particular. Generally, it is the case that the Dharma does deal with the problem that idea Y is supposed to cope with, but does so in a completely different manner that the writer has failed to appreciate.

An area where these tendencies are rife is the field of socially engaged Buddhism. In this area there are many people who are deeply schooled in and committed to certain liberal or socialistic principles — what may generally be termed "progressive thinking" — derived ultimately from Hellenistic or Judeo-Christian sources. Where these people have become Buddhist they have brought many of these ideas with them. The prestige of Western thought is such that some of these ideas have now even fed back into contemporary Asian Buddhism.

A classic examples is the Western concern with a certain idea of justice which is partly derived from Plato and partly from the Old Testament, but which has no roots in Buddhism as far as I can see. Other examples include liberal ideas about tolerance, non-judgmentalism, value relativism, non-dualism, interdependence, and deep ecology. In some of these cases it is possible to find a concept of similar name within Buddhism, but with different meaning.

In order to deal with this issue in a more concrete way I would like to focus upon David Chappell's critique of Honen in his article "Engaged Buddhists in a Global Society: Who is Being Liberated?"[*] The general drift of the article as a whole is that socially engaged ideas are liberating and up-dating Buddhism, so this is a clear example of the trend that I am worried about.

---

[*] In S. Sivaraksa et al. *Socially Engaged Buddhism for the new Millenium* Sathirakoses-Nagapradipa Foundation and Foundation for Children: Bangkok, 1999

Now I can say that, in general, I do find many of Chappell's ideas useful, interesting and stimulating, yet, at the same time, I feel critical in the way that I have explained above. So let's have a look at what he says about Honen specifically.

Chappell prefaces his remarks by acknowledging that

> "Honen is notable for challenging the limits of the traditional Buddhist institutions by bringing Buddhism out of the monastery and into the street, and... attracting commoners and disreputable people, the humble and the outcaste."

He then goes on to list the ways in which Honen was very different from the socially engaged Buddhists of the twentieth century.

POINT ONE: Is Honen Reductionist?

Chappell claims that Honen was reductionist and exclusivist in contrast to the New Buddhism that affirms interdependence, and aims for inclusivity including interfaith dialogue.

Of course, anybody who advances a proposition as more right than others, Chappell included, can be said to be reductionist and exclusive, but this is not the way that these terms are usually understood. Similarly, misguided followers of any creed or philosophy, be it socially engaged Buddhism or whatever, can make a dogma of it and assert it in an exclusionary manner, but, again, we would have to say that the misapplication of something should not be taken as a reflection upon the original idea. So is it true that Honen's approach is reductionist and is it exclusive?

Literally, we can say that Honen "reduced" the whole of Buddhism to devotion to the Buddhas, especially Amitabha, and said that those who follow this path should make a selection of nembutsu as their practice, thus excluding other practices, but this does not imply a condemnation of those who follow other paths. It was simply a means of making the Dharma widely available. It is odd to accuse the person who made Buddhism available to the masses of being exclusivist. It was the fact that Buddhism prior to Honen was limited to an elite that stimulated him to find a way for the ordinary person to practise.

Honen does doubt that other methods actually work, but leaves it to others to make their own judgement. He based his teaching primarily upon a small number of Buddhist texts amongst which the Larger Pureland Sutra features prominently. The Larger Sutra is one of the few religious texts in the world that provides a grounding for and positive injunction toward paying respect to "other Buddhas" in ways that accord with their requirements.

Here we see a different approach to a similar problem. Chappell advocates interfaith dialogue, but Honen's Pureland advocates making offerings to other Buddhas in ways appropriate to them. In fact, in the Pure Land, according to both the larger and smaller sutras, making offerings to other Buddhas appears to be the main occupation of inhabitants of the Pure Abodes — an ultimate validation of respect for other teachers. Arguably, this Pureland approach is actually more respectful of other faith communities than the dialogue approach. The latter preserves distance, whereas the former legitimises Pureland practitioners in participating with other faith communities so long as the practice in question is not blatantly unethical from a Buddhist point of view. A Buddhist practitioner should not participate in animal sacrifice, but can happily go and sing hymns and consider them to be simply other forms of nembutsu.

Interdependence — Dependence

Pureland is not centred on the idea of interdependence. It is more conscious of simple dependence.
Interdependence implies that you need me as much as I need you. In many ways this philosophy overestimates the human existential situation. Planet Earth does not need humans as much as humans need planet Earth. I suggest that the principle of dependence is a better basis for a correction of current human hubris than the idea of interdependence is. Buddha originally taught dependent origination and this is a valid principle that helps us to stay humble and grateful.

On the specific point about interfaith dialogue, when this does occur, and I personally have been involved in a good deal of it over the years, it is generally my impression that this comes much easier to Pureland practitioners than it does to followers of other forms of

Buddhism. Pureland practitioners easily find common ground with other faiths because they do use terms like faith, grace, and other-power that other Buddhists are rather shy of.

POINT TWO: Does Honen Undermine Confidence in Human Activity?

Chappell claims that "Honen rejected hope for salvation in this world and undermined confidence in any human activity" whereas leaders of the New Buddhism are "committed to working in this world to seek relief of suffering through compassion and enlightenment here-and-now."

This criticism misreads Honen and confuses social action and salvation. Affirmation of salvation by faith does not entail passivity as the Protestant work ethic clearly demonstrates in our Western culture. In the West it is precisely those religious groups that rejected the idea of "salvation by works" who went on to generate the industrial revolution. Chappell here makes a mistake that is quite commonly encountered among people who make only a superficial reading of Honen. Honen himself was one of the most active missionaries for the Dharma in the history of Japan and his followers went on to be so active that by a few generations later the Japanese state was worrying that Pureland might displace the government. In China, at an earlier date, the Pureland White Lotus Societies had been one of the mainstays of the Ming Revolution which had displaced the Mongol dynasty and re-established Chinese rule of China. Empirically speaking, Honen's approach tends to generate more social involvement not less and this is understandable from first principles.

All Buddhists, Honen no less, are in favour of compassionate action and Honen is an exemplar. However, most socially engaged Buddhists of the kind praised by Chappell follow a self-power path and believe that the first priority is to get oneself enlightened and that such quietistic practices as silent meditation are somehow the key to social reform, all of which requires a good deal of time in retreat away from the world. On the other hand, followers of Honen, precisely because they do not expect to become enlightened in this lifetime, feel freed up to live socially engaged lives and feel empowered to do so by their faith, not believing that they need to achieve some personal advanced level of spirituality first.

The Pureland practitioner, believing him or herself already "seized by Amida" self-identifies in a different way.

Having already become, in effect, a citizen of the Pure Land, it is quite natural to try and make wherever one is into some reflection of that paradise.

At the same time, the recognition that one will never completely accomplish the creation of a Pure Land in this world by one's own efforts is a strong prophylactic against disappointment. The self-power practitioner is inevitably looking for results and can easily lose heart. The Pureland practitioner simply does what comes naturally whether the results turn out to be great or meagre. Arguably, this latter is a more practical strategy and a more effective spiritual support. In any case, it is certainly the case that Pureland in Japan has given rise to educational systems and universities that are far from undermining confidence in human activity.

A major reason why the approach of Honen became popular and widespread was that the practice of nembutsu does not interfere with other activities. A sailor can say nembutsu while sailing his boat, a farmer while following his plough, a soldier, even, while marching. It was the very compatibility of Pureland with the active life that made it so appropriate to the lay population. Approaches based on silent contemplation needed time out and have an inherent tendency toward a life of non-engagement. Honen's approach also could readily encompass the whole family. Walking and chanting does not exclude children in the way that silent contemplation generally does. I suggest, therefore, that Chappell has got hold of the wrong end of the stick.

POINT THREE: Is individual Buddha Nature the Answer?

> "Honen was impressed by the karmic debt that humans had incurred... that totally obstructed salvation by their own efforts" whereas New Buddhism emphasises people's inherent goodness" and seeks to "empower

> ordinary people by emphasising their Buddha Nature."

What Chappell says is correct, but in taking the latter philosophy to be self-evidently superior, he is, surely, mistaken. The Critical Buddhism movement in Japan has convincingly demonstrated how the Buddha-Nature-of-individuals thesis easily leads to spiritual complacency and the turning of a blind eye to social oppression.

Honen, like Shakyamuni Buddha, emphasised the urgency and difficulty of the situation and thereby injected vigour into the spiritual life.

If people are all inherently good, what need is there for social engagement? Honen had great compassion for the ordinary person, often trapped in an invidious social situation, and showed each how to do whatever they can.

Philosophies of inherent goodness are dangerously close to the atma philosophy that Buddha rejected that culminates in an all's-well-with-the-world-and-nothing-needs-to-be-done complacency. The individual Buddha Nature idea chimes with an aspect of popular philosophy that is found in spiritual systems all over the world and with some ideas in popular psychology. It is a humanistic principle that asserts that what it is to be human must be intrinsically good and right. Teachers like Shakyamuni come along and upset this smug idea. The Buddha pointed out that people in general are deluded in a great many ways, that ignorance is widespread, and that what is normal is not good enough. Popular culture — and contemporary medicine — sees the goal as being to make people normal, but great teachers ask more.

Honen, like most people of his time, was very conscious of the cruelty and greed that was everywhere apparent in the world around him. In this he was just the same as Shakyamuni Buddha. His heart-felt desire was to find a path for the ordinary person who is inevitably caught up in this world-on-fire. This surely is what all great teachers do. When Shakyamuni was confronted by the mad woman Patacara who had gone insane after losing both her children, her husband and both parents in the course of one disastrous week, he did not reassure her that she had Buddha Nature. He said the tears she had locked up inside her were only a small part of the ocean of tears she had shed in her many lives. In other words, he did not reassure her with comfortable wishful thinking but showed her that he appreciated the terrible karmic debt that humankind carries. He understood, but was not crushed, and she thus drew strength from him and regained her sanity.

In my view, the idea of individual Buddha Nature is a departure from proper Buddhist principles and is a form of human self-aggrandisement. Honen seems to have though so too.

POINT FOUR: Is Progress Inevitable? Is Honen Pessimistic?

Chappell accuses Honen of pessimism due to his belief in mappo, the Dharma ending age. Chappell sees that there are individuals of evil tendency and that there is "institutional structural violence here-and-now" but still wants to believe in progress, thus "many examples of the improvement of knowledge, institutions, and technology provide encouragement to believe that the combination of mindfulness and work can reap some positive decrease in suffering." In this section, Chappell sounds less than fully convinced by his own argument. He says, "even when there is no rational hope of improvement one should still try."

Certainly there is a big gap between Honen's idea of mappo and the modern belief in progress. This latter faith is not as widespread or as convincing as it used to seem, of course, now that we are aware of ecological degradation, terrorism and recurrent economic downturns. Times were bad in medieval Japan too. It seems very wide of the mark, however, to call Honen a pessimist. He drew huge support from the population in his own time because he gave them hope in a time when signs of decay and disaster were all around. A philosophy made for bad times can still stand us in good stead in good ones, but a philosophy made for good times is not much use when the good times end.

Chappell seems to me here to suffer from the common tendency to believe that thinking makes it so. If you think times are good they will become so and vice versa. This is a fallacy. Chappell needs examples of progress to give him hope and faith, but Honen has hope and faith even in the complete absence of them. Chappell's New Buddhism seems to be grounded in a results oriented approach, whereas the true spirit of Buddhism and any true religion, I suggest, is virtue for its own sake. Religion should be able to inspire us even and precisely in those dark times when there are no material profits to be had. Honen's philosophy does that. Chappell's does not: it needs external supports.

Honen's message gave people confidence in the midst of disaster, famine, earthquake and war. Chappell wants to ground his philosophy in evidence of progress in this material world. However in this world of conditions, things can go down as well as up, backwards as well as forwards.

Buddhism does not assume that progress is inevitable. Things change according to conditions and our intentional actions.

This is what makes the Buddhist philosophy one of freedom. The Buddha reinterpreted karma to mean that anything is possible, intentional action has consequences. Good intentions bring good consequences sooner or later and bad bad. We do not need to import faith in progress into Buddhism, it is better without it. Nonetheless, by embracing the metaphysical aspect of Buddhism, Honen was able to give people hope that transcended material circumstance.

POINT FIVE: Was Honen Backward Because He Did Not Have Wifi?

Chappell says that "today's Buddhist leaders can seek reform of their institutions by collaborating with more diverse and inclusive institutions, such as education, democracy, and the internet to ensure diversification, maximum participation and fulfilment of one's potential" whereas Honen lived in a society that "was institutionally impoverished by having very few options".

This criticism bundles together a great many prejudices into a small space and there is hardly room here to unpick them all. In general, it seems to continue the drift of Point Four to the effect that progress is a good thing and therefore modern times are superior to historical ones. This is a dubious claim. Modern times may have more wherewithal, but whether we use it for better or worse is a very open question. Certainly our modern society has some options, like the internet, that Honen did not have, but the internet is just as much a highway for spam and corruption as for enlightenment and spiritual uplift. All technical innovations are ethically neutral in themselves — it all depends upon how people use them.

Does modern education make people more spiritual, liberated and enlightened? Honen gave a message that uplifted people whether they were educated or not. Chappell himself seems to recognise that the increasing complexity of modern institutions is not an unmitigatedly good thing since he sees them as one of the main targets for socially engaged reform. I don't think one can have it both ways.

The modern progressive person is committed to democracy, equality, diversification, maximum participation and fulfilment of one's potential, but arguably these goals are often incompatible one with another. There is no fundamental reason to see them as ultimate or self-evident goods or as the highest things that humans are capable of. They are ideals of a particular phase of late industrial culture in economically developed countries. Honen lived in a society in which ideals of loyalty, piety, family cohesion, duty, self-sacrifice, courage, altruism, and modesty carried more weight than they do today. Is it immediately self-evident that his society was always wrong in these particulars and ours always right? I don't think so.

Indeed, I think that by implicitly over-valuing our own (or, at least, American) culture Chappell offends against his own supposed principles of tolerance and inclusivity. If he cannot see the virtues of the society that Honen lived in how can he claim to have a philosophy that "affirms interdependence, and aims for inclusivity"? In his rhetoric, he seems to be saying that he values all societies and all cultures, but this is not borne out by his judgements that value one particular culture above all others. In fact, Honen's philosophy is really more culturally neutral than Chappell's is.

On the question of democracy and participation, Honen's reform did, in fact, make for widespread local forms of co-operation. Nembutsu practitioners met fortnightly all over Japan to practise nembutsu together and these meetings became community gatherings that were a great support to country people, not just in their spiritual lives, but in many practical ways too. When we look at the history of Buddhism we see that it has often been very successful at community development and Pureland Buddhism particularly so. One of the reasons that Honen's approach has this characteristic is that he placed such emphasis upon the ordinary, bombu, vulnerable nature of people.

In the atmosphere of Honen's philosophy it is easier for people to appreciate one another and feel sympathy for one another's misfortunes.

These sentiments are natural building blocks of community. It is not that Honen or Buddhism in general tries to impose a rational ideology of democracy or socialism or anything of the kind. It is rather that it cultivates the kinds of attitude that help people to help and appreciate one another. They may find a multitude of different ways to do so and many of these ways do not conform to any particular ideological correctness, but they do touch the heart.

One of the problems of the modern world has been the attempt to replace virtue with rationality. In a perfectly communistic or socialistic society, generosity would be redundant. In a Buddhistic society, and especially one that followed Honen's style of Buddhism, generosity is fundamental. In the modern world we are constantly substituting form for substance. In a faith based community the opposite occurs.

The advance of technology certainly gives us opportunities, but the message of Shakyamuni and Honen stands up with or without such conveniences.

POINT SIX: Should Buddhism Get with It and Become Postmodern?

Chappell says that "today's [New Buddhist] leaders have a wealth of information... [and] postmodern awareness that no single source is adequate or authoritative" and are "returning to the scepticism of Gautama Buddha who pointed up the relativity of all words and concepts (Sutta Nipata VIII)" whereas, apparently, Honen had total confidence in the authority of the Buddhist scriptures.

Again, even if this were correct, it is not clear that Honen's position would for that reason be inferior. The postmodern sceptic may be paralysed by indecision and lost in a morass of relativistic considerations that lack any power to move the heart. It is not at all clear that postmodern thinking is conducive to social action. It tends rather to the kind of relativism that makes decisive action always suspect.

There is something a bit strange about this section of Chappell's argument. It is the section in which he throws doubt upon the reliability of texts, yet it is the one and only section in which he has reference to a Buddhist text to back up his argument, citing Sutta Nipata 8. However, my translation of the Sutta Nipata has only five sections and none of them speak about the "relativity of words and concepts" so I am not sure what Chappell is relying upon here. In any case, Shakyamuni Buddha's teaching has very little in common with postmodernism.

Buddha uses words in a very clear and defined manner, makes precise distinctions and makes it quite apparent what he favours and what he rejects. I cannot see a basis for Chappell's contention that his view is a return to the teaching of the great sage.

Honen had confidence in the teachings that he received from the scriptures and from the writings of former sages such as Shan Tao. However, this was not a reliance upon a narrow literalism so much as upon the spiritual meaning. It was his genius in bringing out and demonstrating this meaning that made him an inspiring teacher. The same is true of Shakyamuni who also interpreted perennial wisdom in vibrant ways relevant to his audience.

Again, it is very difficult to see how anybody can think that Honen took the texts uncritically. An obvious and salient feature of his message was the fact that he indicated that even though the texts might speak great wisdom, most of them were not capable of implementation in his time and culture. It was because he was critical that he was persecuted. It is true that he was not a sceptic in the modern sense, but modern scepticism largely just leaves people alienated and directionless.

Now I do appreciate modern scholarship and I do value having a great range of sources and comment available. I enjoy scholarly activity. In my lifetime the internet has come along and it is often convenient to be able to google a Buddhist text and find it pop up quite quickly. I imagine Honen would have enjoyed this too. He also was a scholar and had the good fortune to live for much of his life on Mount Hiei where there was probably the best Buddhist library in his country. He had a reputation for being extremely learned. There were times when he was visiting leading people from other schools of Buddhism when he demonstrated a better understanding of their own texts than they themselves possessed. It was the fact that he was so learned that made his adoption of such a simple approach so striking. So I think Honen would have valued some modern equipment, but a postmodern attitude would not have enhanced his philosophy, his appeal or the quality of his life.

POINT SEVEN: Was Honen in Need of Multiculturalism?

Finally, Chappell claims that "Today's leaders recognise... cultural differences not as barriers or failures but as sources of diversity and enrichment. Rather than hoping to copy another culture and its mode of enlightenment that led to... Honen's despair of duplicating Indian Buddhism, today's leaders accept the differences and work interactively for mutual enhancement as a source to stimulate new creativity."

It is difficult to understand how Chappell got hold of this idea of Honen, who himself had disciples who followed several different schools of Buddhism and whose success must have been largely due to his ability to take Chinese wisdom and reshape it into a form that spoke eloquently to the ordinary Japanese people of his own day, people from many different strata of society. He was an adapter of culture. It does not seem accurate to say that he despaired of making Japan like India; what he despaired of was finding anybody who could live up to the super-human standard of perfection required by so many Buddhist texts.

Although Buddhism does adapt as it goes from one culture to another, it does not give up its essence.

A Buddhist needs to understand and be loyal to that essence or they cease to be Buddhist. If Chappell's suggestion is that one should embrace an unlimited degree of creativity and cultural cross fertilisation then he ceases to be Buddhist and while what he advocates might still be interesting it would not warrant the name of engaged Buddhism, it would simply be Western progressive thinking — which, perhaps, is what it actually is. At the same time, there is something ingenuous in this precisely because it does all smack of Western progressive thinking and, therefore, of a bias in favour of one particular culture, and at that, not a Buddhist one. This is my fundamental point. Writings of this kind are not really doing a service to Buddhism by kindly correcting the Buddha's errors and showing how postmodern leftist thinking is superior, but are, in a rather biased way, undermining a profound and noble religion in unjustifiable ways rooted in cultural prejudice.

Now I am confident that Chappell and many others like him sincerely believe that a good dose of postmodernism and so on is just what Buddhism needs in order to bring it up to date. They think that there can be no sound basis for social engagement other than the set of ideas that they have inherited from Western culture. However, in this they are wrong. There are many ways of being socially engaged. If one's aim in being so is to make the world as much like America as possible one would be well advised to think again and consider whether a society that has an unsustainable energy footprint is really what the planet needs at the moment.

Through the ages Buddhism has been socially engaged by building community (rather than the fragmentation of postmodern alienation), by inculcating love and compassion (rather than rights and justice), by giving people confidence in goodness (rather than relativism), by fostering faith (rather than scepticism) and by humanising (rather than institutionalising) society.

Chappell finally advocates that all religious texts should be "interpreted in the light of the Declaration of Human Rights." Leaving aside the fact that Chappell has already declared himself to be against relying on any one text particularly, I think that there is a good deal of scope for questioning whether this particular text should really be considered an ultimate source of wisdom. Surely it is the human insistence upon "rights" rather than responsibility that has contributed massively to the ecological plight that we find ourselves in, one in which the country that holds that text most dear must figure as one of the most blameworthy culprits.

Rights?

Rights is not a Buddhist concept. Kindness is a Buddhist concept. Wisdom is a Buddhist concept. Compassion, patience, energy, and restraint are all Buddhist concepts, but "rights" is a modern, Western legal fiction. The way to be socially engaged from a Buddhist perspective is not to fight for rights but to cultivate communities that embody love, compassion, joy and equanimity. It should not be a matter of campaigning for justice and equality, concepts that can be twisted in a thousand ways to support almost any political agenda, but rather of fostering trust, understanding and co-operation.

If we have a genuinely Buddhist form of social engagement of this kind, then I suggest that both the philosophy and the example of Honen will stand us in good stead. We shall then accept the failings of others, not from a principle of tolerance (a word that does not occur in Buddhist texts) but out of fellow feeling rooted in Honen's fundamental principle of bombu nature. We shall accept the limitations of human achievement and the vulnerability of ourselves and others for similar reasons. Yet, nonetheless, because we have faith that we are recipients of grace, and because our faith is not dependent upon factors like technological progress, we shall naturally contribute to the building of compassionate community that does not even attempt to treat everybody equally, but rather makes allowance for each uniquely frail person in the best way it can as circumstances unfold.

Buddhism is not trying to reorganise the world on rational principles, as though people were machines, or interchangeable units. It is concerned with cultivating living community that is ever evolving in organic ways, guided by principles of kindness, patience and goodness. Sages such as Honen are revered precisely because they embodied this spirit.

So, to return to my original theme, whether we are talking about Honen or any other Buddhist sage, or about Pureland, or any other Buddhist school, I am concerned that there is a tendency as Buddhism comes to the West for it to be reconstructed according to principles that are quite alien to the spirit of Shakyamuni. Mostly this distortion comes about through the actions of people who believe they are doing something good and constructive. I cannot blame them, but I lament the effect of what they are doing. We now see in the West a widespread consensus across many different schools about what Buddhism is that in many particulars owes more to the Western religious tradition and the preoccupations of Western philosophy than to the Eastern one or to the founder's original principles. I hope that this is merely a phase, just as Buddhism entering China was initially greatly infiltrated by Taoist ideas yet later emerged in its own right. I hope that something similar will occur in the West, even if it does not happen in my time.

Training in Buddhism

Training?

The term training is often used in association with Buddhism. My Zen teacher Houn Jiyu used it a lot but was still never totally happy with it. When one is doing Zen what is one doing? Is one 'training'? Training for what? Is one a trainee? On the other hand, what other word will do? The more religious words have gone out of fashion — acolyte, devotee, worshipper.

Convenient Fiction

I have noticed, over my lifetime, a trend toward more and more belief in credentials and, with that, in 'training' as a pathway to qualification. To say that somebody is not properly trained is nowadays taken as a sin. Such a career path is a normal convention and motivates people to stick at something. For this reason offering Buddhism as 'a training course' or a series of short courses 'works' in the sense that it gets people to actually do something. However, there is an element of convenient fiction in all this. 'Course' means, fundamentally, a duration of activity or a space to be run across — like a horse racing course. However, Buddhism is not a race and it is not a credential. It is a profession only in the very old fashioned sense of being something that one professes.

Carkhuff's Research

I was very struck, many years ago, by the research of Robert Carkhuff who investigated the training of counsellors. Comparing the skills, qualities and effectiveness of trained and untrained people in counselling roles, he concluded both that in general the untrained were better than the trained and that even the same person was more often worse after training than before. This heretical discovery gives one pause and should certainly be seriously thought about. The fact that people are trained certainly does not guarantee anything about their human skills. I had a similar impression myself when I used to recruit social workers.

Why?

There are several likely reasons for this. Firstly, training, by imparting techniques, tends to lead the trainee to treat other people somewhat like inanimate objects or mechanisms to be manipulated. Secondly, a training course in human relations often leads trainees to become more rather than less self-preoccupied. Thirdly, training can introduce an element of routine into very human situations: the nurse at the end of her training may have become 'thicker skinned' through vicarious exposure to much suffering. This often manifests as a kind of cynicism about patients. Fourthly, training toward a credential involves a concern with status that strengthens investment in self-identity. I was struck, reading some human relations professional magazines a while back, how many of the courses on offer were actually about how to protect oneself as a worker rather than how to actually be of real use to the client.

Spiritual Professionalism

How relevant is all this to Buddhism? I think it is certainly something to be careful about. There is a danger that we import into our practice attitudes that are not grounded in compassion but are to do with protecting ourselves and strengthening our own egos. Such attitudes are not Buddhism. Buddha was open to all and did not count his own life as a priority. We should remember him going to talk to Angulimala or entering the shrine of the sacred python. Buddhism is not about processing people. It is about waking up the heart. Of course, not all professionals are self-protective and many are compassionate, but there is a distinct difference of ethos between professionalism and real religion.

Aspiring and Postulating

So I do use the terms training and trainee occasionally where it is conventional to do so, but I do so with the same reservations that my teacher had and I prefer other terms when possible. In our order we have aspirants and postulants. These are better terms. An aspirant aspires. A postulant is trying something out. This is closer to the mark.

Some say that Buddhism is an education and there is some truth in this, but, again, education is a word whose meaning has degenerated in modern society.

Education used to be about character and duty. Nowadays it is more and more indistinguishable from training.

The Old Way

The traditional way in Buddhism is a mixture of devotion and apprenticeship. The transmission is heart to heart and mind to mind. The acolyte gives and receives by being with the teacher. Self-preoccupation gradually dissolves. Many skills, techniques, methods and procedures may be used, but one comes to recognise that they are of secondary importance. Nobody who is concerned about their own status is fit to hold power over others and so finding Buddhism is about rediscovering humanity. One needs the innocence of a babe coupled with the experience of years... and a tender heart with it.

These things tend to take time to grow, and this passage of time is a 'course' in the fundamental sense of the word, but it is not a programmatic process of working through a syllabus. It is a matter, more, of engaging with life, with all of its unexpected and often unintended vicissitudes, in a courageous and sensitive way equipped with a willingness to do something about oneself when aspects of oneself get in the way. What might be called 'self' work in Buddhism is not intended to enhance the ego but to release one from it.

A Different Nuance

Progression in this respect is certainly helped by gradually increasing responsibilities and a sense of duty as well as deepening acceptance and appreciation of the love and benefits that one receives, and it is impeded by a sense of entitlement, and by any of the thousand and one varieties of neurosis that one may be bringing along that are, in fact, the material that one prays to be liberated from. One can call all this 'training' and there is nothing intrinsically wrong about doing so, but it is important to realise that 'training' in Buddhism is not the same thing as training has come to mean in society at large.

Domestication

The other context in which we use the word training is in relation to animals. Here, training means domestication. A certain amount of domestication is certainly a valuable thing. In a Zen monastery people get socialised into very precise ways of doing things. This has a value. Liberation, however, does not lie in attachment to these forms. It lies in the experiential learning that one can do them and, therefore, one can also do without them. Learning that one can do more than one thought possible should release one into a confidence to tackle the unknown. In other words to go into the future full of faith. To take such 'training' as being drilled into a way that things must always be done is a strait jacket, not a liberation. True salvation lies elsewhere.

Proceed with Caution

Faith, confidence, courage, attention to deeper duty, kindness, love, compassion, wonderment, awe, joy — these are the kinds of things that Buddhism is about and they cannot be reduced to routines. Much of what is generally conveyed by the word training, therefore, is a little off the mark. We shall continue to use the word, no doubt, but it is important to understand that in Buddhism it has a distinctive nuance of meaning and not to confuse it with some of the other implications that the word tends to be burdened with.

Styles of Buddhist Training

Having given a teaching on the pitfalls of the idea of training, I would now like to give one on its excellences. The Buddhas accept all who turn to them in faith whether they have progressed in this life or not; however, it is also a universal Buddhist teaching that this human life is the best opportunity one is going to get to improve one's character and understanding and to not take that opportunity would be rash indeed. Therefore, Buddhist communities universally include opportunities and encouragement to do so.

Before going into the main points, a caveat. Do not see this as being 'the path to enlightenment'. It is always possible that illumination may strike as one goes along, but it might do so if one were on a completely different track too. I say this because the idea that one can personally get hold of the process of becoming enlightened is one of the biggest obstacles to it actually happening. OK, enough of that.

There are innumerable different modes of training in Buddhism just as Shakyamuni is said to have given 84,000 teachings. However we can broadly distinguish a number of styles.

1. One's Own Petard. There is an English expression 'hoist by his own petard' which refers back to

a rather gruesome historical habit in which failed admirals were executed by being hanged on their own ship using a piece of the rigging called a 'petard'. The expression means that one learns from the unfortunate effects of one's own actions. It is somewhat akin to the American expression 'what goes around comes around'. Another saying of the same ilk is 'if you give a person enough rope he will hang himself'. In relation to training this means that if you give a person freedom to follow their favourite ideas in a context in which nobody else has told them what to do, they may come to face the fact that their preferred way of doing things does not work. When a person first comes to a Buddhist community this may well be the starting point. Until a person has some motivation to learn, nothing much is going to happen except by accident or natural consequence. However, natural consequence is not to be under-estimated. In the final analysis it is reality that is the true teacher. We live in the midst of myriad Dharmas of myriad Buddhas — we just do not see it yet.

2. The Pebble Mill. Living in a community one rubs up against other people. One's rougher corners are bound to get dented and sometimes even knocked off. If you start with a square piece of wood with four corners and knock off the corners, there are then eight corners, though each is less sharp. If you knock those off there are sixteen. Eventually you have a circular column. The same principle works in a pebble mill. Stones churned together eventually all become smooth and round. In a similar way, living with other people forces one to moderate one's

awkwardness. One may have been very square on arrival but one gradually gets worn down into a more pleasing smoothness. This is the effect of living in Sangha. This process is greatly assisted if each person has a habit of self-reflection. This is the meaning of 'to study the self is to forget the self' — self-reflection leads us to the view that the self's view is less important than we thought it was. It is revealed to have been a protection, like a suit of armour. It is much easier to move about fluidly when wearing less armour. However, in order to take armour off one has to believe that it is at least moderately safe to do so. The pebble mill, therefore, should not spin too fast. A certain tolerance and gentleness should be the hallmark of true spiritual community.

3. The Smallest Detail. Some Buddhist centres, especially the Zen ones, are sticklers for detail. How one folds one's robe, how one holds one's spoon, which way round you put it in the drawer, how straight the edges of the cushions are in the meditation hall — all these and a million other details are prescribed. One is told that 'every moment is meditation' and there is a great emphasis on awareness and on remembering how each little thing should be done. Life is a series of details. A perfect life is a life of perfected detail. This sort of behavioural training can be immensely valuable if done with a genuinely kind mind. The danger is that if those who impose such a system are not kindly minded it rapidly becomes an intolerable form of oppression. The medium is the message, so although the trainee might learn the content of the instruction, he or she will

certainly learn the manner of it. If well done, therefore, this type of training can be invaluable in demonstrating how it is possible to give instruction and hold authority from a position of great love. People who can do this are not common, but, then, that is the point.

4. Reparenting. What many people need in addition to or even more than training in right behaviour, or socialisation in community living, is some kind of additional parenting. We have all had parents of some sort and those parents have done their best for us and deserve our gratitude, but they are or were human, beset with all the difficulties of samsara, products of long karma, and we are the heirs thereof. A Buddhist teacher therefore needs 'parental mind' and the ideal teacher is Buddha. It is for this reason that in Japan Buddha is often called 'oyasama' which means, more or less, 'most honourable parent'. In the Tibetan traditions a nun is called 'ani' which means aunt. Sometimes one needs a good aunt to fill in the gaps that mother left. The good parent is infinitely loving and compassionate, accepting everything, but, at the same time, chivvies in small ways, nudging the infant in the right direction. This may take the form of a kind of camaraderie. The parent gives a good example, but, of course, does not do exactly the same as the child. When the relationship is a good one the child wants to 'help' the parent and through this activity learns many things. The child hangs around, not going too far away, but from time to time making a foray on their own. The parent appreciates all this. The good parent showers praise upon whatever the infant brings home

from school class even if it is an indecipherable scribble. Thus, a Buddhist teacher only rarely gives direct orders. More often he or she drops hints or suggestions, often in an oblique way that leaves room for them to be picked up or not. At the end of the day the disciple grows at a pace determined by capacity.

I have described these four as distinct styles, but in reality there is a smooth gradient between them and what the teacher does is a reflection of the need and robustness of the disciple. This is a very 'person centred' process, but it is not guided by the disciple's own self-assessment. The teacher has to make a judgement.

Of course, perhaps in lesser degree, this applies to all of us both ways round. In our dealings with other people we all have to make assessments of what they can take, what will help and what will not, and it is not the same in all cases. If you tell one person the best way to make pancakes they will be delighted. If you tell another they may be offended.

Similarly, when we are in the disciple position, some criticism can be really helpful and some just throws us into resistance and pain, and, again, some tolerance enables us to grow and some just leads us to languish. No two situations are the same. Thus there cannot really be a protocol, but it is possible, in a broad way, to distinguish these types.

The Indian word for 'training' is sekha. The person who is accomplished in the spiritual life is said to be asekha, which means that they are 'beyond training'. Such a person left to their own devices, serves the needs of all sentient beings, which, locally, often means the good of the community, and the results that they see confirm their good intention in the long run; living in community they see what needs doing and get on without fuss, taking care not to offend others unnecessarily and attending to needs as they arise, gradually evolving a more and more deep sense of what the true needs of the collective may be; they are naturally attentive to detail and avoid waste, seeing the potential in things and keeping good order so as to create a pleasing environment for all; and they are truly filial to their elders in the Dharma, seeking to advance their work and making their life easier while being solicitous of those junior to themselves and cherishing them with a warm regard, like younger brothers and sisters. They themselves draw great strength from the merit of all the Buddhas which facilitates equanimity, and, being humble in a genuine way, they have a deep sense of humour.

The Samadhi of Equality

Equality is a religious vision. Nowadays, of course, it has become associated with a secular political agenda, but this agenda lies in the realm of religious ideals. Nobody has ever seen an empirical society of equality. Everything in the secular world is arranged on a hierarchical scale. If, on secular reductionist principles, one should only believe in what one has seen and had evidenced, then nobody should have any faith in equality, yet this faith is widespread and powerful. Take any two individuals and you have difference of power, money, strength, influence, status, intelligence, etc. etc. The secular world is the world of hierarchy — verticalism. Motivation in the secular world is entirely a matter of improving one's position on one or other of the many intersecting vertical scales by which everything is given meaning and standing. This is the nature of samsara.

Equality is a religious vision. It cuts through samsara. Before God we are all equal — nowhere else. For God you can say Allah, Tao, Amida Buddha, the Confucian Mean or whatever. It does not matter what religion we are talking about. Before the divine we are equal and experiencing the divine includes experiencing that complete and perfect equality. In Buddhism this is called the samadhi of equality. It is an ecstasy that leaves an enduring impression that one will be eternally mindful of.

We could say that this must tally with some deep structure or archetype within us which would be why the idea has such power to move people — however the notion of archetypes is just one metaphysic by which we try to explain these things. The experience itself is a religious experience. The writings of many great sages, such as Dogen, for instance, revolve around it. When we are before the divine we experience this equality. Similarly, when we experience this equality we are in the divine. Experiencing it is quite different from having a concept of it, or an agenda about it. To experience it is a mystical state.

When that state is genuinely experienced one is affected, not just at that time, but enduringly. It affects how one relates to others. One sees the light in them. One experiences a clear certainty that, in the eyes of Buddha, all are equally precious.

Although this vision must lie at the back of many political and social agendas, there is no social structure that can achieve or grant such a vision. The imposition of equality in a polity tends only to discourage people as it erodes all worldly motivation, as has been found in the various communistic experiments. Nonetheless, even if one does not subscribe to a communistic agenda, one can still feel the power of the ideal. One is inclined to say, "It is a perfect idea, but it reckons without real human beings," but the very fact that it feels as a perfect idea is a reflection of the religious vision that lies behind it and accounts for the religious fervour with which many people pursue such ideals.

Paradoxically, in the minds of many people, especially in the West, religion has come to be associated with hierarchy and verticalism. I imagine that this is because religion has fallen into disrepute in many quarters because it became too much implicated in non-religious, secular interests. The Church was used as a support for the political establishment and clerics traded authenticity for power and influence. This has not just been a problem in the West. When a religion becomes popular and influential, secular authorities want to appropriate and use that power and greedy people start to see the church as a vertical self-promotion ladder. So God then becomes the validator of the social order which, being secular, is hierarchical. This, however, is the decay of the religious vision.

In the fullness of awakening, all beings are radiant and all are loved. This is a condition of equality that transcends all differences of intelligence, virtue, merit, earning power or whatever. Every blade of grass is a splinter of enlightenment — not even only a splinter — is the whole of it. The whole moon is reflected in every dewdrop. They are all equal in moonshine whether they are big or small, new or old. Even in the smallest dew drop, the whole universe is reflected. That is true equality.

This equality, however, does not inhere in the things themselves. It is a function of the moon. Each drop has the power to reflect, but that is all. In self-power there are many differences of level — the dewdrops are various — but in other-power there is complete equality of beings for it is the very same light that is reflected in every one and this is the essence of religion.

The Robe

The Buddhist robe is made of patchwork. There are many pieces of cloth sewn together. This is because originally the robes were made of rags. The monks took cast away pieces of cloth and stitched them together. In many cases these pieces of cloth were taken from the charnel grounds where dead bodies were cremated. The bodies were wrapped in a shroud and then burnt on a pyre of sticks and logs. Often there were bits of cloth left. In some places bodies were left to be eaten by vultures or other animals. Thus charnel grounds supplied many rags that found their way into monk's robes. The robe would then be dyed yellow or orange.

There is much symbolism in all this and wearing such a robe immersed one in all these meanings and, although the robes nowadays are made from fresh cloth, the symbolic meanings still touch one.

The word for a robe in the Indian languages is a kashaya. This word has the original meaning of 'stained' or 'dyed'.

The bits of cloth were taken from the charnel grounds, so the monk was wearing the clothes of the dead. The monk is dead to the worldly life and, symbolically, is already reborn. He has himself been wrapped in a shroud and the worldliness has been burnt out of him. The purpose of spiritual practice is to bring us to new life. So the monk or nun is living a new life beyond death-to-the-world. She or he is reborn, enlightened and liberated by a new faith and inspiration.

The robe is made of all the bits of our old life — all the dead bits — sewn together and then stained or dyed. It is dyed in the Dharma. The Dharma is the dye that unifies and renews the old. It makes us part of the spiritual community which is the enactment here and now of the new life. This community is a manifestation of love, compassion and wisdom. The old mortal life is ended and eternal life entered.

This dyed cloth envelops the priest. It is what does the job. Inside, I am still the foolish old fellow, but in my robe I can do some good. New members of the Sangha can be abashed when asked to do some holy task — who am I to do such a thing? they think. In fact, indeed, one is nobody, but the robe can do it. When one is in the robe one can perform the part. It does not matter what sort of foolish fellow I am, I can stand before the altar and make offerings to the highest Buddhas.

So this is a little of the meaning of the robe. Traditionally a monk has three. This enabled him to travel in India. The robe was his or her clothing, mattress and sleeping bag. So at all times he was enveloped in these deep meanings and they protected his actions and his dreams.

Overcoming Weakness and Discovering No Birth: The Story of Parsva

The Dharma can radically change your life. We are not just made of flesh and blood and the bones of our life are not just the ones made of calcium. Sometimes something else gets into us and the sick get up and dance. Listening to scriptures recited in the morning air, one can be touched by eternity.

Parsva (Japanese: Barishiba) came from central India. Before he was born his father had a portentous dream of a white elephant with a radiant pearl on its back from which shone four light beams. Later it was thought that these four beams represented the four assemblies of Buddhists to whom Parsva would later minister — ordained and lay, men and women.

His mother was old when he was born. His birth was difficult. He was a sickly child, but of a serious turn of mind. When he was young, a soothsayer made a prediction that he would become a saint.

Everyone said that Parsva was too weak

When the sage Buddhamitra was travelling in central India Parsva's father met him and, impressed by his teaching and remembering the prediction by the soothsayer, agreed to let his son be ordained as a monk.

Everyone said that Parsva was too weak to manage being a monk. To be a monk one had to learn a lot of scriptures and do dedicated meditation and Parvsa, they said, would be incapable of either.

Comments of this kind, however, made Parsva more determined. Soon he was studying all day and meditating all night. It is said that he did not sleep for three years. He served his teacher with extreme devotion. Parsva is held up as a prime example of determination in practice, but this determination did not just come from will power. Parsva felt the presence of Shakyamuni Buddha close at hand. He felt as if the Buddha's very bones had entered into him and given him strength. One day he heard Buddhamitra reciting sutras and explaining the meaning of no-birth. Parsva was enlightened.

The Buddhist teaching of no-birth is that not everything is a result. Birth means one thing born from another. The true nature of Buddha, however, is not born from anything else. This may be called nirvana. So nirvana is not impermanent. The ordinary person thinks that he can become an enlightened being, but it is not he who becomes one. There is no connection between his old self and Buddha nature. Thus enlightenment cannot be the product of a practice or procedure. When Buddha manifests it is unconditional. There cannot be a place or time where the Buddha's voice is not speaking. Master Keizan says: Everyone is a vessel of the Truth; every day is a good day; every place is a sutra.

Entering the teaching of no-birth one comes face to face with the Buddhas of all times and directions. One's purpose transcends circumstance. One no longer minds where one goes or arrives. One is always arriving and departing and worlds appear and disappear, but one is not flustered because one belongs to That which surpasses birth and death. Again, as the Unborn has no favourites, one who knows it lives a life of complete responsibility. We are not talking here about a passive, go with the flow idea. Buddhas are impassioned for peace and electric with compassion.

Once Master Parsva was travelling when some youngsters came up and asked if they could help him by carrying his books. He gave them the books and they ran off with them, making fun of him. An observer noticed that Master Parsva was not in the least disturbed by this bad behaviour and realised that the master must be something special and came to study with him. Through incidents like this the reputation of Master Parsva grew and grew.

At that time there was a King, Kanishka, who was Buddhist. He was from Sri Lanka but also ruled much of India. He convened a Great Council in Kashmir and put Masters Parsva and Buddhamitra in charge. This is sometimes called the Third and sometimes the Fourth Great Council.

The task of the council was to produce an authorised version of the Buddhist scriptures. Theravadins and Mahayanists have different versions of the story and of which scriptures are the real ones. However, it seems that the Council recognised 18 different schools of Buddhism as all being legitimate and true successors to the teachings of Shakyamuni.

Parsva, himself, followed the Sarvastivadin approach to the Dharma. The Sarvastivada school, which no longer exists, can be regarded as intermediate between Mahayana and Sthaviravada. Sarvastivadins took refuge in the dharmakaya, recognised the bodhisattva and arhant paths and believed that women had as much possibility of becoming Buddhas as men. The term sarva-asti-vadin, literally all-existence-school, implies "the school that asserts that the Dharma is everywhere existing throughout the past, present and future".

Thus we see the transformation of Parsva from a weak child to a great spiritual leader. The main features of this story are firstly his devotion to his teacher. Secondly, his great determination to study and practise based on both challenge and inspiration. Thirdly, his arrival at the no-birth state of deep equanimity. Finally, his even-handedness in dealing alike with hooligans, kings and competing sects.

Both Punyayashas and Ashvaghosha benefitted from encounters with Parsva and his legacy comes down to us through many lineages. The ordinary person wants to know what his reward will be before doing good or what the penalty will be before avoiding harm, but when one relies on the Unborn, one needs nothing more. He does not have to know where he is going: wherever he is, it is the same light.

Parsva, who was born a weakling, discovered no-birth and lived to be eighty years old. The spirit of his deeds is still with us.

Mindful Foundation

Short Exposition of the Mahasatipatthana Sutta, Majjhima Nikaya 10

The Buddha strongly recommended four mindful foundations. We establish mindfulness as a fourfold foundation of our existence. Mindfulness means to have your heart or mind full of Dharma — which is to say, love, compassion, joy and peace — or, what, for a Buddhist, amounts to the same thing, to have Buddha ever in your heart.

Mindfulness means to have a heart full of good. It is the faith and courage that one has acquired by being loved by the Buddhas and protected by the gods — which is to say, by the universe. The universe is made up of a myriad gods — unseen powers that protect us. This is the traditional way of seeing it. The modern way is to see the universe as dead matter, as a big, ruthless machine, and even to see the living beings as nothing more than sophisticated machines. In the modern view everything is dead, really. Just a big piece of clockwork. In the traditional view everything is alive, which is to say, in one sense or another, loving.

When I lie on my bed, the bed god is loving me. When I breathe in and out, the air god is loving me. When

I see that it is light and time to get up, the god Sol is loving me. This is mindfulness — to know oneself to be the object of love from every direction, in everything that happens. To know this is to know "what has been known from of old." It is different to the deadness that is propounded nowadays.

Traditionally, they knew about this deadness too. The Buddhist word for it is marana. Marana is the last step of the chain of dependent origination. Buddha said that he was fully enlightened when he fully understood this chain forwards and backwards. Forwards meant that he understood how we become dead and backwards meant that he fully understood how to become alive again, how to be in a fully-alive-again universe, and so, how to be loved. That understanding is mindfulness. We do not have to become fully enlightened Buddhas to have at least a taste of it. When we have a taste of it, then we can apply that taste and Buddha says that we can apply that taste in four ways, particularly.

Mindfulness in Respect to the Body

The first way is body. I have already said a little about this. My body lying in bed is being loved by the mattress god. My lungs are being loved by the good air god. We can begin to establish ourselves upon this foundation by saying thank you to the good air god. Saying "Thank you!" is the best way of 'establishing'.

Perhaps we use our imagination and, as we breathe in we say in our head, "Thank you very much, Good Air God" and after we have breathed out there is a little pause and we imagine the voice of the god saying, "Not at all." Then, naturally, as a reaction, we breathe in again. Breathing in we feel benefitted once more, so "Thank you very much!" Breathing out we disappear. Then, after the breath stops, we hear, as a kind of echo, "Not at all," and so on. Doing it in this English way might seem a bit funny and there is nothing wrong with practice being amusing, however, we might already have an established practice way of saying "Thank you very much." That might be our favourite mantra, such as the nembutsu. Then, as we breathe we say, "Namo Amida Bu" and we hear an echo back, "Namo Amida Bu" in the gaps between breaths.

If we practice in this way, then we shall be naturally aware when the breath is long and when it is short, when it is rough and when it is smooth. More importantly, we disappear. It becomes a kind of rapture or dhyana. This is because we are establishing our body upon the foundation of love. And this foundation of love is freely given — "Not at all," it says. We feel like a baby in mummy's arms. So we can go to sleep, actually. Mummy is quite happy if we go to sleep. She just smiles and thinks how beautiful we are. It does not matter how ugly we are really. We might be completely bombu, but still mummy loves her baby.

That is how we establish our body in the arms of the big mummy of universal love. The same when we go for a walk. We do not have to do breathing practice all the time. The breath goes on quite happily without us paying attention. Mindfulness does not mean paying attention all the time. When the mind is full, it is full whether we pay attention or not. The ultimate is that we do not need to pay attention because we know it. When we know it, that is real mindfulness — unconscious mindfulness — in-the-marrow-of-the-bones-mindfulness. But we can reflect how we are being loved by the sunshine god and the wind god and all the tree gods and the buttercup gods and grass stalk gods and so on, even including all the brick gods, concrete gods, traffic gods, and plumbing gods, the cooker god and the floor mop god. All of these are foundations for the existence of our body — its being and its actions.

Mindfulness in Respect to Life

When we have realised how our body is loved from every direction, we can start to feel how our life is also loved. What is our life? Our life is all the colour of our feelings, moods, plans, cleverness and silliness, smugness and shame, elation and dejection. All this is loved by innumerable gods, in all our flourishing and all our dying. Either we are flourishing or we are dying, though actually we are all the time doing both at once and this flourishing and dying, which is our vitality, really is loved. It is loved by all the gods of the past, future and present, above, below and all around. The feelings and emotions that we have are the colours of this unceasing flourishing and dying that is going on all the time. Our true vitality, flourishing and dying, is immersed in a shimmer of angels. This is what it is to establish our life upon mindfulness rather than upon deadness.

Dogen Zenji says that the most important thing for all Buddhists to understand is flourishing and dying. If you can understand that there is no difference between flourishing and dying, then there is no need to escape from either of them. That is mindfulness. That is dependent origination forwards and backwards, as Buddha said. When he understood this, the great god Sahampati spoke to him and begged him to "go forth". When we have this support from all the gods, then we find courage. Love gives us courage and enthusiasm. As I am loved, so I go forth, full of wonderment, ready for anything.

Mindfulness in Respect to Mind

And when we go forth, everything depends upon mind. Mind leads, mind is chief, mind goes ahead. Mind visualises. If you have no vision you do nothing. Nothing is done without mind doing it first. We say, "I have a mind to do such and such." That is mind. Mind minds about things. Mind activity is also loved by many gods. It is their treasure and they give it to us. It takes many gods to put us in mind of something. They are all contributing, cheering us on, providing ever new dimensions. It is as if the mind were a big pot into which the gods keep throwing new things. And all of these things that the gods toss in are fundamentally love. They sustain, vitalise and move us. This very essay that I am writing right now is an example. I do not know where it is going next, but they will assist. They will assist because they love me. That is love going on, love of my mind, by gods in all directions.

So we can keep this in mind. Our mind can be full of this knowledge of all the love that we are in receipt of. We can rejoice. We can be grateful. We can even go to sleep in the lap of the gods and they will watch over us and say how cute we look.

Mindfulness in Respect to Dharma

So body is supported, life is supported, mind is supported, all with good foundations, and with all this there is naturally endless going forth. How does one go forth? In what does one go forth? One goes forth in Dharma. And when one goes forth in Dharma, then the gods are overjoyed. They are totally inebriated with joy beyond what they can contain. Then the cup of love runneth over.

Mindfulness of Dharma includes all the age old teachings revealed by the great sage. They have come down to us from of old, but they are now ready to be renewed. In each life, in each generation, they are renewed. This is like a spring clean. We get them all out, give them a shake, get all the dust flying, until they look bright and new again. Then we put them back — rehang the curtains, relay the carpets. We shall rebuild the house of Dharma.

We can lay down understanding of the Six Bases as the carpet. We can build seven walls with the Enlightenment Factors, and with the Four Truths we can create an elegant roof. Then into our seven walled house, we can invite all the gods, even including the ugly ones — the wrathful ones, the gluttonous ones, the crazy ones —

and in our well-built house all the common passions will mature as higher wisdom.

With this fourfold mindful foundation we can do this. In fact, with our body so loved, our life so loved, our mind so loved, setting out the great display of Dharma comes quite naturally. It is just what we need. To think the Dharma, speak the Dharma and enact the Dharma feels quite appropriate. It gives a great sense of rightness. Furthermore, now that one is overflowing with such love, all the teachings appear in new light — the five hindrances, the skandhas, the powers and faculties — all appear fresh and clear. Their colours are bright because all the dust of self has been shaken out.

The Buddha says that one who is established in this fourfold foundation will attain final knowledge, either here and now or in the Pure Land to come — so, absolutely nothing to worry about.

Ju-Nen Contemplation

This morning, leading the service at Oasis*, I explained our practice of chanting 41 nembutsu, which we sometimes call "Four Tone Nembutsu" though it is rather different from the original Chinese Four Tone Nembutsu, due to our difference of language and culture.

The core of our practice is the invocation of Amitabha Buddha. There is nothing exclusive about this — to invoke one is to invoke all, since there is no quarrel between Buddhas. We do it in many ways, but one is the chanting of the nembutsu — Namo Amida Bu. Amida is Amitabha. "Bu" here is short for Buddha.

Ten nembutsu is called JU-NEN. The way to do Ju-nen is as follows:

Na-mo-a mi-da-bu

Na-mo-a mi-da-bu

Na-mo-a mi-da-bu

Na-mo-a mi-da

Na-mo-a mi-da-bu

Na-mo-a mi-da-bu

---

* Oasis is a residential retirement community for Buddhists near Dharamvidya's home in central France.

Na-mo-a mi-da-bu

Na-mo-a mi-da

Na-mo-a mi-da-buddha

Na-mo-a mi-da-bu

These can be recited slowly or fast, as plain speech or with a tune or intonation. When I was in Japan I heard people interrupt their work every so often, do Ju-nen rapidly all together, then carry on with whatever they had been doing.

Often, here, we do four lots of Ju-nen at the beginning of a period of contemplation, in which case we may use a particular intonation and accompanying visualisation. The intonation is a rising and falling note with "Na-mo-a" rising and "mi-da-bu" falling. Usually there is a single nembutsu at the end, making 41 altogether.

In the visualisation, with the first Ju-nen one imagines anticipating Amitabha coming as a vast cloud of power in the sky before you. In the second Ju-nen, the initial "Namo" is omitted from each line, which gives the sound of the chant a greater power. With this second Ju-nen one imagines Amitabha fully arrived, vast, towering above, regarding the world with compassion.

The third Ju-nen follows on. This time the full line is said, including "Namo" but the whole is done faster, maintaining the urgency and power of the second Ju-nen. Now one imagines myriads of rays of light from Amitabha cascading down upon the world, reaching into every place and home.

Then, in the last Ju-nen, the "Namo" is again dropped, but the recitation remains rapid. One imagines Amitabha's blessing has fallen into every place and one feels gratitude.

Finally, there is one single slow soft "Na-mo-a mi-da-bu" as peace settles upon the world. In this great peace one settles into one's period of contemplation, all the while feeling oneself to be in receipt of the grace, merit and saving-power of Amitabha.

The Night of Enlightenment

When Buddha sat under the tree, he had a series of experiences.

One

He remembers that, as a child, he had entered a state of reverie or rapture while sitting beneath a rose apple tree while everybody else was enjoying themselves at the Spring Ploughing festival. He thinks to himself, why can't I just enjoy such an experience now? So he does so and this is called the First Dhyana. He then passes through seven more dhyanas. It is clear from several texts, however, that this ability to enjoy the dhyanas is not considered to be enlightenment. In fact, Buddha says in the very first sutra of the Majjhima Nikaya that one can experience all these dhyanas and still be completely deluded. So I think we should try to understand this.

Really, dhyanas are states of enjoyment that are independent of any extra stimulus. This is enjoyment that does not depend upon having a movie to watch or other form of entertainment, does not require alcohol or drugs, does not require a sex partner, does not require anything other than simply joy in being alive. We can imagine the Buddha asking himself, "Why not? Why not just enjoy being alive?" It is a good question. The dhyanas are available to anybody. Secluded from all unwholesome thoughts, all unwholesome stimuli, the Buddha was able to enjoy all eight dhyanas.

I remember that when I first got involved in Buddhism it was in the late sixties. It was the time of "flower power". People were "dropping out and turning on". The people who were promoting meditation at that time often said that meditation is the way to get everything that drugs can give you but with no bad side effects and without it costing you anything. This was a strong argument and it was not so far from what Buddha said to himself. The dhyanas were, and indeed are, tranquil and delightful abidings.

Two

However, hot on the heels of this pleasant abiding, Mara arrives with all his host. What does this mean? It means, in psychological terms, that the attempt to simply push the unwholesome thoughts, fantasies and urges aside and enjoy life without them, provoked a reaction on a large scale. What is pushed aside goes for a time, but then it comes back, perhaps in even greater force.

This is how the mind works. We can impose rules upon it and it will follow them for a time, but it does so by holding back the things that don't fit. This only works for a limited time and, as Freud said, "arguments are of no avail against... passions". Whatever rule we impose upon ourselves, there will be times when it comes undone. So, on the rebound from the happy thought that he could simply enjoy peace, secluded from the passions, the passions return in force.

Three

It says that Buddha was able to turn all of Mara's host into celestial flowers. I take this to mean that this time, rather than resisting, destroying or setting them aside, he was able to receive, accept and honour the passions without them leading him into unwholesome action. This was an act of sublimation. Instead of putting the fire out, he was able to contain and direct it.

Four

It was after this that he had insight into dependent origination. Looked at in this context we can take dependent origination to be, broadly, the idea that the passions appear in different form according to whether they are built upon avidya or not. Buddha had been able to turn them into flowers by not being caught in avidya. So what is avidya? Avidya is something that we could call wilful ignorance. The Buddha concluded that wilful ignorance is a function of personal conceit. These two, thereafter, were the main objects of his attack and criticism — conceit and its derivative wilful ignorance. These two are the root of all evil in Buddhism.

So we can say that the essence of Buddhism is to transform avidya into vidya and conceit into a non-self attitude. This, however, cannot be done by the conceited, wilfully ignorant mind and herein lies the problem of self-power. The conceited, wilfully ignorant mind can do many things — enter all the dhyanas, practise awareness, be in the present moment, at least every now and again, and can use all the Buddhist methods and practices, but when it does so it will turn them to its purpose of self-aggrandisement, self-abasement, self-definition, self-projection, self-esteem, self-love, self-centredness and so on.

The best method available, therefore, is to despair of self — cultivate a sense of humour about oneself — and baffle self-power by worshipping what is mysterious and gracious beyond. This is why Mahayana Buddhism developed such a panoply of sambhogakaya Buddhas. Such an approach asks the Buddhas for their help. It says, "I see that I cannot do this. Please help." Thus, there is no method by which one can ensure arrival at enlightenment except complete reliance upon a Buddha or all the Buddhas. Their Dharma will save one — one can take refuge in that even without knowing really what it is. In fact, one never really knows and it is that essential ignorance that makes such reliance real. This means that ignorance is essential for its accomplishment and that this is the only way for conceited, wilfully ignorant beings to have a chance of fully entering the grace.

It does not really matter whether you take as your object of refuge Amida Buddha, Quan Shi Yin, the Lotus Sutra, Samantabhadra, the Buddha's relics or whatever, so long as it is a symbol or manifestation of what is totally wholesome. In the Amida Shu we turn to Amitabha, but that does not mean we are in opposition to those who turn to some other manifestation of Buddhadharma. To be so would just be another demonstration of conceited wilful ignorance.

So one of the things that Buddha is telling us by this story of his own experience is that, yes, it is possible, by will, to put unwholesome states aside temporarily and enjoy coasting through the dhyanas, however, you can expect a comeback. Mara will return. However, armed with this knowledge, you can be ready for him. This means that as passions arise, you are ready to investigate their true nature — celestial flowers — and see how them affecting you one way or the other way depends upon the functioning of self.

You might think that seeing in this way would then free you from self, but it doesn't. Insight into the cause of a disease does not cure it. It permits wiser management of the condition, but it does not cure. A person can know all the reasons why and how he is an alcoholic and he still goes on drinking. It takes something else. It takes faith that something beyond oneself can help. Entrusting to that is the real liberation.

Sila, Samadhi and Prajna

In many sutras, Buddhism is presented as sila, samadhi and prajna.

Sila refers to the moral precepts and right behaviour, samadhi is meditation and prajna is wisdom. That's all! But how should we understand it?

There is a superficial level and there is a deeper level. The precepts indicate the superficial behaviour, how the things appear in the world. So the Buddha says, "What would an ordinary person who knows nothing about Buddhism notice? They will notice the good behaviour." So it is said the behaviour is what appears on the surface. We can say that meditation, samadhi, is what is underneath, what supports the good behaviour. Meditation is the cultivation of the mind. In this way, we can understand Buddhism quite simply.

Then Buddha says that that there is something else, beyond this: there is prajna, wisdom — though wisdom may not be quite the right term. Wisdom is 'wise'. If I am wise, I know a lot. I have got a lot. I have a lot to give. But in Buddhism, prajna is emptiness. I have got nothing. So, in a way, sila and samadhi are states of fullness, they are the same. But prajna is a state beyond these two. With the cultivation of behaviour — sila — you can go on and on and on. There is no end to it. You can always do better. However good you are, improvement is always possible, you can always do better. There is no natural end. This is like 'gradual cultivation'. The same is true for meditation. You can train your mind. It may be even more difficult. Training your behaviour is like training an ox, training your mind is like training a monkey. You can go on and on. You can always do better.

Prajna is not like that. It is like switching the light on and off again. Prajna is emptiness. Empty is empty, it cannot be more. So we have these two aspects. In a sense there are three aspects of Buddhism — sila, samadhi and prajna — but in an important sense, there are only two: sila and samadhi on one side and prajna on the other side. Normally people cultivate sila and samadhi and maybe they have prajna. But some people have prajna, without having done the other side at all. They are kind of natural. They have that all-acceptance, or, we can say, complete faith, complete trust. Emptiness is like that. Whatever comes along, you receive it. It is like the great earth. The earth doesn't mind what you put on it: you can put gold on it, or you can put rubbish on it, it just accepts it. It is all alright. You can put the most delicious food on it, or excrement. So, in this sense, the earth is empty. It is all the same. It doesn't matter. Emptiness is like that. Spaciousness.

You might have heard about a monk being asked about his sickness who says: "Sun face Buddha, moon face Buddha". Sometimes sun face, sometimes moon face. Sometimes you are well, sometimes you are sick. Whatever comes, from the position of emptiness —

sunyata — it is all the same. Sometimes monkey face Buddha, sometimes ox face Buddha, sometimes Buddha is the cat. From the Buddhist point of view, emptiness — prajna — is the most important. When we read the text, Tan Butsu Ge it says: there are many excellences such as meditation, virtues, but prajna is at their head.

Prajna is the spirit of Mahayana. Prajna paramita goes beyond, it is that which goes to the other shore. On this shore, we can cultivate meditation, many meditations, we can do many things but when on the other shore, you have a different perspective. Everything appears in a different perspective. When you are trying to be good, you are all the time measuring how good, you tend to be a bit judgemental, you tend to be a bit proud or sometimes demoralized: "Oh! I didn't mean to do that! Terrible!" But from the point of view of prajna, sometimes you are terrible, sometimes you are good, sometimes bad, it is human.

There is the famous story of Takuan and Baso: the tile and the mirror. "You can't make a mirror with a tile" and "You can't make a Buddha by meditation." This is a challenge to Zen people, because Zen is all about meditation. So this is the one side of the river. Baso thinks: "If I do enough, I can accumulate enough merit to be a Buddha." It is not like that.

Enlightenment of the Buddha cuts through. It is not a matter of getting a bigger stack of merit, it just cuts through, and Baso is enlightened. In a way, we can say that the tile is a mirror because the tile shows Baso his nature. Baso looked at the tile and he saw himself. So, it is a mirror. When you are in a state of emptiness, you are a mirror and everything else is a mirror. We are all mirroring each other. My stupidity shows you your stupidity and as for your stupidity, well, let's not talk about that...

So emptiness, wisdom, faith, mirror-mind are all the same thing.

Kyo Ju Kai Mon: Ten Precept Teaching

There are various versions of the moral precepts of Buddhism. The following is based, with very slight variation, upon the version offered by my teacher Jiyu Kennett Roshi. The precepts themselves are from the Mahayana Brahmajala Sutra. The phrases that follow are from Keizan Zenji, a successor of Dogen. The paragraphs headed 'comment' are my own.

The Three Pure Precepts

Cease from evil: This is the house of all the laws of Buddha; this is the source of all the laws of Buddha.

Do only good: The Dharma of the Sammyakusambodai is the Dharma of all existence.

Do good for others: Be beyond both the holy and the unholy. Let us rescue ourselves and others.

The Ten Great Precepts

1. Do not kill: No life can be cut off. The life of Buddha is increasing. Continue the life of Buddha. Do not kill Buddha.

Comment: When one does not recognise the life, love, freedom and faith of the other, one cuts of his or her life, whether one kills the body or not. Buddhism is about waking up and seeing — seeing the whole life of all sentient beings. One liberates oneself by liberating others to liberate yet others. This is to give and enhance life.

2. Do not steal: The mind and its object are one. The gateway to enlightenment stands open wide.

Comment: When illumined by the light of the Dharma, all things reveal themselves as Dharma. Possessiveness and grasping hide the Dharma nature of the object. Mind always has an object. When the object is illuminated, we are illuminated. As Dogen says, when we forget ourselves we are illuminated by everything.

3. Do not covet: The doer, the doing and that which has the doing done to it are immaculate, therefore desire is empty. This emptiness is the same as that of the Buddhas.

Comment: Covetousness includes all kinds of abusive desire, greed and licentiousness. Such fantasy can have karmic consequences that reverberate for aeons. However, it is still all empty from beginning to end. On the one hand, we live in the world of conditions and it is good to create good conditions. At the same time, Buddhism points beyond conditions to infinite immaculacy, which cannot be disturbed by any conditions at all. Having faith in the latter, we are better placed and inspired in relation to the former.

4. Do not say that which is untrue: The Wheel of Dharma rolls constantly and lacks for nothing yet needs something. The sweet dew covers the whole world and within it lies the truth.

Comment: To live by what it true, without putting on airs through pride or self-pity is to be natural and by being natural in such a way one implicitly expresses the Dharma. Dharma is Dharma, beginninglessly and eternally, but it still calls for expression. In itself, the Dharma needs nothing, yet it needs you and me to give it expression.

5. Do not sell the wine of delusion: There is nothing to be deluded about. If we actualise this we are enlightenment itself.

Comment: This refers to anything that colludes with or encourages delusion. Most basically it refers to alcohol and mind altering drugs. Beyond that to whatever undermines faith. People take to drugs and compulsive habits in flight from life. However, it is in this very human life that the great illumination is to be found. There is no need to be afraid of one's real life.

6. Do not speak against others: In Buddhism, the truth and everything are the same: the same law, the same enlightenment and the same behaviour. None should speak of another's faults. None should make such a mistake in Buddhism.

Comment: How we see and frame the acts of others reverberates throughout the community. Adding energy to quarrels or blackening another's character is like wiggling in quicksand — one sinks ever deeper. Finding the way to true companionship is the samadhi in which Buddhas appear in all directions.

7. Do not be proud of yourself and devalue others: Every Buddha and every ancestor realises s/he is the same as the limitless sky and as great as the universe.

Comment: There is no need to inflate oneself and even less to diminish others, nor, indeed, the converse. Nothing is added to reality, nothing subtracted thereby. Merely we add to our foolishness.

8. Do not be mean in giving either Dharma or wealth: There is nothing to be mean with: one phrase, one verse, the hundred grasses, one Dharma, one enlightenment, every Buddha, every ancestor.

Comment: What is all this for except to use in the service of the Dharma? Truly we own nothing. We have things in trust for a while — possessions, reputation, money, status, life — then they go. Did we use them well? This is not me, this is not mine, this is not my self.

9. Do not be angry: There is no retiring, no going, no truth, no lie; there is a brilliant sea of clouds, there is a dignified sea of clouds.

Comment: Why lose your dignity? What point is there in impugning that of others? Life is a pageant of many colours. Others have their reasons; they get results in their own way. Life is the teacher of us all.

10. Do not defame the Three Treasures: to do something by ourselves, without copying others, is to become an example to the world and the merit of doing such a thing becomes the source of all wisdom. Do not criticise, but accept everything.

Comment: Taking refuge is true faith and it brings independence of the best kind. With Buddha as one's friend what need one fear? The Three Treasures appear in many forms casting their radiance upon our lives. By ourselves we are nothing, but in that light everything.

Overall Comment: These great precepts of Mahayana Buddhism describe the life, form, mind and heart of Buddha. We can try to keep them and in the attempt we shall learn many things. In particular, we shall, on the one side, become acquainted with our own weakness, error and vulnerability, and on the other with the excellence of the objects of refuge. May this deepen our faith.

Each of the precepts implies all the others. The first nine are all injunctions against defaming the Three Treasures in different ways. If one deeply understands and respects life in all its forms, the other precepts follow naturally. If one takes the things given to one in this life as being simply the means to live an innocent life and help liberate others, pride, anger and covetousness will not arise. All are thus within all.

However, while admiring and being inspired by these high ideals, it is important to remain grounded in the reality of one's own life and karma. They give us humility as well as ecstasy.

Reflecting the Ocean of Truth: The Koan of Kapimala

Kapimala (lived approx. 100AD) was a native of Pātaliputra in the Indian state of Magadha. As a young man he taught a form of Brahmanism and he had three thousand disciples. He had magical powers and was ambitious. His powers enabled him to change his form and appearance and thereby impress people.

One day he encountered Ashvaghosha. Ashvaghosha was not impressed by Kapimala's powers. Although Kapimala said that he had the power to change the great ocean, Ashvaghosha said he was more interested in the ocean of the truth which Kapimala could not change.

The question is, does one seek the power to change the world or the facility to be changed and enriched by it? Does one really encounter the other or does one subvert it? When one really encounters the other one lives the other, even though one never ceases to live one's own life thereby. The ocean of truth flows into one yet one does not thereby become something fixed and notable. In the samadhis of Buddhism, everything becomes the truth, everybody becomes a Buddha, just for the time being. Sometimes a Buddha, sometimes a fool, sometimes a foreigner, sometimes a friend. This is emptiness. There is no need to change others into disciples and dominate them. They become true disciples by becoming themselves. Yet, when one is truly oneself, one is a mirror of everything else and such a mirror is empty. Yet, although the mirror is always empty there is always something in it. Not only is there something in it, without the mirror making any effort, the whole universe can be found within it. So it is with ourselves. The greatest teacher is the best learner.

Kapimala ceased to be ambitious and selfish and came to Ashvaghosha as a disciple. He no longer cared about being powerful, yet, for that reason, he received the power of the ocean of truth. Being happy to be a servant he became the master.

Later Kapimala propagated Buddhism in southern and western India. When Kapimala went to see Nagarjuna he simply went in order to meet an interesting man. He had no ambition or selfish intention. Paradoxically, this led to Nagarjuna becoming his disciple because it was exactly this emptiness that Nagarjuna needed.

Dialectic Within the Teaching and Within the Sangha

My teacher often talked about the danger of quietism. By this she meant that it is no good thinking that one has arrived at the perfect understanding, or the perfect organisation, or the perfect practice. There has to be an endless dialectical process to re-invigorate the practice, or things become stale and then become narrow. Wherever we have got to, there is always a next step. It is not that that next step takes us closer to the goal, it is that taking next steps is the goal. As soon as we stop doing so, we fall out of the Dharma creating a gap "as great as that between heaven and earth".

In a spiritual community there should always be some grit, or it does not produce pearls. The Buddha Shakyamuni had many disciples and his leading ones were very different personalities. There was plenty of dynamic between them. Honen Shonin also had many disciples and after he died there were many different ideas about the precise meaning of his teaching. Different groups were in competition. The result was that Pureland in one or another shape or form spread all over Japan and became the most popular form of religion in the country. Since the Second World War, Nichiren Buddhism has approached similar status and, again, we see many different Nichiren groups in competition.

Competition, debate, and airing of different perspectives can become conflict and go over into a destructive mode. There is, therefore, a middle path to be found between quietism and conflict — between death and destruction, one could say. On the middle path there is life, joy, respect and a continual 'going beyond'. If we lose this spirit of adventure and exploration, then the Dharma decays. When we have it there is a vibrancy and the Dharma continues — we are all young at heart.

Although I have retired to the country, I am by no means retired in any other sense. We talk about going 'on retreat', but perhaps we sshould be talking about 'advance'. Rather, instead of talking about it, we should be living it. There is no end to this path. The Dharma is not bland — there is always some pepper and salt and sometimes a dash of curry powder too.

Too many people are looking for the one right answer, or the one right way. When you find it, give it a good kick and see if it says anything. If it gives a shout, then ask it the direction to somewhere it has never been.

Dharma Based Alternative Society

One way of understanding Buddhism is as an attempt to create an alternative society. Groups of Buddhists are cells in what is intended in the long run to be a quiet revolution, gradually transforming society partly from within and partly from without.

What sort of alternative are we talking about? Evidently one based upon a rather different scale of values from those of materialism, nationalism and militarism that prevail at present. How are people to live in peace together?

Many people have been drawn to Buddhism by seeing it as a force for peace in the world and it certainly has this potential. Small groups of people living in peace tend to have an effect out of all proportion to their numbers. By demonstrating an alternative, they give hope even to those who themselves do not participate.

A Buddhist community is an experiment in creating harmony with minimum resort to coercion. If one considers the vast number of laws in a modern country and the huge number of people whose jobs consist essentially of regulating others or preventing them from doing dysfunctional things, one can see that a huge amount of energy and person power could be released if people were more trustworthy. However, for them to be so, they need greater faith than is common in society at large, both faith in one another and a faith that transcends immediate person advantage.

All of this is partly a problem of scale. Small Is Beautiful: A Study of Economics As If People Mattered is a collection of essays by German born British economist E. F. Schumacher which comes close to spelling out a Buddhist approach to economics. The slogan "small is beautiful" stands against "bigger is better". Schumacher suggests that we need an ethic of enoughness. Buddhism advocates simplicity, fewness of desires and contentment.

However, the Buddhist ideal does not neatly correspond to any of the major modern Western ideologies. It is not communist, socialist, capitalist, nor liberal and it is not an aggressive crusade for 'freedom, justice and democracy'. Many so-called engaged Buddhists have not really thought through their Buddhism, but have, rather, imported into it many supposedly 'progressive' modern ideas that do not really have much grounding in Buddha's Dharma.

In practice, most Buddhist communities have been rather in the nature of villages or small towns centred on a monastic establishment of some kind. This is not totally unlike Plato's idea of philosopher kings. Even in these small societies there has to be authority of some kind or the crops do not get grown and harvested. Somebody has to organise and take responsibility.

In practice, a Buddhist group is a select one. Only people who fit in are recruited. The community might carry some members who do not contribute, but there is a practical limit. The Buddha's mission can be seen as having been basically to recruit and train such people who could then act as a leaven in society and make the possibility of genuinely peaceful communities more widespread. This is a long term strategy, but it is a noble cause. Those who become part of it gain the satisfaction of being part of the solution, rather than part of the problem, and have a way of life that contributes to inner and outer peace.

Singularity and Community

Buddha taught ekagata. Eka means 'one'. 'Gata' is from the verb 'to go'. Thus ekagata refers to going alone or going as a single one. What does this mean?

We can take it externally and internally. Externally, at the very least, it means that a Buddhist practitioner is at ease in solitude and the knowledge that he or she is at ease when in solitude means that when in company she or he has no need to 'cling'. It also means that it is good to seek a good teacher, but if you can't find one then it is better to plough your own furrow than to follow somebody who will lead you astray. Of course, 'ploughing your own furrow' does not mean following some foolish fashion. To do so would be the same as following a bad teacher. It is important to say this because many people nowadays — and perhaps in all ages — construct a kind of 'individualism' that is really just adoption of currently fashionable ideas. Just to be against the establishment because all of your friends are is not real individuality.

This consideration leads us easily onto the internal aspect. This internal aspect is the more fundamental. Examining it we can see that fulfilling the Buddha's prescription is not so easy. Essentially it means to be free of all our 'internalised others'. When we examine our life we can often see that we are living out an imaginary relationship with an imagined audience. This audience may be one or both of our parents or might be society at large. In this imaginary relationship, we may have several habitual scripts which are like vows that we have made at various crucial points in life. Such scripts might be "I'll show them!" or "I'll get my revenge," or "I hate you for being better than me, but I'm familiar with my repertoire of hateful thoughts, so I'll go on playing this part," or "I'm the sick member of the family," or whatever.

We can readily see that these scripts and imaginary relationships constitute a fantasised identity for oneself. Dropping them may leave one in unfamiliar territory. This leads us to the, perhaps startling, conclusion that the truly and authentically individual person does not know who or what they are. Their nature is something that they are continually discovering. Furthermore, they do not really discover it so much by paying attention to themselves, but more by their involvement with fresh encounters in the world.

It is not so much that one uncovers a true identity as that one simply plays one's part, does one's duty, and notices what is necessary and gets on with it. Then one is being a 'fully functioning person' without having to have any particular or strong awareness of the fact.

In the play, A Man for All Seasons, Sir Thomas Moore is asked whether he fears for the fate of his soul and he says not and when this is questioned, he says that the Lord will not refuse one who comes to Him so blithely.

The Buddha is saying something similar. The true life is lived blithely. It is not tortured by endless introspection. Some introspection once in a while can be valuable, but the main stuff of life is to be found in engagement. However — and here we meet what seems like paradox, again — it is only the one who is free who can really engage. Only when one recognises and respects separateness can one have a fully healthy relationship with others. Only when one is singular, in the Buddha's sense of ekagata, can one play one's part in community in a fully responsible manner.

Teachers, Disciples and Students

In Buddhism, and in many spiritual communities, a key role is ascribed to teachers and to those who study and train with them. The former are transmitters of the Dharma and the latter are receivers of it. However, the terms transmitters and receivers does not here mean exactly what the worldly mind tends to make of it. Disciples are also vitally important supports to the life and work of the teacher.

Darshan

The Dharma is not simply a set of ideas. It is a lived life and a mystic way, a Tao. Nor is it a stereotyped life. Not all teachers sit under bodhi trees. We could say that it is a fullness of life. This fullness is transmitted, but in such a transmission there is no thing that is given — no commodity is involved. The traditions of India, whether Hindu, Jain, Sikh or Buddhist all emphasise darshan. Darshan means being in the presence of the teacher. One acquires the Dharma directly from being with the teacher just as he or she has acquired it by contact with other former teachers. It is a contagion of spirit.

Teacher-Disciple and Teacher-Student

For this reason there is a crucial difference between students and disciples. Students are consumers of what a teacher teaches. They do seek and receive a commodity. Furthermore, they take what they like and leave the rest. Their commitment is temporary and instrumental. There is nothing wrong about this, but it is a limited function. Typically a student is somebody who does a course. There is a beginning and an end to the course. When the course is over the student goes his own way. I have been a student on many courses. Mostly I cannot remember the names of the teachers. I acquired knowledge or skills and I, or somebody else, paid for me to study. Essentially the relationship is similar to a customer in a shop.

A disciple is something else. A disciple is an adopted child. When the scriptures refer to "a man or woman of good family" they mean the family of the Dharma. The child will carry on the family farm. His or her investment is different from that of a hired hand.

Just as there are students and disciples, there are two different meanings to the word teacher. There are teachers who teach, perhaps in schools or universities, who might not even be Buddhist, but who teach Buddhism in an academic way. A student going to such a teacher may learn a lot about Buddhism. This is quite different from having the Dharma transmitted to one. It is an academic exercise. It may even be an advantage for such a teacher to not be a Buddhist. From the point of view of the academy, one can do religious studies more objectively if one is not a devotee or believer.

Since the word guru has been debased by popular usage and the term lama is restricted to the Tibetans, we currently have no good single word noun for a spiritual Buddhist teacher. For learners, the term disciple does still work. We can describe the two modes, therefore, as teacher-disciple relationship and teacher-student relationship.

The relationship between disciple and teacher lasts forever — "through all bardos, through all lives". This is true even if, in this life, there were to be only one meeting between the two people. It is a heart to heart connection in which Dharma is transmitted. Once there has been such, there is karmic affinity. Of course, when such a connection exists, the disciple wants to be with the teacher as much as possible, but what really is possible depends on circumstances. The idea of contagion is a good analogy, though. One can get infected by a short encounter, or a long one.

Teachers are Each Unique

Teachers are not all the same. When I think of my teachers, Kennett Roshi established an order of celibate monastics and used the terminology of medieval Christianity. Saiko Sensei ran a three generation family temple and stressed always the close connection between Dharma and psychology. Trungpa Rinpoche made massive adaptations to Tibetan tradition in order to make the Dharma available to people living in the materialist society of contemporary America. Nai Boonman taught tranquil abiding. Thich Nhat Hanh reformulated the whole of Buddhism into the idiom of mindfulness.

My heart to heart connection with each of these great figures was in each case different, yet, in another sense, always the same. The inspiration was the same. The style was always different. There is not one single way of being Buddhist and Buddhism is not a standard from of institution. Buddhism generates many institutions — organisations of many kinds — but they are vehicles, not a destination. Those who think that the vehicle is the important thing may play a part, but they have missed the essence of what is happening. The purpose of a teacher is not to create a perfect organisation. Teachers may, therefore, create many organisations, or none at all, and what they create may follow a pattern, or might not, but, whether it does or not, the Dharma is not the pattern — that is merely superficial.

Lectures are a Lesser Part of Teaching

So, as a teacher, my role and mission is to live love and thereby transmit the contagion that I received from my teachers. However, one transmits to different people in different ways. There is a story about a man who goes to a monastery where there is a teacher that he wants to learn from. He is given a job in the temple. After some time he goes to the teacher and says, "Why do you never teach me?" and the teacher says, "When was I ever not teaching you?"

"Teaching" may even not be the most suitable word, except that I do not know another better one. In a sense the teacher is always transmitting Dharma in the same sense as an infectious person is always spreading their disease. Some may catch it and others not. It depends how much immunity they have. Some may come as students and go on to become great disciples and wonder how that happened. Some may fancy themselves as disciples, but never really be anything more than students, gleaning only for personal advantage.

The Koan of Being a Disciple

If the trainee is not seeking personal advantage, what is she doing? Good question! This is an important koan for anybody who gets caught up in this business. "Why am I here?" Of course, "Why am I here with this teacher?" is also, "why am I here in this life?" Now this is a koan because the person has got hold of the wrong end of the stick. When Shakyamuni was enlightened he turned the stick around. Or, to change the metaphor slightly to one that he used, he got hold of the other end of the snake and, doing so, stopped getting bitten and poisoned. The teacher would like the student to get hold of the right end of the Dharma. He has several means at hand for helping the disciple to do so, but can never force or guarantee results. One method is to give the newcomer plenty of rope. Another is to give the disciple responsibilities so that life teaches. Another is that the disciple cares for the teacher and so learns altruism and compassion. Another is through the example of the teacher's life.

Unconventional Life

This does not necessarily mean that the teacher exhibits a life of conventional morality nor conformity to the role expected of a guru. Often they don't. However, they exhibit being fully alive. This can lead to problems. Observers are liable to judge a teacher on the basis of conventional ideas, but the teacher is in a process of experimenting with life and may take risks with it that most people would be frightened of. Trungpa Rinpoche is a prime example, but there are many others. A teacher is likely to live a life that is unconventional in one way or another. Kennett Roshi was extraordinary in going, as an English woman, to an all male monastery in xenophobic, chauvinistic, immediately-post-war Japan and also in defying the trends of Western Buddhism when she got back.

Handling Personal Neurosis

A fifth way of showing the Way is that the teacher never comes to the end of the Dharma — he is always demonstrating it through his own koan which is his own encounter with impermanence and frailty. Reality is always presenting new situations and the teacher is a human being with a karmic history. These two currents mixing together generate the personal neurosis. Thus everybody is continually in process of giving rise to new neurosis. It is not the presence or absence of neurosis that distinguishes the awakened from the non-awakened — it is how they respond. To the person who is in the stream, the arising of the personal neurosis is a koan, because it arises in the midst of already established mindfulness, which is to say, religious consciousness. When this happens, it naturally leads to investigation of Dharma. By penetrating the neurosis, Dharma is revealed. If there is no pre-established religious consciousness, the arising of personal neurosis leads to a hardening of the sense of self. One's problem is mistaken for one's identity.

The would-be disciple might think that a teacher should be completely sorted out and not show any sign of neurosis. If you meet such a person, they are pretending. Neurosis is like dust settling. The worldly person accumulates the dust and builds castles with it. Walking the path is not a matter of being beyond the world. To use Dogen's analogy, it is not like being so far out in the ocean that you lose sight of land.

Motivation

A seeker may come to a teacher thinking to learn a particular technique. They think that Buddhism is meditation or mindfulness, or a particular sadhana or empowerment. They might want to acquire this spiritual property as a credential, or as a road to power of some kind, or as a solution to a personal supposed problem, such as stress. The teacher might offer something of the kind. This, however, is window dressing. It might get the passing stranger to enter the shop. The real Dharma, however, is hidden in a nondescript box on the third floor. In that box the seeker will discover her attachment to her own identity-agenda and burst out laughing.

There are as many motives as people. As the neurosis arises it brings with it the slightest hint that there is a hidden way, a way that is limitlessly mysterious and wonderful, a hidden treasure. The seeker has that treasure sewn into his garment. If he comes as a pauper he will go on to realise riches. If he comes with the air of somebody who knows something, well, they have their reward already - there is nothing for them in Heaven.

The Perfect Way

"The Perfect Way lacks for nothing, yet needs something," said Master Keizan. It needs that we enact it. We enact it by ceasing with our acting. We enact it in the dance between a teacher and a disciple.

Teacher and disciple together are manifesting the Dharma. The love between them is the Way. Being a teacher is not an act, as on the stage, and no more so is being a true disciple. A really true disciple is already a teacher of gods and humans. A real teacher is a good disciple. This is a karmic affinity that endures beyond birth and death. It manifest in cleaning the dishes and stoking the fire, in translating a text or buying oranges.

> The sun shining fills the yard.
>
> The cherry tree does not know that it is happy.
>
> The disciple is sweeping up the dust
>
> - How wonderfully it sparkles!

Respecting Difference

It is not true that believing that all people are part of one another will necessarily make somebody a better person. People are often careless of themselves.

The idea that we are each and all part of one another is sometimes said to be a central idea of Buddhism. It is not.

The idea seems to rest upon the assumption that fundamentally all people act selfishly and therefore if they can be made to think that other people are part of themselves they will act in the interests of all and not just of themselves separately. This is, surely, a clever piece of double think based on false premises.

If it is really true that everybody is always fundamentally selfish, why would one want them to think of others anyway? Either one is being inconsistent in wanting this, or one has the Machiavellian idea that if others think of others then one does not need to do so oneself. Or, to say the same thing the other way round, if one is sincere in advocating altruism, then one does not believe that people are necessarily selfish.

In fact, it is not true that we always think of our own interest. Sometimes we are selfish and sometimes we aren't. Often people will do something for others when they would not stir themselves on their own account.

Doing something for others tends to give one a sense of purpose that is often stronger than pursuing a personal gain. One will prepare a proper meal for a guest and eat chips when alone. People abuse themselves in all kinds of ways and there is no virtue in extending this to others. The drive to love others may, in fact, often be stronger than the drive to reap personal benefit.

These drives are already part of us and do not need rationalising. Rationalising the altruistic element by grounding it in the selfish one is counter-productive in that it actually gives the selfish one a more fundamental status. This is the opposite of what is required.

There is an intrinsic satisfaction in being involved with and for others and the fact that they are 'other' is an important element in this. It provides an escape from self. From a Buddhist perspective, it is self that is the problem and the solution is not to make all others into self, but quite the opposite, to appreciate otherness more.

Thus separation is just as important as, and is the other side of the coin of, connection. When we recognise that our parents are separate people with lives and motives and meanings of their own, it becomes possible to respect them and thus have a mature love for them that is very different from the immature, dependent-cum-resentful attachment that one may have as an adolescent, or the complete dependency one has as an infant when the separation is less fully appreciated.

The motive behind the advancement of the idea that we are all part of one another is essentially respectable in that it is intended to make people care more for one another, but while mutual care is good, the way to arrive at it is not through an extension of the idea of self-centredness. Peace in the world will not come through recognition that 'we are all one', nor even that 'we are all the same', but by recognition and appreciation of difference.

I have been to many interfaith meetings. A common strategy of the organisers of these meetings is to create an agenda in which the first item is, "Let's find out what we all have in common." This almost always misfired, leading to all kinds of unnecessary conflict and misunderstanding that then has to be passed over or hushed up so that we can get on. A much more effective strategy is to get people to take an interest in difference. Then the things that in the previous approach had seemed to be causes for discord, now became things that people can offer to one another without there being any pressure to agree or take on the contrasting material.

Neither of the extreme positions on this issue work. Ordinary people are neither completely selfish nor completely not so. Maturity does involve expanding the mind to encompass a greater range, but this means a range of differences. It is the very fact that things are not self that makes them capable of being Dharma and a source of liberation. A philosophy that eliminates such separation seems well meaning, but actually points in the wrong direction.

Dualities and Nondualities

There is a passage…

> 銀碗盛雪 明月藏鷺 類而不齐 混則知處

> "A silver bowl full of snow / a white egret hidden in the moonlight / these are not the same / comparing them we can appreciate [our own] place"

This comes from the Jewel Mirror Samadhi, a medieval Chinese text. My own teacher gave a teaching upon this text back in September 1981. Her translation is:

> "The white snow falls upon the silver plate, / The snowy heron in the bright moon hides; / Resembles each the other yet these two are not the same; / combining them we can distinguish one from other."

Here is what she said about this passage:

> "Snow is white, a silver plate is white, but they are not the same whiteness. Herons and bright moons are the same colour, but they are not the same thing. Do not discriminate between the value of the silver and

> the apparent lack of value of the
> snow."

In other words, in her view, it is a teaching about non-discrimination, which is one variant on nonduality. Non-discrimination of this kind is valuable, but I think that there is a more important teaching contained in these lines. The dualistic element is more important.

This text specifically says, in both translations, "These two are not the same". If two are not the same, then they are dual, and the purpose of the text is evidently to get us to "distinguish one from other," and this is for a reason.

The teaching not to discriminate values has some grounding in Buddhism, but, I suggest, it is a subordinate to that of honouring the Three Jewels as supremely radiant (the moon). Since the nondual idea is much promoted it has taken me some time and effort to see that often what is taken as teaching on nonduality is actually nothing of the sort.

This particular extremely famous passage is telling us to appreciate our proper lesser place in the scheme of things. That may not be a popular message these days, but there it is. However white a heron or egret one may be, one can never be the moon. Egret means an individual creature standing in the light, i.e. oneself. Moon means the source of the light, i.e. Buddha. We are held by the Dharma as a bowl holds snow. The contrast intended here is that the bowl endures while the snow is ephemeral. We are ephemeral and the Dharma endures. Because it endures, we are held.

If there is a non-discrimination aspect to this teaching it is that the bowl does not mind what kind of snow falls and the moon does not discriminate between birds.

This is a text about not pretending to be Buddha and not thinking that when Buddha acts on, in or through oneself that that is by one's own power. It sets the Buddha and oneself apart and this separation is necessary in order that one be able to receive. When we look closely we see that there is a world of difference between ourselves and the Buddha, our own mind and the Dharma. The notion that one is oneself Buddha already is a sad distortion. We should not be minimising the difference; we should be realising the majesty.

What would my teacher have thought of this? There are those who say that one should never disagree with one's teachers. This idea is wrong. Buddhism is a dialectical process. If my disciples are not capable of debating with me then they have missed the point. To follow the Dharma is also to wrestle with the Dharma. Thus it becomes real. We stand on giants' shoulders and should always try to see further than they — that's why they lifted us up.

Nonetheless, I think that my beloved teacher would have appreciated this interpretation. Perhaps she would have taken the whole idea even further, and such a conversation would itself have been the Dharma in motion — sparks of compassion flying off the wheel. I have been very blessed with great teachers and this is my way of honouring them.

www.ingramcontent.com/pod-product-compliance
Lightning Source LLC
Chambersburg PA
CBHW070527010526
44118CB00012B/1071